全国翻译专业资格（水平）考试指定教材

英语口译综合能力（2级）

（修订版）

主 编 王立弟

图书在版编目（CIP）数据

英语口译综合能力. 二级 / 王立弟主编. —北京：外文出版社，2009
全国翻译专业资格（水平）考试指定教材
ISBN 978-7-119-03629-8

Ⅰ. 英… Ⅱ. 王… Ⅲ. 英语-翻译-资格考试-教材 Ⅳ. H315.9

中国版本图书馆 CIP 数据核字（2004）第 010250 号

全国翻译专业资格（水平）考试指定教材
英语口译综合能力（二级）（修订版）

主　　编　王立弟
责任编辑　王　蕊　夏伟兰
封面设计　吴　涛
印刷监制　张国祥

出版发行　外文出版社
地　　址　北京市西城区百万庄大街24号　　邮政编码　100037
网　　址　http://www.flp.com.cn
电　　话　（010）68320579/68996067（总编室）　68995875/68990283（编辑部）
　　　　　（010）68995844/68995852（发行部）　68995852/68996188（邮购部）
印　　刷　北京中印联印务有限公司
经　　销　新华书店/外文书店
开　　本　16开
印　　张　14.5
印　　数　70001-76000
字　　数　220千
装　　别　平
版　　次　2016年1月第2版第14次印刷
书　　号　ISBN 978-7-119-03629-8
定　　价　43.00元

版权所有　侵权必究　有印装问题可随时调换

前　言

　　本书是专门为全国翻译专业资格（水平）考试之英语口译综合能力考试（二级）编写的。口译综合能力考试的目的是测试应试者的英语水平和操作能力是否达到专业口译的要求。该考试分为短篇判断、短句选择、篇章选择和听力综述四项内容，应试者要通过听来完成这几项。显然，要做得好，听力能力一定要很强才行，这也是口译的特点决定的。当然，听力和其它的技能是相辅相成的。试想一下，没有丰富的词汇和语法知识，没有流畅的表达能力，没有很好的阅读和写作能力，要想把口译工作做得很出色几乎是不可能的。因此，本书设计的训练和练习既有针对性又有综合性，包括了听说读写诸方面的内容。本书采用的语言材料都取自英语国家的权威刊物、杂志、报章、书籍和国际组织的出版物，内容真实鲜活，语言文字地道流畅，用词简练精确，对考生的语言能力要求很高，这与二级专业口译的要求相一致。做好翻译，要具备多方面的知识。本书在有限的篇幅内提供了涉及政治、经济、科技、法律、能源、社会等方面的阅读材料，目的就是扩大考生的知识面和相关的语言知识。可是，大千世界纷繁复杂、变幻无穷，语言同样也是一个具有丰富创造力的开放系统，任何的努力也只能做到沧海之一粟。考生应尽量做到举一反三，以一斑而窥全豹，才能够达到较好的学习效果。

　　做好翻译除了要有广博的知识外，还要系统地认识和掌握两种语言特别是外语的规律。说到语言知识，人们最容易想到词汇和语法。当然，这是语言最基础的元素，是必不可少的。但是，语言的表达不是这些材料的简单堆砌。语言表达最核心的东西是"意义"，语言的功能在于表达思想，在于对事物的分门归类和表述。人的语言之所以能够做到这一点，一方面是它的创造性和开放性，另一方面在于它的系统性。离开了这两点，语言表达是无法实现的。正是基于上述考虑，本书在练习材料的编写过程中，既没有按照语法结构的顺序，也没有采用按内容分类的方法，而是参照系统功能语言学的理念，按照语言表达的功能体系进行划分，同时照顾口译综合能力考试的特点。

　　按照这一体系，本书分为16个单元，每个单元突出一项功能和任务。前14个单元分四个部分。第一部分是听力练习，共两组。第一组是10个正误判断题。第二组是10道单项选择题。

　　第二部分是阅读，长度在600到900字，内容涉及国际政治、经济、贸易、法律、社会、科技等不同领域。文章前面有一段英文的提示，帮助考生掌握要点。文章后面对难点做了注释，并附有词汇表。

　　第三部分的问答帮助考生进行口语练习，考生可以先阅读课文，读完再回答问题。

第四部分是写作练习，要求考生将课文的内容加以总结，用200到250字的篇幅写出一篇短文。考生可以先读文章，读懂之后，写一篇短文。

其中，第15单元的第一部分是由几组篇章构成的听力练习，每段约有200到250个词，每段听力都配有5道选择题。第16单元的练习是由两段各为500词左右的较长文章组成，听后各写出一段短文。第15和16单元的其余部分与前面的单元一样，配有阅读和问答等内容。

本书除了这16个单元的课文和练习之外，还编写了5套全真模拟试题供考生参考练习，为参加考试做好充分的准备。

在本书的编写和修订过程中，得到张连江、韩俊梅、杨清珍等同志的协助和支持，编者在此表示感谢。

目　录

Unit 1　A World in Action
Section Ⅰ　Listening Comprehension …………………………………………………… 1
Section Ⅱ　Reading: Rebuilding Valuable Soil ………………………………………… 3
Section Ⅲ　Speaking up …………………………………………………………………… 7
Section Ⅳ　Summary Writing ……………………………………………………………… 7

Unit 2　The Inner Self
Section Ⅰ　Listening Comprehension …………………………………………………… 8
Section Ⅱ　Reading: Arnie's Uphill Climb ……………………………………………… 10
Section Ⅲ　Speaking up …………………………………………………………………… 14
Section Ⅳ　Summary Writing ……………………………………………………………… 14

Unit 3　Well-Connected
Section Ⅰ　Listening Comprehension …………………………………………………… 15
Section Ⅱ　Reading: None So Deaf As Those That Will Not Hear …………………… 17
Section Ⅲ　Speaking up …………………………………………………………………… 21
Section Ⅳ　Summary Writing ……………………………………………………………… 21

Unit 4　When, where and how?
Section Ⅰ　Listening Comprehension …………………………………………………… 23
Section Ⅱ　Reading: Monk's Best Friend ……………………………………………… 25
Section Ⅲ　Speaking up …………………………………………………………………… 29
Section Ⅳ　Summary Writing ……………………………………………………………… 29

Unit 5　Putting the Horse before the Cart
Section Ⅰ　Listening Comprehension …………………………………………………… 30
Section Ⅱ　Reading: The End of Oil Age ……………………………………………… 32
Section Ⅲ　Speaking up …………………………………………………………………… 36
Section Ⅳ　Summary Writing ……………………………………………………………… 36

Unit 6 The Other Side of the Coin

Section I Listening Comprehension 37
Section II Reading: Carmakers see the future in China 39
Section III Speaking up 42
Section IV Summary Writing 42

Unit 7 Lending an Ear to Numbers

Section I Listening Comprehension 44
Section II Reading: Sustaining our future 46
Section III Speaking up 49
Section IV Summary Writing 49

Unit 8 Being Indirect and Probable

Section I Listening Comprehension 50
Section II Reading: Rethinking Protectionism 52
Section III Speaking up 55
Section IV Summary Writing 56

Unit 9 Speaking in Quotes

Section I Listening Comprehension 57
Section II Reading: Light Heavy Lifters 59
Section III Speaking up 62
Section IV Summary Writing 62

Unit 10 Speech Acts

Section I Listening Comprehension 63
Section II Reading: Justice Takes its Time 65
Section III Speaking up 68
Section IV Summary Writing 68

Unit 11 Traveling to Other Lands

Section I Listening Comprehension 69
Section II Reading: Budapest's Pride of Palace 71
Section III Speaking up 74
Section IV Summary Writing 75

Unit 12 The Flowers

Section I Listening Comprehension 76

Section II   Reading: Poppy Glut Brings Crash in Opium Prices ········· 78
Section III   Speaking up ········· 81
Section IV   Summary Writing ········· 81

Unit 13   In Search of Life's Origin

Section I   Listening Comprehension ········· 83
Section II   Reading: The Case for a "Grand Bargain" ········· 86
Section III   Speaking up ········· 89
Section IV   Summary Writing ········· 90

Unit 14   The Little Guy

Section I   Listening Comprehension ········· 91
Section II   Reading: A New Biofuel from Fruit Sugars ········· 94
Section III   Speaking up ········· 96
Section IV   Summary Writing ········· 97

Unit 15   Stretching the Limits

Section I   Listening Comprehension ········· 98
Section II   Reading: The Child is Father of Patient ········· 100
Section III   Speaking up ········· 103
Section IV   Summary Writing ········· 103

Unit 16   Getting the Gist

Section I   Listening Comprehension ········· 104
Section II   Reading: I Google, Therefore I Am ········· 105
Section III   Speaking up ········· 108
Section IV   Summary Writing ········· 108

Sample Test One ········· 110
Sample Test Two ········· 116
Sample Test Three ········· 122
Sample Test Four ········· 128
Sample Test Five ········· 133

Answer Key ········· 139
Transcripts ········· 143

全国翻译专业资格（水平）考试问答 ········· 214

Unit 1
A World in Action

Section I Listening Comprehension

I. Listen to the following passages and then decide whether the following statements are true or false.

1. While using a computer or cell phone, we are completely cut from the world around us.
   ○ True
   ✓ False

2. Other countries surrounding the ocean are strongly opposed to Russia's claim to a large part of the ocean.
   ○ True
   ✓ False

3. Smoking can raise people's risk of atherosclerosis.
   ✓ True
   ○ False

4. More than 30 states in the U.S. have turned against the federal government's ban on importing beef from Canada.
   ○ True
   ✓ False

5. Sheep near Guildford are likely to get infected by the disease.
   ✓ True
   ✓ False

6. The reality of today's world is mundane as compared with the world of the Internet.
   ✓ True
   ○ False

7. The design of modern airplanes has nothing to do with Wright brothers' craft first flown at Kitty Hawk in 1903.
   ○ True
   ✓ False

8. The Federal Reserve was confident about the value of the dollar even as it continues to fall.

○ True
○ False

9. Developing countries are being cautious on the free flow of capital because it can lead to unemployment, bankruptcies and other economic woes for the country.
   ○ True
   ○ False

10. The agricultural economy as well as the fabric of society in the United States will be subject to change as a result of shifts in public values and needs.
    ○ True
    ○ False

II. Choose the one answer that best fits the meaning of the statement you have heard.

1. The elements that determine a national foreign policy consist in _____.
   a. the various grades of oil
   b. the links between oil and foreign policy
   c. the benchmarks that are used to negotiate prices
   d. the general availability and overall price of oil

2. Who does the author think shall be sent to Mars?
   a. A group of women.
   b. A group of men.
   c. A mixed team made up of women, men and robots.
   d. Robots.

3. According to the passage, _____.
   a. terrorists have deployed 756 vehicle bombs in Britain since 1970
   b. the consortium aims to study terrorism and responses to terrorism
   c. terrorists would rather figure out a way to solve problems than attack a target
   d. car bombs seldom happen in Britain

4. Douglas Kennedy _____.
   a. is a French author
   b. has written at least 7 novels
   c. is going to publish his sixth novel worldwide
   d. is supposed to be an experienced salesman

5. Which of the following statements is true to women athletes?
   a. They are more likely to get hurt than males in football.
   b. They suffer 240% more concussions than male players in basketball.
   c. They run 40% higher risks than males in sports.
   d. They are more competitive than males in sports played by both sexes.

6. Which of the following statements is true according to the passage?

a. The holding of the first round of UN World Summit on the Information Society was a controversial one.
   b. It took two years for countries to negotiate their positions before the first World Summit on the Information Society was convened.
   c. The rich and the poor countries reached an agreement on the division of labor on the Internet.
   d. The conference demonstrated a harmony of global interconnectedness among countries, rich or poor.
7. Which of the following statements is closest in meaning to what was said above?
   a. Vietnamese farmers abandoned coffee growing during the mid-1990s.
   b. Vietnam is one of the world's major coffee exporters nowadays.
   c. The Vietnamese has helped coffee price to soar in the world market.
   d. Coffee price has been plummeting in the world market since the mid-1990s.
8. Which of the following the author thinks is essential to a healthy economy?
   a. Foreign banks entering local markets.
   b. Domestic banks channeling more fund on the international market.
   c. Local banks lending more to businesses.
   d. Banks avoiding risky investments.
9. The development of science offers satisfaction of demands in which of the following areas?
   a. Continued productivity gains, more and varied products and better health.
   b. Reduction of animal disease.
   c. Animal welfare.
   d. All of the above except (b).
10. Which of the following statements is closest in meaning to the passage you have just heard?
    a. The new vision of agriculture will support U. S. expansion of power overseas.
    b. The new vision will enhance public health and social well-being.
    c. The new vision embraces technologies for the cloning of rare species of wildlife.
    d. The new vision promotes agriculture as a political, economic, social and environmental force.

Section II Reading

Rebuilding Valuable Soil

Prompts: Perhaps the soil underneath our feet is the most common and often neglected thing on earth except the air. Yet these days it is as important to protect the soil as protect the air. The article introduces methods of soil conservation and efforts made in America, Africa and Asia to protect the soil from erosion, desertification, overgrazing and other forms of soil degradation.

The 1930s Dust Bowl that threatened to turn America's Great Plains into a vast desert was a traumatic experience[1] that led to revolutionary changes in the nation's agricultural practices, including the planting of tree shelterbelts[2] (rows of trees planted beside fields) and strip-cropping (the planting of wheat on alternate strips with fallowed land each year). Strip-cropping permits soil moisture to accumulate on the fallowed strips, while the alternating planted strips reduce wind speed and, hence, erosion on the idled land.

Terracing, a time-tested method for dealing with water erosion, is common in rice paddies throughout the mountainous regions of Asia. On less steeply sloping land, contour strip farming, as found in the American Midwest, works well. Another utensil in the soil conservation tool kit — and a relatively new one — is conservation tillage, which includes both no-till and minimum tillage. In addition to reducing erosion, this practice helps retain water, raises soil carbon content, and reduces the energy needed for crop cultivation. Instead of plowing land, discing or harrowing it to prepare the seedbed, and then using a mechanical cultivator to control weeds, farmers simply drill seeds directly through crop residues into undisturbed soil, controlling weeds with herbicides[3]. In the U.S., where farmers were required to implement a soil conservation plan on erodible cropland to be eligible for commodity price supports, the no-till area went from 7,000,000 hectares in 1990 to 25,000,000 in 2004[4]. Now widely used in the production of corn and soybeans, no-till has spread throughout the Western Hemisphere, covering 24,000,000 hectares in 2004 in Brazil, 18,000,000 in Argentina, and 13,000,000 in Canada. Australia, with 9,000,000 hectares, rounds out the five leading no-till countries.

Algeria, trying to halt the northward advance of the Sahara Desert, announced in December 2000 that it is concentrating its orchards and vineyards in the southern part of the country, hoping that these perennial plantings[5] will halt the desertification of its cropland. In July 2005, the Moroccan government, responding to severe drought, announced that it was allocating $778,000,000 to cancel farmers' debts and to convert cereal-planted areas into less vulnerable olive and fruit orchards.

There are similar concerns about the expanding Sahara on the southern edge of the desert as well. Nigeria has proposed planting a Great Green Wall[6] of trees, a band five kilometers wide stretching 7,000 kilometers across Africa, in an effort to halt the desert's advance. Senegal, which is on the western end of this proposed wall and is losing 50,000 hectares of productive land each year, strongly supports the idea.

In Inner Mongolia, efforts to halt the advancing desert and to reclaim the land[7] for productive uses rely on planting desert shrubs to stabilize the sand dunes. In many situations, sheep and goats have been banned entirely. In Helin County, south of the provincial capital of Hohhot, the planting of desert shrubs on abandoned cropland has stabilized the soil on the county's first 7,000-

hectare reclamation plot. Based on this success, the reclamation effort is being expanded. The Helin County strategy centers on replacing the large number of sheep and goats with dairy cattle, increasing the number of these animals from 30,000 in 2002 to 150,000 by the end of 2007. The cattle are kept in enclosed areas, feeding on cornstalks, wheat straw, and the harvest from a drought-tolerant forage crop resembling alfalfa, which is grown on reclaimed land[8]. Local officials estimate that this program will double incomes within the county during this decade.

To relieve pressure on China's rangelands, Beijing is asking herders to reduce their flocks of sheep and goats by 40%. In communities where wealth is measured in livestock numbers and where most families are living in poverty, such cuts are not easy or, indeed, likely, unless alternative livelihoods are offered pastoralists along the lines proposed in Helin County.

The only viable way to eliminate overgrazing on the two-fifths of the Earth's land surface classified as rangelands is to reduce the size of flocks and herds[9]. Not only do the excessive numbers of cattle — particularly sheep and goats — remove the vegetation, but their hoofs pulverize the protective crust of soil that is formed by rainfall and that checks wind erosion. In some situations, the only viable option is to keep the animals in enclosures, bringing the forage to them. India, which successfully has adopted tills practice for its thriving dairy industry, is the model for other countries.

Protecting the Earth's remaining vegetation also warrants a ban on the clearcutting of forests in favor of selective harvesting as, with each clearcut, there are heavy soil losses until the forest regenerates[10]. Thus, with each subsequent cutting, productivity declines further. Restoring the Earth's tree and grass cover protects soil from erosion, reduces flooding, and sequesters carbon. It is one way we can restore the Earth so that it can support our children and grandchildren.

Words and Expressions

traumatic 痛苦的；极不愉快的
shelterbelt 防风林
strip-cropping 间作
fallow 使（土地）休闲；休整
alternating 交替的；轮流的
terracing 梯田
rice paddy 稻田，水田
contour （农）沿等高线作业的
tool kit 工具箱
tillage 耕耘；耕地
no-till 免耕法
plow 耕；犁
disc (=disk) 用圆盘耙耙地

harrow 耙掘；用圆盘犁犁地
crop residue 作物（收获）残余
herbicide 除草剂
erodible 可侵蚀的；易蚀的
perennial 四季不断的；终年的
sand dune [地] 沙丘
forage 草料
alfalfa [植] 紫花苜蓿
rangeland 牧场，放牧地
pastoralist 放牧人；牧场主
viable 切实可行的
overgrazing 过度放牧
flocks and herds 牛羊

hoof 蹄

pulverize 粉碎；摧毁

warrant 使有必要

sequester 使隐退，使隔绝

Notes

1. traumatic experience: 一种给人心灵带来创伤的，磨灭不掉的经历和记忆，像战争、瘟疫和天灾人祸等。30年代美国中西部地区的沙尘暴，惊心动魄，让人记忆犹新。几年前在东南亚发生的海啸（tsunami），给当地的人们带来的经历和记忆也可以形容为 traumatic experience。2008年3月发生在西藏的暴乱，对于亲历这场灾难的人们来说，无疑也是 traumatic experience。

2. shelterbelts: 防风林带。下文中还提到了一些农业上常用的技术，例如 strip-cropping 间作，terracing 梯田，no-till 免耕法。

3. Instead of plowing land, discing or harrowing it to prepare the seedbed, and then using a mechanical cultivator to control weeds, farmers simply drill seeds directly through crop residues into undisturbed soil, controlling weeds with herbicides: 农民们没有对土地进行耕作，如耙平苗床，用机器除草，他们只是将种子点播在尚有庄稼秸秆未曾翻过的地里，而且用灭草剂除草。这种简单的耕作方式对土壤的培护极为不利。

4. In the U.S., where farmers were required to implement a soil conservation plan on erodible cropland to be eligible for commodity price supports, the no-till area went from 7,000,000 hectares in 1990 to 25,000,000 in 2004: 在美国，农民必须在易流失土地上执行保护水土计划，这样才有资格获得商品价格补贴；免耕区从1990年的700万亩增加到2004年的2500万亩。be eligible for 是形容词短语，有……资格的，具备……条件的。

5. perennial planting: 多年生植物。

6. a Great Green Wall: 非洲的尼日利亚提议建设一道绿色长城以防止撒哈拉沙漠的进一步扩大。

7. reclaim the land: 在我国的内蒙古，人们种植沙棘来防沙治沙，人进沙退，从沙漠中夺回失去的土地，这一过程就被称为 land reclamation。

8. The cattle are kept in enclosed areas, feeding on cornstalks, wheat straw, and the harvest from a drought-tolerant forage crop resembling alfalfa, which is grown on reclaimed land: 牛群被圈养在固定地方，用玉米杆、麦秆以及长在沙漠中被夺回的土地上像紫花苜蓿一样的耐旱牧草来喂养。drought-tolerant 耐旱的，类似的结构还有 water-proof 防水的，light-sensitive 感光的，等等。

9. The only viable way to eliminate overgrazing on the two-fifths of the Earth's land surface classified as rangelands is to reduce the size of flocks and herds: 在占全球五分之二的牧区消除过度放牧的唯一有效的方法就是减少牛羊的数量。overgrazing 过度放牧，草原上的草被羊、牛等畜牧动物食用过量，整个草原系统不能马上恢复，会造成草场退化、植被干枯、土质疏松。

10. Protecting the Earth's remaining vegetation also warrants a ban on the clearcutting of forests in

favor of selective harvesting as, with each clearcut, there are heavy soil losses until the forest regenerates: 要保护地球上尚存的植被就必须严令禁止滥伐树木，而实行有计划采伐，因为在树木重新长出之前，每次滥伐都会造成严重的水土流失。clearcutting of forests: 对森林的滥伐，这将导致水土流失，防治水土流失的方法是采用 selective harvesting，即有计划采伐。

Section III Speaking Up

Try to answer the following questions after you have read/heard the above passage.

1. Can you list the reasons why the soil on Earth is badly degraded?
2. What measures must be taken to eliminate soil erosion?
3. With population explosion, the earth has to feed too large a population. How to solve the contradiction between population and environmental protection?
4. In northern China, every spring sees too many sand storms. If you are the mayor of Beijing, what will you do to prevent this phenomenon?

Section IV Summary Writing

Write a short summary of the passage you have just read/heard.

_____
_____
_____
_____
_____
_____
_____
_____
_____
_____

Unit 2
The Inner Self

Section I Listening Comprehension

I. Listen to the following passages and then decide whether the following statements are true or false.

1. The speaker of the passage believes that the world is still safe as long as the nuclear weapons are not falling into the hands of the terrorists or ruthless dictators.
   ○ True
   ✓ False

2. Globalization is helping us to understand that we all belong to one and the same race on this planet.
   ✓ True
   ✓ False

3. France and Germany lagged behind in recent years because they were reluctant to take reform measures in their labor and product markets.
   ✓ True
   ○ False

4. Hollywood studios are jealous of the profits Cannes makes over the film festival and they want to hold the event in the United States.
   ○ True
   ✓ False

5. The Iranian people are much afraid of earthquakes, because of the lack of proper education.
   ○ True
   ✓ False

6. Beyond the year of 2009, no country may claim to exploit any continental shelf under the 1982 Law of the Sea.
   ✓ True
   ○ False

7. The Europeans, and among them, the Britons, believe that university education should be free for all in their countries today.

○ True
✓ False

8. Wright, the American architect, was influenced by his uncle when he was a young man.
   ✓ True
   ○ False

9. With more people aspiring to go to college, it is possible to each college student to pay less for his tuition fees.
   ○ True
   ✓ False

10. French students recently took to the street to protect against deteriorating educational facilities in their universities.
    ○ True
    ✓ False

II. Choose the one answer that best fits the meaning of the statement you have heard.

1. Which of the following statements is true of Asian women and young girls?
   a. They like to read science fiction.
   b. They follow Western standards of beauty at the expense of disfiguring their own looks.
   c. They are not as attractive as women in the Western countries.
   d. They aspire the life style of the leisure class in the West.

2. The IT industry _____.
   a. is facing cut-throat competition
   b. is full of jargons understood by very few people outside the profession
   c. has put out many new gadgets recently
   d. is an highly innovative area of development

3. According to the speaker, _____.
   a. the Japanese imported industrial silicon for breast implants after World War II
   b. the invading forces sold silicon to Japanese women working in factories
   c. plastic surgery is also very popular with women in Western countries
   d. Asian women undergoing plastic surgery are eager to emigrate to the U. S.

4. Which of the following does the speaker thinks is a worthier cause to pursue?
   a. Boosting the domestic economic growth.
   b. Strengthening international friendship.
   c. Changing the current trend in fashion.
   d. Helping the poor and the needy in less developed areas.

5. The speaker of the passage _____.
   a. believes that women in Asia need plastic surgery
   b. is surprised by the number of women urge to do plastic surgery

c. wants to have plastic surgery

d. believes that plastic surgery are too expensive

6. Brazilian motorists today _____.

   a. can buy fuel very cheaply at their local garage

   b. are running their cars on ethanol because they can't afford the petrol

   c. are not allowed to buy alcohol at their local garage

   d. are using ethanol as a substitute for petrol

7. Replacing petrol with ethanol _____.

   a. remains a dream for many people

   b. requires great steering skill of the driver

   c. is environment-friendly

   d. makes the engine more fuel efficient

8. What happened to the Time magazine reporter?

   a. He was killed in the battle field.

   b. He was wounded by an explosion in the vehicle he was riding in.

   c. He covered the fighting of two American soldiers and took pictures of them.

   d. He was trying to throw a grenade at the enemies but failed.

9. Which of the following is true of Spain and Australia?

   a. Both countries suffered casualties during the war on Iraq.

   b. Both have been targeted by terrorists for attacks on civilians.

   c. They both have their own separatist forces to deal with.

   d. Both countries have been attacked by Islamic extremists.

10. Why was the last decade a time for travel agents?

    a. It was because fuel price was soaring.

    b. It was because the tickets prices were reduced.

    c. It was because there was a competition from rivalry companies using the Internet.

    d. It was because the concern for air travel safety was demanding.

Section II Reading

Arnie's Uphill Climb

Prompts: The super-movie-star-turned governor Arnold Schwarzenegger has morphed into a different type of fighter. The environmentally pro-active Arnie is all out against a new enemy — the worsening climate change. California's confident approach to climate change has inspired

America and the world, but things do not look so good in the state itself.

In most parts of the world, climate change is a worrying subject. Not so in California. At a recent gathering of green luminaries — in a film star's house, naturally, for that is how seriousness is often established in Los Angeles — the dominant note was self-satisfaction at what the state has already achieved. And perhaps nobody is more smug than Arnold Schwarzenegger. Unlike Al Gore, a presidential candidate turned prophet of environmental doom, California's governor sounds cheerful when talking about climate change. As well he might: it has made his political career. [1]

Although California has long been an environmentally-conscious[2] state, until recently greens were concerned above all with smog and redwood trees[3]. "Coast of Dreams", Kevin Starr's authoritative history of contemporary California, published in 2004, does not mention climate change. In that year, though, the newly-elected Mr. Schwarzenegger made his first tentative call for western states to seek alternatives to fossil fuels. Gradually he noticed that his efforts to tackle climate change met with less resistance, and more acclaim, than just about all his other policies. These days it can seem as though he works on nothing else[4].

Mr. Schwarzenegger's transformation from screen warrior to eco-warrior[5] was completed last year when he signed a bill imposing legally-enforceable limits on greenhouse-gas emissions[6] — a first for America. The bill, which is just 13 pages long, obliges California to cut its emissions to 1990 levels by 2020. That alone is ambitious, considering that the state's population is expected to increase by 42% in the period. But Mr. Schwarzenegger has set up two other targets[7]. He wants the state to reduce greenhouse-gas emissions to 2000 levels by 2010, and to slash them to 80% below 1990 levels by 2050.

Thanks mostly to its lack of coal and heavy industry, California is a relatively clean state. If it were a country it would be the world's eighth-biggest economy, but only its 16th-biggest polluter. Its big problem is transport — meaning, mostly, cars and trucks, which account for more than 40% of its greenhouse-gas emissions compared with 32% in America as a whole. The state wants to ratchet down emissions limits on new vehicles, beginning in 2009. Mr. Schwarzenegger has also ordered that, by 2020, vehicle fuel must produce 10% less carbon: in the production as well as the burning, so a simple switch to corn-based ethanol is probably out.

Californians of the future will also be expected to use cleaner electricity. The state subsidizes solar power[8], with the intention of creating a million power-generating roofs within ten years. It has, in effect, banned electricity companies from signing long-term contracts with coal-fired power stations, and plans to buy from cleaner sources. In 2002 Gray Davis, then the Democratic governor, signed a bill that committed the state to obtaining[9] a fifth of its power from renewable sources, not including nuclear or large hydro-electric power stations, by 2017. Last year, in a typically cocky gesture, the deadline was brought forward to 2010. [10]

All of which is a welcome change from business as usual. [11] California has not just inspired other states; it has created a vanguard that ought to be able to prod the federal government into stronger national standards than it would otherwise consider. But California is finding it easier to export its policies than to put them into practice at home.[12]

The state's first hurdle, which requires it to generate a fifth of its electricity from renewable sources in three years' time, now seems impossibly high. Last year it managed just 11%. Although the energy companies are eagerly signing up wind and sun farmers, there is simply not enough supply out there — at least, at the price the companies want to pay. Meanwhile, the plan to install solar roofs on houses has been stymied by the high cost of photovoltaic panels[13], red tape[14] and a requirement, temporarily suspended, that customers buy additional power at rates that vary according to demand. That would have increased some households' energy bills.

Despite making some optimistic assumptions about future contracts, the public utilities commission has concluded that the state will miss its target for renewables. And the aim of cutting emissions from electricity production to 1990 levels by the end of the next decade may be just as unrealistic.

It is a bad sign that California's electricity suppliers are struggling, because electricity is something over which the state wields considerable control. It has less power over carmakers, who are fighting to prevent California imposing emissions standards on them. If they succeed, even temporarily, California's goals will become unreachable. Thanks partly to the lack of rain and snow in California, vehicles stay on the road for a long time. It takes 16 years for half the cars made in a given year to be retired from service.

In one way, California's self-confidence is fully justified. It has done more than any other state — let alone the federal government — to fix America's attention on climate change. It has also made it seem as though the problem can be solved, which is why failure would be such bad news. At the moment California is a beacon[15] to other states. If it fails, it will become an excuse for inaction.

▶▶ Words and Expressions

luminary 杰出人物
smug 自鸣得意的
tentative 试验性的
acclaim 称赞
eco-warrior 环保卫士
emission （光、热、气等的）排放
ratchet 一步步推动
subsidize 资助
hydro-electric 水电的

vanguard 先锋
prod 促使
hurdle 障碍
stymie 阻碍
photovoltaic 光电的
panel 控制板
public utility 公用事业
wield 行使，支配
beacon 灯塔

Notes

1. 文章开头就点题说，气候变化这一令世人忧心忡忡的事情，在加州却是另一番景象，故意制造悬念，吊人胃口。在这里热心环保的人士成了绿色明星，也难怪连他们集会的地方都选在了电影明星的寓所。会场上的气氛是自我陶醉，而其中最为神气活现者当然是大名鼎鼎的施瓦辛格。文字诙谐调侃，略带一点酸酸的讥讽，为整篇的文章定下了基调。接着又抬出另一位令美国人和地球人都熟知的环保明星，美国前副总统戈尔为这位加州州长当陪衬。但是与戈尔的悲观相比，更让施瓦辛格显得踌躇满志。

2. environmentally-conscious: 形容环境保护意识强，同一类型的搭配还有 environmentally-sound 环境未遭到破坏的，以及 environment-friendly 有利于环境的。

3. … until recently greens were concerned above all with smog and redwood trees: 最近，环保人士对烟雾及红木林格外关注。在这里，greens 指环保人士，也称 the green party（绿党）；smog 烟雾，是一种烟与雾的混合物，尤见于城市。

4. These days it can seem as though he works on nothing else: 最近，他似乎心无旁骛。简短的一句话，使得施瓦辛格州长全力以赴治理环境，阻止气候变化的形象跃然纸上。

5. Mr. Schwarzenegger's transformation from screen warrior to eco-warrior: 施瓦辛格曾在电影中扮演英雄战士一类的形象，家喻户晓，现在摇身一变成了环保卫士。

6. greenhouse-gas emissions: 造成温室效应的主要原因是向大气中排放过多的二氧化碳，这类气体被称为 greenhouse gas。气体的排放用 emission，这里用的是复数，也就是说有不止一种气体的排放。

7. But Mr. Schwarzenegger has set up two other targets: 注意本句与前面的 That alone is ambitious，两句话为州长未来的失败埋下了伏笔。

8. solar power: 太阳能，还有其它类的能源如 hydro-electric power 水电和 wind power 风力发电，他们都是可再生能源 renewable energy。而石油、天然气和火力发电 coal-fire power generation 则被称为 fossil fuel 化石燃料，因为他们都是由古生物化石形成的。

9. committed the state to obtaining: 加州保证……，注意 commit... to doing 保证，承诺。

10. Last year, in a typically cocky gesture, the deadline was brought forward to 2010: 去年，最后期限又被非常狂妄地提前到 2010 年。本句中 cocky 一词用得生动形象，看来，州长的失败是在所难免的。

11. a welcome change from business as usual: 上文中说到的种种措施在作者看来都是可喜的变化，这是和一成不变的那种事不关已的态度进行比较。所谓 business as usual 指的就是这样一种处之泰然，以不变应万变的态度。

12. But California is finding it easier to export its policies than to put them into practice at home: 然而加州发现，推广宣传其政策远比在本州具体实施政策容易得多。

13. photovoltaic panels: 太阳能光伏发电板（简称太阳能 PV 板）。

14. red tape: 官僚作风，源自用红色或粉红色的袋子捆扎公文的习俗。

15. beacon: 灯塔。美国在全球环境保护方面施行的是损人不利己政策，自不待言。加州对于其他州来讲在环境保护措施上具有引领的作用，假如加州都办不成的事情，其他州就更做不成了。

Section III Speaking Up

Try to answer the following questions after you have read/heard the above text.

1. What do you know about Mr. Schwarzenegger? Have you ever seen a film starring him?
2. In your opinion, what causes climate change?
3. What influence does climate change cast on the earth?
4. Why is Mr. Schwarzenegger's ambition doomed to failure?
5. What measures can be taken to fight climate change?

Section IV Summary Writing

Write a short summary of the passage you have just read/heard.

_____
_____
_____
_____
_____
_____
_____
_____

Unit 3
Well-Connected

Section I Listening Comprehension

I. Listen to the following passages and then decide whether the following statements are true or false.

1. Modern cyberspace provides an escape from the drudgery of daily life.
   ○ True
   ✓ False

2. Cluster bombs cause massive damage to enemies to keep them from advancing.
   ✓ True
   ○ False

3. Michael Weisskopf won the Pulitzer Prize for his coverage of the War on Iraq.
   ○ True
   ✓ False

4. American troop in South Korea, like their counterparts in Japan are stationed in the high-profile locations of the country.
   ○ True
   ✓ False

5. Wright finished his college education at the University of Wisconsin.
   ○ True
   ✓ False

6. Agricultural research will lend support to agriculture in improving production and enhancing public health and community well-being.
   ✓ True
   ○ False

7. Development in the hi-tech areas will benefit the developed countries more than it benefits the poorer nations.
   ○ True
   ✓ False

8. Inventive and creative practices are the sole results of development of IT.
   ○ True
   ✓ False

9. Creativity is found in many different fields and contexts and brings benefits of various forms to the society.
   ✓ True
   ○ False

10. Ground-breaking discovery is admired purely as a stroke of genus.
    ○ True
    ✓ False

II. Choose the one answer that best fits the meaning of the statement you have heard.

1. Systems for monitoring fires have values in _____.
   a. deploying fire-fighters and equipment
   b. deciding which areas should be evacuated
   c. predicting how a wildfire is to behave
   d. all of the above

2. Earth-observation satellites circle in their orbits _____.
   a. to help put out wildfires
   b. to measure the extent of damage done by wildfires
   c. to measure the moisture of plants
   d. to forecast rains that may stop the burning of wildfires

3. Hector Berlioz is regarded _____.
   a. as a man that breaks all rules of composition in music
   b. as a music genius that no other musician rivals
   c. as a self-disciplined fellow countryman by the French
   d. as someone difficult to be classified

4. Which of the following statements is true of learning?
   a. Learning is a very basic primitive function of humans.
   b. Learning mathematics is more difficult than learning the history of a society.
   c. Much of learning is done in schools where teaching was systematic.
   d. Humans are more clever at learning than any other species.

5. Research on infants' behavior has shed lights on _____.
   a. their relations with their parents
   b. their emergent dispositions
   c. their abilities to organize and coordinate information
   d. how they solve problems on their own

6. The speaker advocates which of the following methods?
   a. Student centered.
   b. Knowledge centered.
   c. Assessment and community centered.
   d. Different approaches for varying goals.

7. Freshwater fish stocks are vulnerable or endangered because of _____.
   a. shortage of freshwater
   b. pollution and changes in their living environment
   c. fertilizer run-off
   d. closed chemical works

8. Which of the following constitutes a challenge for water in the developing countries?
   a. Shortage of clean bottled water.
   b. Lack of flushing toilet.
   c. Lack of underground sewage pipes.
   d. Lack of tap water.

9. How do some students categorize the people in Northern Europe?
   a. Fierce warriors, pillagers and traders.
   b. Invaders of Paris.
   c. Greedy psychopaths.
   d. Raiders of Baghdad.

10. The process of nuclear weapons is seen as _____.
    a. a source of global influence
    b. providing deterrence
    c. a source of global insecurity
    d. all except (c)

Section II Reading

None So Deaf As Those That Will Not Hear

Prompts: The article describes changes in the public attitudes and behavior towards smoking and drinking and notes the patterns along social orders. It is true that the government's health messages are becoming increasingly strident, but are they any more effective by simply shouting louder?

Time for a quick one?[1] If you smoke, you'd better hurry. From July 1st pubs all over

England will, by law, be no-smoking areas. So will restaurants, offices and even company cars, if more than one person uses them. England's smokers are following a well-trodden path.² The other three bits of the United Kingdom have already banned smoking in almost all enclosed public spaces, and there are anti-smoking laws of varying strictness over most of western Europe. The smoker's journey from glamour through toleration to suspicion is finally reaching its end in pariah status.³

Michael Marmot, a professor of epidemiology at University College London, recalls that during his medical training in the 1960s, his teachers would say: "What's the point in telling people about the dangers of smoking?⁴ You can't get anyone to give up." How wrong they were. Most smokers have already heeded public-health messages and stubbed out.⁵ In the 1950s two-thirds of British men smoked, and they lit up all over the place. Now only a quarter do, and most enclosed public places went smoke-free voluntarily years ago.

But behind this public-health success story lies a darker tale. Poorer people are much more likely to smoke than richer ones — a change from the 1950s, when professional and laborers were equally keen. Today only 15% of men in the highest professional classes smoke, but 42% of unskilled workers do. Despite punitive taxation — 20 cigarettes cost around £5.00 ($10.00), three-quarters of which is tax — 55% of single mothers on benefits smoke. The figure for homeless men is even higher; for hard-drug users it is practically 100%. The message that smoking kills has been heard, it seems, but not by all.

Having defeated the big killers of the past — want, exposure, poor sanitation — governments all over the developed world are turning their attention to diseases that stem mostly from how individuals choose to live their lives. But the same deafness afflicts the same people when they are exhorted to abjure other sorts of unhealthy behavior.⁶ The lower down they are on practically any pecking order — job prestige, income, education, background — the more likely people are to be fat and unfit, and to drink too much.⁷

That tempts governments to shout ever louder in an attempt to get the public to listen — and nowhere do they do so more stridently than in Britain. One reason is that pecking orders matter more than in most other rich countries: income distribution is very unequal and the unemployed, disaffected, ill-educated rump is comparatively large. Another reason is the frustration of a government addicted to targets,⁸ which often aim not only to improve something but to lessen inequality in the process. A third is that the National Health Service is free to patients, and picking up the tab for those who have arguably brought their ill-health on themselves grows alarmingly costly.⁹

The smoking ban is an example of the official excess of zeal.¹⁰ Many of the places covered by the new law are already smoke-free — churches, for example. But they all must display prominent no-smoking signs, or else face penalties that are far heavier than those for lighting up. Sign-miscreants may have to pay as much as £1,000, against £200 for a rebel smoker.¹¹

Warnings about the dangers of drinking are likewise becoming more shrill.[12] On June 5th, the Department of Health published a "national alcohol strategy", which sets out to make drunkenness as socially unacceptable as smoking has become in most circles. At the end of May it told booze producers to put health warnings on bottles and cans, and threatened legislation if they did not comply. A few days earlier it toughened its advice to pregnant women, though no medical research dictated a change. The message had been that a couple of small drinks a week were all right; now women are told to avoid alcohol entirely from the day they start trying to conceive until their babies are born.

That stridency may be pointless, even counter-productive. There is no reason to believe that those who ignore measured voices will listen to shouting. It irritates the majority who are already behaving responsibly, and it may also undermine all government pronouncements on health by convincing people that they have an ultra-cautious margin of error built in.[13]

Such hectoring may also be missing the root cause of the problem. According to Mr. Marmot, who cites research on groups as diverse as baboons in captivity, British civil servants and Oscar nominees, the higher rates of ill health among those in more modest walks of life can be attributed to what he calls the "status syndrome"[14]. People in privileged positions think they are worth the effort of behaving healthily, and find the will-power to do so. More directly, higher status itself protects people's health, he argues, not just by reducing their propensity to behave riskily, but also by changing their body chemistry in ways that protect them against disease.

The implication is that it is easier to improve a person's health by weakening the connection between social position and health than by targeting behavior directly. Some public-health experts talk of changing an environment where the worst choices are the easiest to make, especially for those without the time and money to seek out better ones — supermarkets crammed with ready meals, happy hours in pubs, roads too dangerous for children to walk to school. Others speak of social cohesion, support for families and better education for all. These are bigger undertakings than a bossy ad campaign; but more effective, and quieter.

Words and Expressions

well-trodden 常被踩踏的；经常有人出入的
glamour 刺激；诱惑力
toleration 容忍；默许
suspicion 怀疑
pariah 贱民；受歧视的人
epidemiology 流行病学
heed 留意；注意
stub 掐灭
punitive 苛刻的；极严厉的

sanitation 卫生设备；公共卫生
afflict 使苦恼；折磨
exhort 规劝，告诫；恳请
abjure 戒去；改掉
stridently 刺耳地；尖声地
arguably 按理，可论证地
miscreant 歹徒；无赖
booze 酒
conceive 怀胎；怀孕

stridency 尖声大叫
hector 威吓；虚张声势
baboon 狒狒

captivity 囚禁；羁绊
nominee 被提名者；被提名为候选人
propensity 倾向；习性

Notes

1. Time for a quick one? 在酒吧里常听到的用语，相当于：要不要来一杯（酒）？要不要来一根（烟）？

2. a well-trodden path: 指一条老路。这里指英格兰烟民也逃脱不掉最终被禁，四处封杀的厄运。

3. The smoker's journey from glamour through toleration to suspicion is finally reaching its end in pariah status: 烟民的历史，从魅力四射，到被宽容忍受，再到引起怀疑，最终落得个贱民的下场。作者在这里连用四个名词 glamour，toleration，suspicion 和 pariah 降序排列了烟民的身份历史。

4. What's the point in telling people about the dangers of smoking? 告诉人们吸烟的危害又有什么用呢？What's the point（in）的意思是"有什么用呢？"

5. Most smokers have already heeded public-health messages and stubbed out: 多数吸烟者听从公共健康方面的告诫，把烟戒掉了。stub...out 把……弄灭，例如：The moment the boy saw his mother entering the room, he stubbed the cigarette out. 男孩一看到妈妈走进房间，赶紧把烟掐灭了。

6. But the same deafness afflicts the same people when they are exhorted to abjure other sorts of unhealthy behavior: 不断让这样一群人戒掉一个又一个的不良习惯，他们也只是充耳不闻。

7. The lower down they are on practically any pecking order — job prestige, income, education, background — the more likely people are to be fat and unfit, and to drink too much: 人们所处的社会地位越低，包括工作地位，收入，教育以及家庭出身，他们就越有可能身体肥胖，不健康，而且酗酒。pecking order，指排序，阶层划分。

8. Another reason is the frustration of a government addicted to targets, which often aim not only to improve something but to lessen inequality in the process: 另一个原因就是醉心于完成目标的政府必然遭遇挫折，因为在这一过程中，政府不但要有所改善，而且还要降低不平等感。addict to 对……上瘾，对……入迷。

9. A third is that the National Health Service is free to patients, and picking up the tab for those who have arguably brought their ill-health on themselves grows alarmingly costly: 第三个原因就是国家卫生机构免费接纳患者，而为那些按理说是自作自受把身体搞垮的人买单是相当昂贵的。这里 tab 是账单的意思，pick up the tab 意思是结账，结算费用。

10. The smoking ban is an example of the official excess of zeal: 作者认为这一轮的禁烟宣传又是政府发高烧的表现，批评的态度溢于言表。

11. Sign-miscreants may have to pay as much as £1,000, against £200 for a rebel smoker: 不遵守戒烟令的吸烟者将被罚款200英镑，而不贴告示的业主要被罚1000英镑。从这句

话可以看出，政府工作重点在于宣传作秀，为自己大捞政治资本，而非真正关心是否戒烟。

12. 对于政府的宣传造势，作者用 shouting，shrill，stridency 和 hectoring 等词语表示让人听起来极不舒服，但是和风细雨不能让有些人回心转意，急风暴雨就能够奏效吗？这也是作者提出的疑问。

13. It irritates the majority who are already behaving responsibly, and it may also undermine all government pronouncements on health by onvincing people that they have an ultra-cautious margin of error built in. 使人们深信给他们留了极端小心犯错的余地，这让那些令行禁止的绝大多数人感到不安，同时有损于政府的各种卫生公告。

14. ... the higher rates of ill health among those in more modest walks of life can be attributed to what he calls the "status syndrome": 生活在较低社会阶层的人健康不佳的比例较高，这是由于他所说的 "身份综合症" 造成的。attribute to 意思是 "把……归因于，认为……是由于"。例如：The eminent film star attributed her success to hard work and a little luck. 这位著名的电影演员认为她的成功来自努力工作和一点点运气。

The angry candidate attributed his failure in the presidential election to the inefficiency of his staff. 愤怒的候选人认为自己之所以在总统选举中失利是由于工作人员的不力。

Section III Speaking Up

Try to answer the following questions after you have read/heard the above passage.

1. According to the text, why does the British government have to shout ever louder in an attempt to get the public to listen?
2. What kind of people do you think tend to be addicted to smoking? And why?
3. In your opinion, what measures must be taken by the government to help the smokers stop smoking?
4. One of your close friends is a chain-smoker, try to find out some ways to help him withdraw from smoking.

Section IV Summary Writing

Write a short summary of the passage you have just read/heard.

_____
_____
_____

Unit 4
When, Where and How?

Section I Listening Comprehension

I. Listen to the following passages and then decide whether the following statements are true or false.

1. The construction work in Kuwait and Qatar will be supported by 20 people from Japan's Air Self-Defense Force arriving there in late December.
   - ○ True
   - ◉ False

2. China is trying to help find a peaceful solution to the nuclear showdown in North Korea by sponsoring the six-nation talks.
   - ◉ True
   - ○ False

3. Except the Inuit people, nobody can lay claim to the Arctic.
   - ◉ True
   - ○ False

4. China's economy will be twice the size of that of India within the next six years.
   - ○ True
   - ◉ False

5. India's economy is expected to grow at a fast pace of 8 percent in the years to come.
   - ○ True
   - ◉ False

6. The Japanese ships are sent to the Indian Ocean to provide logistical support in combat.
   - ◉ True
   - ○ False

7. The Liberal Democrats believe that people earning more than £100,000 a year should donate extra money.
   - ○ True
   - ◉ False

8. So far, Arctic has been a demilitarized, nuclear-free area devoted to science.

○ True
○ False

9. AgustaWestland is an innovative company and a market leader in making helicopters.
   ○ True
   ○ False

10. Alfred Marshall thought that businesses in Germany seized the scientific fruits from universities.
    ○ True
    ○ False

II. Choose the one answer that best fits the meaning of the statement you have heard.

1. Which of the following has the resistance force done?
   a. Toppling the American-led new Iraqi government.
   b. Killing several people holding important positions in the new Iraqi government.
   c. Re-electing their own mayor of Baghdad.
   d. Capturing several American soldiers of the occupying force.

2. How do the European countries compare with the United States in terms of spending money on education?
   a. They spend as much as the United States.
   b. They spend more than the United States.
   c. They spend 5 time less than the United States.
   d. They spend nearly as much as the U. S. government, but there is more private money going into education in the U. S. .

3. What's happened in August?
   a. Four students were killed in the bombing of the Marriott Hotel in Jakarta.
   b. Four students were deported from Jakarta.
   c. The Marriott Hotel in Jakarta was bombed by terrorists.
   d. Four students participated in the Jakarta bombing.

4. What's the reason for potential tax increases in the U. S. ?
   a. The economy is overheating.
   b. The baby boomers are reaching retirement age and making huge claims on pension.
   c. Huge federal deficits.
   d. The growing number of new-born children.

5. Two main processes that determine oil prices are _____.
   a. media accounts and oil markets
   b. economic fundamentals and irrational fears or the actions of shadowy governments
   c. consumers' fears and suppliers' political decisions

d. the forces of supply and demand and constraints on those forces created by political risk and cartel behavior

6. What did U. S. Secretary of Agriculture do last week?
   a. It banned McDonald from using meat from unhealthy cattle.
   b. It stopped the selling of meat from unhealthy cattle.
   c. It lost the trust from the public.
   d. It issued a recall of the meat from unhealthy cattle sold last month.

7. Why is it better to eat fish than to avoid it?
   a. There is still plenty of seafood that remains pure.
   b. The fish that have been contaminated are still safe to eat.
   c. Mercury in fish might not harm healthy adults.
   d. All of the above.

8. What is the best way to reduce the amount of soot?
   a. Installing exhaust filters on all trucks and buses.
   b. Better managing forest fires.
   c. Getting Americans to give up SUVs.
   d. Melting snow and ice.

9. What do we learn from this message about online gambling?
   a. It is becoming a thriving business in the U. S. .
   b. The federal government is turning a blind eye on it.
   c. It is threatening U. S. business abroad.
   d. It leads to many crimes committed in the U. S. .

10. Several big media operations in the U. S. stopped broadcasting advertisement for online gambling because _____ .
    a. they are losing money in the business
    b. they are afraid of being sued against by the government
    c. they know it is doing harm to the young children
    d. they are bankrupt

Section II Reading

Monkey's Best Friend

Anna Kuchment

Prompt: This article reports recent findings of scientists through their study of the social behaviors of animals in the wild. It is interesting in several aspects. First, it offers close-up observations of wild animals, which are beyond our sphere of life and naturally raise our curiosity. Second, the discovery seems to shed new light on the role of socializing in human society. Last, in describing the animal behavior, the author has made extensive use of the "circumstantial" elements: when, where and how, which provide an anchorage for the story she is telling.

Prudy is one of the most popular baboons in her group. When her fellow monkeys pass by, they raise their tails in deference.[1] When her fur grows dusty there's always a volunteer to give it a good grooming.[2] For eight years, she's even had that rare thing in the baboon world: a steady male companion. Rocky would carry her children on his back and accompany her on foraging expeditions through the savannah at the foot of Kenya's Mount Kilimanjaro.[3] Even though Rocky left the group in August, Prudy still has female friends and relatives she can count on.[4] In 23 years, she's given birth to 11 kids, of which eight have survived.

Viva, a female from a nearby group, is a social pariah.[5] When she approaches her fellow baboons, they often lunge at her threateningly or raise their eyebrows, flashing the pale pigment of their eyelids, to scare her off. She's also been less fortunate in childbirth. In 18 years, she delivered eight children, but only four have survived.[6]

One of the biggest clichés in psychology is that in times of crisis, women turn to friends, while men either withdraw or curse and gesticulate.[7] The male response — a manifestation of the "fight or flight" survival instinct — has been rigorously studies. A paper published last week in the journal Science now sheds some light on the female response.[8] Scientists studying baboon populations have found that the mothers who develop the most elaborate social networks tend to raise children with lower mortality rates. The findings suggest that a woman's social network is more than just a diversion: it's basic to the survival of the species.

The study focused on 108 female baboons in Kenya's Amboseli basin, who had been observed continually from 1984 to 1999. A group of scientists studied the baboons in their natural habitat,[9] living in tents and following them on foot and by[10] car from sunrise to sundown. They were struck in general by how much time female baboons spend socializing — about 10 percent of their day. "It's a very expensive activity," says one researcher. Baboons need all the time and energy they can muster to forage for food, care for their offspring and guard against predators. "The phenomenon begs the question of why evolution constructed an organism that's so sensitive to social contact," says the scientist. "Ultimately, it has to be because it affects Darwinian fitness. It affects how well you propagate your lineage."[11]

Knowing that socializing plays a role in the evolution of a species is one thing, but exactly how it works remains a mystery. The scientists have several guesses: proximity to fellow baboons is known to discourage predators, especially if a female teams up with a male. And because most of baboons socializing involve grooming — picking dirt or insects out of each other's fur — it may promote better health. (A lonely baboon will self-groom, but there are always those hard-to-reach areas, like the back and ears.)

The leading theory, though, is that socialization relieves stress.[12] Data gathered on baboons in captivity have shown that grooming reduces the animals' heart rate and promotes the release of endorphins. Human studies have also linked social ties and good health. Researchers have found a correlation between the social network of an expectant mother and the birth weight of her baby. The more support a woman receives, the more healthy her pregnancy is. Friends and family will pitch in[13] with everything from helpful advice to transportation and money for prenatal visits. But the benefits of friendship go far beyond material support. The sociologists who think about relationships use the term "social capital". And they use it in the sense of: OK, how many people in an emergency can you borrow money from or have watch your kids? How many people would you trust with keys to your house? That's a collective measure of stability, and there's an enormous literature that shows every aspect of health gets better as a result of more social capital. Scientists may need more time to nail down exactly how socializing confers an evolutionary advantage.[14] In the meantime, let's just assume that meeting friends for a drink is a biological necessity.

Words and Expressions

deference 敬意
grooming 梳理毛发
forage 觅食
savannah 大草原
Mount Kilimanjaro 乞力马扎罗山
lunge at 猛冲
pigment 颜色
gesticulate 张牙舞爪
shed light on 说明
social network 社交网络
diversion 嗜好
basin 盆地
natural habitat 自然栖息地
be struck by 对……惊讶

predators 猛兽
begs the question 靠……解释
propagate 繁衍
lineage 世系
proximity 亲近
discourage 阻止
endorphin 内分泌
correlation 相关性
expectant mother 预产妇
pitch in 出力
prenatal visit 围产期就诊
social capital 社会财富
confer 赋予

Notes

1. When her fellow monkeys pass by, they raise their tails in deference: 她的同伴猴子从她身旁走过，都将尾巴翘起以示敬意。to do sth. in deference/out of deference，表示出于敬意而做某事。

2. When her fur grows dusty there's always a volunteer to give it a good grooming: 她的毛发脏

了，总有同伴自愿为她梳理一番。猴子在一起时，常常会为同伴梳理毛发，这是猴群相互示好的一种方式。汉语里的歇后语"猴儿拿虱子——瞎掰"，就是源出于此。

3. Rocky would carry her children on his back and accompany her on foraging expeditions through the savannah at the foot of Kenya's Mount Kilimanjaro: 那个被称为"大块头"的猴子会帮她背孩子，陪她在肯尼亚乞力马扎罗山下的大草原四处觅食。乞力马扎罗山是非洲最雄奇的一座大山。海明威曾写过一片中篇小说《乞力马扎罗山的雪》，为世人所熟知。

4. Prudy still has female friends and relatives she can count on: Prudy 还有一些靠得住的雌性的亲朋挚友。Someone you can count on 是指那些可信赖的、可依赖的人。

5. Viva, a female from a nearby group, is a social pariah: 邻近的一个猴群中有个叫 Viva 的母猴，是只被遗弃，无人理睬的猴子。social pariah 原是指（在印度）生活在社会最底层的贱民。

6. In 18 years, she delivered eight children, but only four have survived: 十八年里，他生了八个儿女，只有四个活了下来。devilver 这里是指生产，也可以用 give birth to 来表示。

7. One of the biggest clichés in psychology is that in times of crisis, women turn to friends, while men either withdraw or curse and gesticulate: 心理学中人们最常说的就是遇到危难，女人会去找朋友，男人或者闷闷不乐或者高声叫骂、挥拳擦掌。这里描述女性和男性在遇到困难时的不同表现，用了 turn to friends, withdraw 和 gesticulate 等几个词和短语，值得玩味。

8. A paper published last week in the journal Science now sheds some light on the female response: 上周在《科学》杂志上刊载的一篇文章有助于我们了解女性的反应。shed some light on 表示在一片黑暗中带来些许光明，比喻能让人明白其中的奥妙。

9. A group of scientists studied the baboons in their natural habitat: 科学家研究在野外栖息地中生活的狒狒。habitat 一般指的是动物的栖息地，不过，近来也有用这个词来指人类居住环境的。例如，联合国有一个最佳人居奖的评比项目就用了这个词，彰显了天人合一的理念。

10. They were struck by…: 他们对某件事表示惊讶。

11. Ultimately, it has to be because it affects Darwinian fitness. It affects how well you propagate your lineage: 最终，这一现象肯定会影响到物种的进化，影响到后代的繁衍。这个句子里的 it 都是指猴子广泛的社交活动这一现象。说这种现象一定会影响到 Darwinian fitness，这里需要解释一下。19 世纪达尔文提出了生物进化论，其核心就是 natural selection 和 survival of the fittest，严复把这两条译作"物竞天择，适者生存"。因此，课文里所说的 Darwinian fitness 就是指达尔文生物理论中生物的进化。

12. socialization relieves stress: 社交活动可以减轻压力。

13. Friends and family will pitch in…: 朋友和家人都会加入进来帮忙。美国人喜爱棒球，pitch 是投球的意思，pitch in 是加入进来一起干的意思。

14. Scientists may need more time to nail down exactly how socializing confers an evolutionary advantage: 科学家尚需更多时间来确定社交如何带来进化上的优势。nail down 是找到确凿的证据，使之成为无可辩驳的东西。confer 是赋予、授予的意思。

Section III Speaking Up

Try to answer the following questions after you have read/heard the above passage.
1. How do you know that Prudy is one of the most popular baboons in his group?
2. How many children has the female baboon, Viva raised over the last 18 years?
3. Why is women's social network so important, according to the latest findings of scientists?
4. Baboons need all the time and energy they can muster to forage for food, care for their offspring and guard against predators so they have little time for socializing. Is that correct?
5. Do the scientists know for sure the role of socializing in the evolution of an animal species?
6. Why is it important that friends and family should provide advice and visits to a woman when she is pregnant?

Section IV Summary Writing

Write a short summary of the passage you have just read/heard.

Unit 5 Putting the Horse before the Cart

Section I Listening Comprehension

I. Listen to the following passages and then decide whether the following statements are true or false.

1. The British universities cannot maintain its educational standards without increasing tuition fees.
   - ☑ True
   - ○ False

2. The 1998 Good Friday Peace Agreement has led the city of Belfast to prosperity and peace.
   - ☑ True
   - ☑ False

3. Berlioz produced great music and his talents were appreciated by his fellow countrymen during his lifetime.
   - ○ True
   - ☑ False

4. There are questions with regard to the usefulness of the computer-based technologies for they have never been tested before.
   - ☑ True
   - ☑ False

5. Currently, the Swedes are paying a high price for its welfare system.
   - ☑ True
   - ☑ False

6. Mr. Mubarak has recently hand-picked his successor, whom he found very suitable.
   - ○ True
   - ☑ False

7. The Standard Chartered is certain that the Emirates' GDP will grow by 8% this year despite price increases in the country.
   - ○ True
   - ☑ False

8. Janos Noll distributed his translation job using web-based tools to speed up the work and in so

doing created more leisure time for himself.

○ True
☑ False

9. The new BCI device won't work because it is too slow for real-time applications.

○ True
☑ False

10. Recent scientific breakthroughs will make it easier for agriculture to focus on improving its productivity to supply more food and fiber to the world market.

○ True
☑ False

II. Choose the one answer that best fits the meaning of the statement you have heard.

1. Which of the following aspects form the basis for a new vision in agricultural research?
   a. Lessons in the past and changing American values.
   b. Increasing demand for food production.
   c. Globalization and scientific progress.
   d. All of the above except (c).

2. In engineering, and in technology-based industry, the results of creativity _____.
   a. are often intangible
   b. are difficult to identify in terms of the social and economic benefits
   c. translate into social and economic progress
   d. are often left unprotected due to lack of intellectual property arrangements

3. Which of the following statements is closest in meaning to the passage?
   a. There are very few technologies that are currently held as controversial.
   b. Critics object to genetically modified (GM) crops grown in many different countries in Europe.
   c. A main objection against GM food is that it is not naturally produced.
   d. The transportation of such crops across the Spanish borders is difficult.

4. What do we learn about maize from this short passage?
   a. It is an important crop for food supply for the people in Latin America.
   b. It contains low levels of methionine (蛋氨酸), which is good for the health of animals.
   c. Farmers have to add man-made methionine to their food in order to keep themselves healthy.
   d. Farmers use the maize they produce to feed animals.

5. Which of the following statement is true about Sony?
   a. Sony is making a new effort for more technological and marketing innovations.
   b. Its revenue and profits have improved recently.

c. Sony is trying to make friends with Microsoft, another player in this industry.

   d. Microsoft has been making computer games for the last 20 years.

6. According to the passage, what was the main cause of terrorism?

   a. A feeling of oppression, humiliation and marginalization.

   b. Islamic extremism.

   c. An explosion of violence.

   d. Poverty and despair.

7. How could the cure be worse than the disease?

   a. Human rights groups could sabotage the war on terrorism.

   b. Terrorism could infringe upon human rights.

   c. The terrorists may take revenge and harm innocent people.

   d. The government may use anti-terrorism as an excuse to arbitrarily execute people it does not like.

8. Why does Microsoft allow the users to decide the price?

   a. Some people in the poor countries can't afford the high price.

   b. Microsoft plans to fight against software piracy.

   c. Microsoft is magnanimous.

   d. Microsoft wants to make an immediate profit.

9. All units of the first batch were to be recalled due to the design flaws in _____.

   a. its color   b. its shape   c. its quality   d. all of the above

10. What's the objective of Germany?

    a. Maintaining friendly ties with France and the United States.

    b. Keeping good relations with eastern European countries.

    c. Voicing support for the United States.

    d. Keeping quiet to protect its strategic and economic interests.

Section II Reading

The End of the Oil Age

Prompt: The dependence on oil has not only dramatically changed the economic and political scenes of the world thanks to the oil embargo by the OPEC countries over the past three decades but also produced devastating impact on the natural environment. The cost is huge in both aspects. With the advance of new technology today, there is hope that new sources of energy such as hydrogen fuel cells and bioethanol can offer alternative ways of energy supply. The author discusses such possibilities and their consequences. In making his argument, the author expounds on the cause and effect relations between oil embargo and the political and economic changes, between the concentration of oil supply and the likelihood of its disruption, and between the use of renewable energy and the freedom from air pollution and from war over energy.

"The Stone age did not end for lack of stone, and the Oil Age will end long before the world runs out of oil." This intriguing prediction is often heard in energy circles these days. If greens were the only people to be expressing such thoughts, the notion might be dismissed as Utopian[1]. However, the quotation is from Sheikh Zaki Yamani, a Saudi Arabian who served as his country's oil minister three decades ago. His words are rich in irony. Sheikh Yamani first came to the world's attention during the Arab oil embargo of the United States[2], which began three decades ago and whose effects altered the course of modern economic and political history. Coming from such a source, the prediction, one assumes, can hardly be a case of wishful thinking.

Yet a generation after the embargo began, the facts seem plain: the world remains addicted to Middle Eastern oil[3]. So why is Sheikh Yamani predicting the end of the oil age? Because he believes that something fundamental has shifted since the first oil shock — and, sadly for countries like Saudi Arabia, he is quite right. Finally, advances in technology are beginning to offer a way for economies especially those of the developed world, to diversify their supplies of energy and reduce their demand for petroleum, thus loosening the grip of oil and the countries that produce it[4].

Hydrogen fuel cells and other ways of storing and distributing energy are no longer a distant dream but a foreseeable reality[5]. Switching to these new methods will not be easy, or all that cheap, especially in transport, but with the right policies it can be made both possible and economically advantageous. Unfortunately, many of the rich world's biggest oil consumers are reluctant to adopt the measures that would speed the day when the Saudi's worst fears come true.

If treating the West's addiction to oil will be costly, is it worth doing? To be sure. Petro-addiction imposes mighty costs of its own. First, there is the political risk of relying on the Organization of Petroleum Countries (OPEC). Oil still has a near-monopoly hold on transport.[6] If the supply is cut off even for a few days, modern economies come to a halt[7], as Britain discovered when tax protestors blockaded some domestic oil depots two years ago. And despite what sounds like large investments in the new oil fields in Russia and elsewhere, Saudi Arabia's share of the world oil market will actually grow over the next two decades simply because it has such huge reserves of cheap oil. Geology has granted two-thirds of the world's proven oil reserves to Saudi Arabia and four of its neighbors.[8] Because of this continuing concentration of supply, the risk of a disruption to oil flows will continue to be a threat, and may even rise.

That points to a second sort of cost. According to one American government estimate, OPEC has managed to transfer a staggering $7 trillion in wealth from American consumers to producers over the past three decades by keeping the oil price above its true market-clearing level. That estimate does not include all manner of subsidies doled out to the fossil-fuel industry, ranging from cheap access to oil on government land to the ongoing American military presence in the Middle East.

The disguised cost of oil is the damage it does to the environment and human health. Unlike power plants, which are few in number and so easier to regulate, cars are ubiquitous and much more difficult to control. The transport sector is a principal source of global emissions of green house gases.[9]

The only long-term solution to this connected set of problems is to reduce the world's reliance on oil. Achieving this once seemed pie-in-the-sky.[10] No longer. Hydrogen fuel cells are at last becoming a viable alternative. These are big batteries that run cleanly for as long as hydrogen is supplied, and which might power anything in or around your home — notably, your car. Hydrogen is a fuel that, like electricity, can be made from a variety of sources: fossil fuels such as coal and natural gas, renewables, even nuclear power. Every big car maker now has a fuel-cell program, and every big oil firm is busy investigating how best to feed these new cars their hydrogen.

Another alternative likely to become available in a few years is "bioethanol". Many cars already run on a mixture of petrol and ethanol. The problem is cost. At the moment, the ethanol has to be heavily subsidized. But that might alter when biotechnology delivers new enzymes that can make ethanol efficiently from just about any sort of plant material. Then, the only limit will be how much plant material is available.

Such changes will not occur overnight. It will take a decade or two before either fuel cells or bioethanol make a significant dent in the oil economy[11]. Still, they represent the first serious challenges to petrol in a century. If hydrogen were made from renewable energy, then the cars and power plants of the future would release no local pollution or greenhouse gases. Because bioethanol is made from plants, it merely "borrows" its carbon from the atmosphere, so cannot add to global warming. What is more, because hydrogen can be made in a geographically distributed fashion, by any producer anywhere, no OPEC cartel or would-be successor to it could ever manipulate the supplies or the price[12]. There need never be another war over energy.

Words and Expressions

intriguing 发人深省的
dismiss 不当回事
embargo 禁运
wishful thinking 异想天开
fuel cell 燃料电池
pretro-addiction 对石油的依赖
blockade 阻拦

oil depot 油库
staggering 高耸的
dole out 派送
enthanol 乙醚
dent 减少
cartel 卡特尔

Notes

1. **If greens were the only people to be expressing such thoughts, the notion might be dismissed as Utopian:** 如果只是一些环保人士这样说，人们也许会觉得这些想法都是子虚乌有。绿色已成为环境保护的代名词，这里的 greens 指的也是环境保护主义者。在欧洲还有这类人士组成的政党，赢得越来越多人的支持。他们的名字就叫 green party。Utopia 理想国，有人把它译成"乌托邦"，意思是子虚乌有的国家。Utopian 一词也就用来表示一些无厘头的想法。下文中的 wishful thinking，同样也是指一厢情愿而无法实现的想法。

2. **Sheikh Yamani first came to the world's attention during the Arab oil embargo of the United States:** Sheikh Yamani 这个人头一遭让世人瞩目，是阿拉伯国家对美国实行武器禁运。当时，他是沙特阿拉伯的石油大臣。

3. **... the world remains addicted to Middle Eastern oil:** 全世界一直都依赖中东地区的石油。addict to 通常用来形容那些对烟、酒、毒等上瘾的东西变得依赖，不能自拔。这个词还可以作名词用，指那些上了瘾的人，例如 drug addict 一词的意思就是瘾君子。

4. **... advances in technology are beginning to offer a way for economies especially those of the developed world, to diversify their supplies of energy and reduce their demand for petroleum, thus loosening the grip of oil and the countries that produce it:** 技术进步正在为各国经济提供更加多元化的能源供给和减少对石油的依赖。这样，他们可以摆脱石油和盛产石油国家的束缚。economy 原是指经济，但是这里指的是实体，即国家或者地区，汉语中被译成"经济体"，逐渐被媒体和大众接受。既然是实体，是可数的，因此用复数也就不奇怪了。loosen the grip of 中的 grip 是牢牢抓住的意思，to loosen the grip 就是挣脱，摆脱束缚的意思。

5. **Hydrogen fuel cells and other ways of storing and distributing energy are no longer a distant dream but a foreseeable reality:** 氢燃料电池和其它贮存和配送能源不再是遥不可及的梦想，而是在不远的将来可以变为现实的。这里用了 a distant dream 和 a foreseeable reality 相对应，非常工整，值得欣赏。

6. **Oil still has a near-monopoly hold on transport:** 石油还几乎垄断着运输业。这里的 hold 跟上面的 grip 一词有异曲同工之妙，都有"占有"的意思。monopoly 是垄断的意思，near-monopoly 就是近乎垄断的意思。

7. **If the supply is cut off even for a few days, modern economies come to a halt:** 即使（石油）供应被切断仅仅几天，也会阻断现代国家的经济运行。come to a halt 是突然停下的意思。

8. **Geology has granted two-thirds of the world's proven oil reserves to Saudi Arabia and four of its neighbors:** 沙特阿拉伯和四个邻国的天然地理位置，使其占有了世界探明石油储量的三分之二。这句中的动词 grant 有"赐予"、"赋予"的意思，而赐予的主体竟然是 geology "地理"，这样直译过来显然有些说不通。其实，这里 geology 是一个上位词，具体是指这些国家优越的地理位置。

9. **The transport sector is a principal source of global emissions of green house gases:** 运输业是全球排放温室气体的一个主要源头。温室效应主要是因为二氧化碳的超量排放而形成的。

10. **Achieving this once seemed pie-in-the-sky:** 以往要想做到这一点那简直是空中楼阁。pie-in-

the-sky 直译过来是"天上的馅饼",似乎与汉语中说的"天上掉馅饼"很接近,可是两者的意思却相去甚远。"天上掉馅饼"英语里与之意思相近的是 free lunch,"免费午餐"。

11. It will take a decade or two before either fuel cells or bioethanol make a significant dent in the oil economy: 还要花上十年二十年的时间,燃料电池或者生物乙醚才能让石油经济大幅衰减。

12. … no OPEC cartel or would-be successor to it could ever manipulate the supplies or the price: 石油输出国组织或者它今后的继承者都无法操控石油供给或者价格。cartel 是一种从事垄断经营的经济组织。

Section III Speaking Up

Answer the following questions after you have read/heard the above passage.

1. Did the oil embargo three decades ago produce any impact on the world economy?
2. Why are the words from Sheikh Yamani ironic?
3. What are some of the political risks of the world's dependence on oil-rich Saudi Arabia?
4. Does the author of this article think that the price for oil has been fair over the last three decades?
5. What are the best solutions to these oil-related problems?
6. What is the current problem with bioethanol?
7. What are some of the advantages of bioethanol over oil as a new form of energy?
8. OPEC has managed to transfer a staggering ＄7 trillion in wealth from…

Section IV Summary Writing

Write a short summary of the passage you have just read/heard.

Unit 6
The Other Side of the Coin

········· **Section I Listening Comprehension** ·········

I. Listen to the following passages and then decide whether the following statements are true or false.

1. Nigerians suspect that their government will not make good use of the money saved out of lifting the price cap on fuel.
   ○ True
   ○ False

2. The "war on terror" should make it absolutely necessary for global security to rely on nuclear weapons.
   ○ True
   ○ False

3. Alaska Pollock, an inexpensive whitefish, is not worth the attention of the State Department.
   ○ True
   ○ False

4. U. S. plans to reduce its military presence in Seoul due to public pressure from South Korea.
   ○ True
   ○ False

5. Space programs in Russia and America failed in the past because of shortage of funding.
   ○ True
   ○ False

6. Japan increased its tax on cigarettes in the past few years resulting in reduced sales volume.
   ○ True
   ○ False

7. Many new materials have no chance of reaching the market because it takes too long to produce commercial products.
   ○ True
   ○ False

8. Effective comprehension and thinking are based on structured representation of knowledge and meaning.
   ○ True
   ○ False

9. Scientists study the development of expertise in different areas so that their findings can help children in becoming experts in these and other areas.
   ○ True
   ○ False

10. Corruption and inflation are rampant in Nigeria's capital Abuja.
    ○ True
    ○ False

II. Choose the one answer that best fits the meaning of the statement you have heard.

1. European foreign ministers met in Naples _____.
   a. to work out the details of the EU constitution
   b. to discuss the expansion of EU to include more eastern European countries
   c. to settle the disputes between Germany and the United States
   d. to discuss issues related to climate change

2. China plans to double its gas use in the next decade _____.
   a. to bolster the sales of its natural gas
   b. to cut pollution
   c. to reduce its reliance on the imports
   d. all of the above except (a)

3. China has the greatest number of _____.
   a. fatal instances of respiratory diseases
   b. cars fueled by natural gas in the world
   c. oil companies in the region
   d. oil pipelines that feed into major cities like Beijing and Shanghai

4. The gas reserves in the far west and off the eastern and southern coasts of China _____.
   a. have been tapped for more than 50 years
   b. have an output that is falling
   c. are just beginning to be tapped
   d. are not nearly enough to provide for the nation's fuel consumption

5. Which of the following is appropriate in describing the current state in Afghanistan?
   a. Much of the country is too mountainous for aid works to visit.
   b. The country prospers on the sale of opiates in the international market.

c. Afghanistan is torn by in-fights between the warlords and it is not safe to travel.

d. The country is on the road of reconstruction and revival thanks to international aid.

6. Which of the following statements is true about Japan?

    a. It has a very short life-expectancy on average.

    b. It has the lowest infant mortality rate in the world.

    c. Young people want to have more children.

    d. The number of young people fit for work is decreasing.

7. The public pension system in Japan _____.

    a. is making huge profits

    b. is heavily in debt

    c. wants to attract more young people

    d. is affected by the nation's slow growth of the GDP

8. Investments in developing holiday resorts _____.

    a. have yielded profits for the state-run pension fund

    b. are faced with a shortfall of 6 trillion *yen* at the end of March

    c. have turned wasteland into hot properties

    d. have incurred great losses for the ministry of welfare in Japan

9. What difficulty is the national pension scheme facing?

    a. It can only attract the self-employed, farmers, fishermen and farmers.

    b. It will soon go into bankruptcy.

    c. 37% of those supposed to contribute become retired at an earlier age.

    d. Many of its contributors stopped paying for their pension schemes.

10. The new general of leaders in South Korea _____.

    a. pay more heed to their voters at home than to the U. S. government

    b. are on good terms with the government of the United States

    c. respect the veteran American soldiers who have fought in the last Korean War

    d. hate the past military dictators that ruled the country

Section II Reading

Carmakers See the Future in China

Prompt: Ten years ago, stories about China would rarely appear in major western newspapers, but now you scarcely find them without reporting on China, especially on the business pages. The text is such a news report on the burgeoning Chinese car market. It is based on interviews with top executives of the major carmakers in the global market, and that is why you find many big names here like Daimler Chrysler, General Motors and Bayerische Motoren Werke better known by its shorthand name BMW. Amid much of the euphoria, the writer also sounded a cautious note, which makes his story more balanced.

Canvass the top executives at the Frankfurt International Motor Show about what gives them hope for their industry's future, and the answer is the same: China. With their home countries currently in the doldrums and the outlook for 2004 scarcely better, the eyes of the world's automakers are fixed firmly on the Chinese market, where sales on cars and trucks are rocketing. [1]

"Growth in China is absolutely amazing," G. Richard Wagoner, the chairman of General Motors, said here Wednesday. "The Volkswagen brand sold more vehicles during the first quarter of 2003 in China than they did in Germany. Last month, GM sold more vehicles in China than we did in Germany." To understand what that means, consider that GM owns one of Germany's major car companies, Adam Opel.

Wagoner's theme was echoed by Daimler Chrysler's chief executive, Jürgen Schrempp, who increasingly regards China as the cure to what ails his trans-Atlantic colossus. [2] China is also on the mind of BMW's chairman, [3] Helmut Panke, who likened his company's foray there to its landmark decision to open an assembly plant in Spartanburg South Carolina in 1994. Automobile sales in China are growing at an annual rate of more than 50 percent, compared with about 3 percent in the United States and Europe. By 2013, Schrempp predicted, China will be the world's second-largest car market, after the United States, with 8 percent of global sales. In trucks, where it already accounts for a quarter of the worldwide demand, China will be the world's largest market within a decade.

"The auto industry certainly hopes that China will be the cavalry pouring over the hilltop, with bugle blaring,"[4] said Garel Rhys, the director of the automotive industry research institute at Cardiff university in Wales. But, he added, "The industry would be very foolish if they thought China was the answer to all their problems." Rhys said the euphoria masked a range of potential threats: a glut of foreign carmakers entering China, the lack of a genuine used-car market, the development of consumer credit in a country with debt-laden banks and the simple question of whether torrid growth in China is inevitable. "In 1976, it was confidently predicted that Brazil would be an eight-million-car-a-year market by 1996," he said. "It didn't happen."

Car manufactures look at China and see a burgeoning middle class of perhaps 400 million people, with rising incomes and a taste for consumer goods. Bayerische Motoren Werke's new assembly plant in Shenyang, in northeastern China, will be equipped to turn out 30,000 5-series sedans per year. Chinese drivers, Panke noted, tend to favor cars with the most powerful engines. He expects China to become BMW's best market for 12-cylinder engines.

Daimler Chrysler signed an agreement Monday to produce its Mercedes Benz C-class and E-class cars with a Chinese Partner, Beijing Automotive Industry Holding. Mercedes also has a thriving business in China importing its top-of-the-line S-class sedans.[5] Daimler Chrysler's investment in trucks in China may prove as important as its venture in cars.[6] It agreed to buy a stake in Beiqi Futian, a truckmaker controlled by Beijing Automotive. The venture, Cordes said, will allow Daimler Chrysler to produce a full range of commercial vehicles.

To some extent, Daimler Chrysler is playing catch-up in China, where most global carmakers already have joint ventures.[7] Volkswagen, an early entrant, controls nearly half the Chinese passenger car market. GM has a factory near Shanghai. Even Rolls-Royce has set up dealerships.

Words and Expressions

canvass 走访
in the doldrums 停滞不前
General Motors 通用汽车
Volkswagen 大众
Adam Opel 欧宝
Daimler Chrysler 戴姆勒-克莱斯勒
colossus 巨人
cavalry 骑兵
pour over the hilltop 冲上山顶
bugle 号角

blare 吹响
Cardiff 卡迪夫
euphoria 欣快症
mask 掩饰
glut 过剩
torrid 炙热的
burgeoning 萌芽的
sedan 轿车
cylinder 汽缸
venture 企业

Notes

1. With their home countries currently in the doldrums and the outlook for 2004 scarcely better, the eyes of the world's automakers are fixed firmly on the Chinese market, where sales on cars and trucks are rocketing: 世界各汽车制造厂商本国目前都困难重重，2004年的前景也不容乐观，所以他们都盯住中国市场，去年中国市场轿车和卡车的销售都在飞速增长。in the doldrums 意思是陷于困境，难有起色。用 rocketing 来形容销售，说明增长势头之猛，像火箭一样一飞冲天。

2. Wagoner's theme was echoed by Daimler Chrysler's chief executive, Jürgen Schrempp, who increasingly regards China as the cure to what ails his trans-Atlantic colossus: Wagoner 先生的这番话，同样在戴姆勒-克莱斯勒的总裁 Jürgen Schrempp 先生那里也得到了回应。他的汽车企业规模庞大，横跨大西洋，目前却疾病缠身，他越来越觉得中国是他的一剂良药。echo 本意是指回声，这里是说他响应前面的看法。文章形容戴姆勒-克莱斯勒公司是跨大西洋的巨人，却又有些病病歪歪，身体欠佳。中国的汽车市场为他提供了新的机遇，使企业健康发展。

3. China is also on the mind of BMW's chairman: BMW 的主席也在打着中国的主意。on the

mind of 是说心里想着，搁不下。

4. The auto industry certainly hopes that China will be the cavalry pouring over the hilltop, with bugle blaring: 汽车制造业当然希望中国成为一马当先、冲锋陷阵的骑兵。这里引用了一研究者形象的比喻，把中国形容成军号嘹亮、马蹄声疾、勇往直前的骑兵。下文中说这恐怕也是难以实现的事情。

5. Mercedes also has a thriving business in China importing its top-of-the-line S-class sedans: 戴姆勒-克莱斯勒旗下的梅赛德斯-奔驰还在中国进口顶级的S-级轿车，生意兴隆。a thriving business 是指生意做得很好，日渐兴隆。

6. Daimler Chrysler's investment in trucks in China may prove as important as its venture in cars: 戴姆勒-克莱斯勒在中国卡车生产方面的投资将会与它的轿车企业一样重要。英语里习惯把投资办企业称为 venture，我们通常说的合资企业就叫 joint venture，近些年在高科技领域又出现了所谓的风险投资 venture capital，大概这是因为投资兴办企业是有风险的。

7. To some extent, Daimle Chrysler is playing catch-up in China, where most global carmakers already have joint ventures: 多数全球大的汽车制造企业都已在中国建立了合资企业，从某种意义上讲，戴姆勒-克莱斯勒在中国是要奋起直追的。playing catch-up 是要补上一课，赶上别人。

Section III Speaking Up

Try to answer the following questions after you have read/heard the above passage.

1. Why do carmakers all look to China for their business growth?
2. How did the Chinese market perform during the first quarter of 2003, according to Richard Wagoner?
3. What is the current rate of growth for car sales in China?
4. Can you name some of the problems faced by China's automobile industry mentioned in this report?
5. What is Daimler Chrysler's next move in China in order to produce more commercial vehicles?

Section IV Summary Writing

Write a short summary of the passage you have just read/heard.

Unit 6 The Other Side of the Coin

_____
_____
_____
_____
_____
_____
_____

Unit 7
Lending an Ear to Numbers

Section I Listening Comprehension

I. Listen to the following passages and then decide whether the following statements are true or false.

1. The cost of parking will rise dramatically in London from next week.
   ○ True
   ○ False

2. It is estimated that if the current system is not changed, people will have to give more than half of their pay to the social security payment in 2030.
   ○ True
   ○ False

3. In France and Germany, the majority of the people are in favor of increased social protection.
   ○ True
   ○ False

4. The number of people using mobile phones in India is increasing rapidly with the total exceeding 20 million.
   ○ True
   ○ False

5. Competition in the mobile phone service has boosted profitability of the business in India.
   ○ True
   ○ False

6. Only a small fraction of the animals slaughtered in the past have been tested for possible infections because people assume that animals are safe to eat in America.
   ○ True
   ○ False

7. The new Iraqi Army suffers serious casualties in fighting against pro-Saddam elements inside the country.
   ○ True
   ○ False

8. Air France Flight 68 flew out at 7 p. m. when all the 350 passengers had boarded the plane as scheduled.
   ○ True
   ○ False
9. The earthquake in June 2002 in Iran killed more than 1,000 people there.
   ○ True
   ○ False
10. Currently, there are about two third of the world's population living in countries where water supply falls short of consumption.
    ○ True
    ○ False

II. Choose the one answer that best fits the meaning of the statement you have heard.

1. Food and fiber production have _____.
   a. been the major concern of the U. S. government of the last 50 years
   b. been more than doubled over the last half century
   c. reduced dramatically
   d. been the main source of export for U. S. agriculture
2. Belfast has benefited _____.
   a. from Jackson's investment
   b. from European Union's aid and investment
   c. from the old days of violence
   d. from the city's past
3. Northern Ireland _____.
   a. has a relatively minor problem with unemployment
   b. is enduring great economic loss at the moment
   c. is receiving more aid from EU
   d. is economically better off than the eastern European countries
4. American taxpayers pay _____.
   a. more money on R&D than their European counterparts
   b. less money on defense research
   c. more on the war against terror
   d. more on higher education
5. The Paris-based Lafarge group _____.
   a. is a world leader in car making
   b. spends very little money on research
   c. invests nearly 150 million euros a year on R&D

d. wastes a lot of its resources

6. In North America _____.

   a. consumers cut down two and half million hectares of forest each year

   b. the Forest Service spends a huge sum of money trying to repair the damage caused by consumers

   c. deforestation has caused huge amount of loss

   d. fires have caused steep loss to the forests

7. In Europe, fires _____.

   a. have resulted from a combined weather condition of drought, winds and high temperatures

   b. have destroyed the homes of at least 500,000 people

   c. have killed 500 people

   d. have created many tinderboxes

8. How does the engine adjust itself to different formulas of fuel?

   a. By piping in more oxygen for ethanol.

   b. By sensing the amount of oxygen in a car's exhaust.

   c. By burning in a less-than-optimal mode.

   d. By stopping and checking the fuel tank.

9. How did the Brazilian government encourage the use of ethanol?

   a. By planting more sugar canes.

   b. By importing more sugar from abroad.

   c. By banning the use of petrol.

   d. By cutting oil imports.

10. The market for ethanol fuel in the United States _____.

    a. is known to very few people

    b. limited due to technological problems

    c. may expand many times its present size with technological advancement

    d. is run by the National Ethanol Vehicle Coalition

Section II Reading

Sustaining Our Future

Prompt: This piece is taken from UN Secretary General Kofi Annan's Millennium Report — We, the People. Its focus is on one of the daunting tasks human kind has to face: sustainable development. The speech equates the task for sustainable development with two others written in the UN Charter *half a century ago: freedom from want and freedom from fear to highlight its importance. The author points out the dangers of environmental degradation and the urgent need for world to take up actions to save our world.*

The founders of the United Nations set out, in the words of the Charter, to promote social progress and better standards of life in larger freedom — above all, freedom from want and freedom from fear.[1] In 1945, they could not have anticipated, however, the urgent need we face today to realize yet a third: the freedom of future generations to sustain their lives on this planet. We are failing to provide that freedom. On the contrary, we have been plundering our children's future heritage to pay for environmentally unsustainable practices in the present. The natural environment performs for us, free of charge, basic services without which our species could not survive. The ozone layer screens out ultraviolet rays from the sun that harm people, animals and plants. Ecosystems help purify the air we breathe and the water we drink. They convert wastes into resources and reduce atmospheric carbon levels that would otherwise contribute to global warming. Biodiversity provides a bountiful store of medicines and food products, and it maintains genetic variety that reduces vulnerability to pests and diseases.[2] But we are degrading, and in some cases destroying, the ability of the environment to continue providing these life-sustaining services for us.

During the past hundred years, the natural environment has borne the stresses imposed by a fourfold increase in human numbers and an eighteenfold growth in world economic output.[3] With world population projected to increase to nearly 9 billion by 2050, from the current 6 billion, the potential for doing irreparable environmental harm[4] is obvious. One of two jobs worldwide — in agriculture, forestry and fisheries — depends directly on the sustainability of ecosystems. Even more important, so does the planet's health — and our own. Environmental sustainability is everybody's challenge. In the rich countries, the by-products of industrial and agribusiness production poison soils and waterways. In the developing countries, massive deforestation, harmful farming practices and uncontrolled urbanization are major causes of environmental degradation. Carbon dioxide emissions are widely believed to be a major source of global climate change, and the burning of fossil fuels is their main source. The one fifth of the world's population living in the industrialized countries accounts for nearly 60 percent of the world's total consumption of energy, but the developing world's share is rising rapidly. Our goal must be to meet the economic needs of the present without compromising the ability of the planet to provide for the needs of future generations.

We have made progress since 1972, when the United Nations convened the first global conference ever to address environmental issues. That conference stimulated the creation of environmental ministries throughout the world, established the United Nations Environment Program[5] and led to a vast increase in the number of civil society organizations promoting environmental concerns. Twenty years later, the United Nations Conference on Environment and Development provided the foundations for agreements on climate change, forests and biodiversity. It adopted an indicative policy framework intended to help achieve the goal of sustainable development — in rich and poor countries alike.

Perhaps the single most successful international environmental agreement to date has been the Montreal Protocol, in which states accepted the need to phase out the use of ozone-depleting substances. Nevertheless, we must face up to an inescapable reality: the challenges of sustainability simply overwhelm the adequacy of our responses. With some honorable exceptions, our responses are too few, too little and too late.

Words and Expressions

screen out 过滤
biodiversity 生物多样性
irreparable 不可修复的
agribusiness 农副产品加工

deforestation 森林减退
indicative 指导性的
ozone-depleting 破坏臭氧层的

Notes

1. The founders of the United Nations set out, in the words of the Charter, to promote social progress and better standards of life in larger freedom — above all, freedom from want and freedom from fear: 联合国的创立者在宪章中规定促进社会进步，提高生活水平，争取更加广泛之自由——首先是免于匮乏和免于恐惧。freedom 一词可做抽象的解释，也就是我们一般所说的"自由"，也可以做具体的解释，表示"摆脱、不受束缚"之意，如 free of charge 免费，就属于第二种。这一段里，前面提到的 freedom 可以表示抽象的"自由"，后面再次提到 freedom 是与"免于饥寒，免遭战祸"相提并论。

2. Biodiversity provides a bountiful store of medicines and food products, and it maintains genetic variety that reduces vulnerability to pests and diseases: 生物多样性提供了丰富的药物和食品，以及保持了遗传的差异从而降低遭受害虫和疾病的侵袭的可能。这里指出了生物多样性的作用，这本是一个生态学的概念，现在也逐步为人们所接受。

3. During the past hundred years, the natural environment has borne the stresses imposed by a fourfold increase in human numbers and an eighteenfold growth in world economic output. 在过去的一百年里，自然环境承受的人口增加 4 倍和经济产出增加 18 倍所带来的压力。bear the stress 意思是承受压力。同样，我们还可以说 bear the burnden 承受负担。承担责任，英语说 bear responsibility。a fourfold increase 是 4 倍的增长，后面又出现了 eighteenfold growth 那是说增加了 18 倍。

4. the potential for doing irreparable environmental harm: 造成不可挽回的环境破坏的潜在危险。irreparable 是不能修复的，不能弥补的意思。下文中提到了几个方面的问题包括 massive deforestation 大面积的森林退化，harmful farming practices 破坏性的耕作方法，

uncontrolled urbanization 失控状态下的城市发展和 carbon dioxide emissions 造成温室效应的二氧化碳排放等等，都带来了 environmental degradation 环境的破坏。我们可以从中学到这方面很有用的词语。

5. United Nations Environment Program：文章后面提到联合国对环境保护做出的贡献，包括建立环境署 UNEP，在巴西的里约热内卢召开环发会议 the United Nations Conference on Environment and Development 和发起保护臭氧层的蒙特利尔议定书 the Montreal Protocol。另一项保护环境，防治全球气候变暖的国际公约是京都议定书 Kyoto Protocol。

Section III Speaking Up

Try to answer the following questions after you have read/heard the above passage.

1. What are some of the services nature perform for us that are essential for our survival?
2. How much did the world population increase in the last 100 years?
3. What are some of the damage done to our environment?
4. What has the United Nations Conference on Environment and Development accomplished in terms of protecting our environment?
5. What is the name of the international agreement to phase out ozone-depleting substances?

Section IV Summary Writing

Write a short summary of the passage you have just read/heard.

Unit 8
Being Indirect and Probable

Section I Listening Comprehension

I. Listen to the following passages and then decide whether the following statements are true or false.

1. The speaker is certain that there will be quieter and more fuel-efficient supersonic passenger jets for long-haul flights in the future.
   ○ True
   ○ False

2. People knew that the treaty was imperfect at the time it was first conceived.
   ○ True
   ○ False

3. The speaker suggests the immigration policy should allow people from the developed world to travel in and out of the country more freely.
   ○ True
   ○ False

4. In the rich countries, immigration policy should favor people speaking the same language and having similar legal systems.
   ○ True
   ○ False

5. People from different religious and racial background would find it more difficult to be accepted by the host countries, according to what is proposed.
   ○ True
   ○ False

6. The U. S. has exported large quantities of wine in the last 10 years.
   ○ True
   ○ False

7. Norway is reluctant to join the EU at the moment and so is Iceland.
   ○ True
   ○ False

8. Sweden is a country that is very popular with immigrants.
   ○ True
   ○ False
9. It is likely that a new Iraqi government will be formed mostly by people who served under the Saddam regime.
   ○ True
   ○ False
10. Tomorrow's aircraft may employ principles of flying fundamentally different from the Wright Brothers' pioneering effort.
    ○ True
    ○ False

II. Choose the one answer that best fits the meaning of the statement you have heard.

1. What does this passage say about the C-17?
   a. It is a new generation of passenger air planes designed by Boeing.
   b. It is equipped with a missile-launching device.
   c. It is designed to dodge missiles coming in its direction.
   d. It can misguide missiles for possible attacks.
2. The American and British armies _____.
   a. have experimented with cluster bombs in the recent war in Iraq
   b. have suffered great casualties from cluster bombs used by its enemies
   c. have been the use of cluster bombs in future war fairs
   d. has been accused by the human rights group for using cluster bombs in the past
3. Progress in modern aviation _____.
   a. would make the Wright Brothers envious of the achievement
   b. has helped the colonization of western powers in past 100 years
   c. has created heavier aircrafts than those invented by the Wright Brothers
   d. would have astonished the Wright Brothers by what had happened to flying over the past hundred years, if they were still alive today
4. Which of the following statements is NOT true?
   a. A North Korean and his colleagues have found two sound-sensitive genes in rice.
   b. Plants have a sense of light.
   c. Plants have a sense of touch.
   d. Plants can taste.
5. The accepted time that hominids had been distinct from other apes started from _____.
   a. 5 billion years ago   b. 40 years ago
   c. 5 million years ago   d. 25 million years ago

6. The purpose of this passage is to _____.
   a. frighten people with the rapid melting of the Greenland ice sheet
   b. urge people to take some measures to curb the melting of the Greenland ice sheet
   c. promote people's environmental protection consciousness
   d. let people know the time the Greenland ice sheet will take to melt

7. Which of the following descriptions about mitochondria is NOT true?
   a. Mitochondria can be taken as the power plants of the cell.
   b. Mitochondria can be used to cure some diseases.
   c. Mitochondria can result in many incurable diseases.
   d. Mitochondria accelerates the course of ageing.

8. Architectural work in Californian _____.
   a. bears little resemblance to mainstream American architectural design
   b. is diversified in form
   c. is primitive compared with the work accomplished in the East Coast areas
   d. represents the future of architectural style

9. Europe's industrial base _____.
   a. has no potential for more creative development
   b. is spending large sums of money in order to keep up with the knowledge-economy
   c. is mature and robust as ever
   d. has an unproportionally large share of capital-intensive industries

10. What challenge does the European industry face?
    a. Investing in the hi-tech industries.
    b. Shifting to more innovative production.
    c. Manufacturing products.
    d. Marketing.

Section II Reading

Rethinking Protectionism

Charles Schumer and Paul Craig Roberts

Prompt: Charles Schumer is the senior senator from New York and Paul Craig Roberts was assistant secretary of the Treasury economic policy in the Reagan administration. Their article reflects some of the thinking shaping the American policy toward "off-shore" economy today. It provides examples of job loss from the United States to the developing countries. More fundamentally, it questions the validity of the long cherished notion of "*free trade*" *in a changed world in an effort to protect the American interests from being undermined by a globalized labor market.*

"I was brought up, like most Englishmen, to respect free trade not only as an economic doctrine which a rational and instructed person could not doubt but almost also a part of the moral law," wrote John Maynard Keynes[1] in 1933. And indeed, to this day, nothing gets an economist's blood boiling more quickly than a challenge to the doctrine of free trade[2]. Yet in the essay of 70 years ago, Keynes himself was beginning to question some of the assumptions supporting free trade. The question today is whether the case for free trade made two centuries ago is undermined by the changes now evident in the modern, global economy.

Two recent examples illustrate this concern. Over the next three years, a major New York securities firm plans to replace its team of 800 American software engineers, who each earns about $150,000 per year, with an equally competent team in India earning an average of only $20,000. Second, within five years the number of radiologists in the United States is expected to decline significantly because MRI data can be sent over the Internet to Asian radiologists capable of diagnosing the problem at a small fraction of the cost.[3]

These anecdotes suggest a seismic shift in the world economy brought on by three major developments.[4] First, new political stability is allowing capital and technology to flow more freely around the world. Second, strong educational systems are producing tens of millions of intelligent, motivated workers in the developing world, particularly in India and China, who are as capable as the most highly educated workers in the developed world but available to work at a tiny fraction of the cost. Last, inexpensive, high-bandwidth communications make it feasible for large work forces to be located and effectively managed anywhere.[5]

We are concerned that the United States may be entering a new economic era in which American workers will face direct global competition at almost every job level — from the machinist to the software engineer to the Wall Street analyst. Any worker whose job does not require daily face-to-face interaction is now in jeopardy of being replaced by a lower-paid, equally skilled worker thousands of miles away.[6] American jobs are being lost not to competition from foreign companies, but to multinational corporations, often with American roots, that are cutting costs by shifting operations to low-wage countries.

Most economists want to view these changes through the classic prism of "free trade[7]", and they label any challenge as protectionism. But these new developments call into question some of the key assumptions supporting the doctrine of free trade. The case for free trade is based on the British economist David Ricardo's principle of "comparative advantage" — the idea that each nation should specialize in what it does best and trade with others for other needs. If each country focused on its comparative advantage, productivity would be highest and every nation would share part of a bigger global economic pie. However, when Ricardo said that free trade would produce shared gains for all nations, he assumed that the resources used to produce goods — what he called the "factors of production" — would not be easily moved over international borders. Comparative advantage is undermined if the factors of production can relocate to wherever they are most productive[8]: in today's case, to a relatively few countries with abundant cheap labor. In this situation, there are no longer shared gains — some countries win and others lose.

When Ricardo proposed his theory in the early 1800's major factors of production — soil, climate, geography and even most workers — could not be moved to other countries. But today's vital factors of production — capital, technology and ideas — can be moved around the world at the push of a button. They are as easy to export as cars. This is a very different world than Ricardo envisioned. When American companies replace domestic employees with lower-cost foreign workers in order to sell more cheaply in home markets, it seems hard to argue that this is the way free trade is supposed to work. To call America's economic recovery "jobless" is inaccurate. Lots of new jobs are being created, just not in the United States.

In the past, we have supported free trade policies. But if the case for free trade is undermined by changes in the global economy, American policies should reflect the new reality.[9] While some economists and elected officials suggest that all America needs is a robust retraining effort for laid-off workers, we do not believe retraining alone is an answer, because almost the entire range of "knowledge jobs" can be done overseas. Likewise, we do not believe that offering tax incentives to companies that keep American jobs at home can compensate for the enormous wage differentials driving jobs offshore. America's trade agreements need to reflect the new reality. The first step is to begin an honest debate about where the American economy really is and where the United States is headed as a nation.

Old-fashioned protectionist measures are not the answer, but the new era will demand new thinking and new solutions. And one thing is certain: real and effective solutions will emerge only when economist and policy maker end the confusion between the free flow of goods and the free flow of the factors of production.

Words and Expressions

MRI data 磁共振成像数据
radiologists 放射学家
seismic 地震性的；震动的
high-bandwidth 高速宽带
in jeopardy 处于危险之中

prism 棱镜；棱柱
comparative advantage 比较优势
tax incentive 税收优惠
wage differentials 工资级差

Notes

1. John Maynard Keynes: 约翰·M·凯恩斯（1883—1946），英国著名经济学家，开创了所

谓"凯恩斯革命",对战后建立起来的布雷顿森林经济体系和创建国际货币基金组织发挥了重要作用,其著作《货币论》是西方经济学的经典。文章中提到的另一英国的著名经济学家 David Ricardo 大卫·李嘉图（1772—1823）,曾被看作是马克思经济思想的来源之一,以其地租理论和国际贸易中的比较优势的观点著称,倡导自由贸易。

2. And indeed, to this day, nothing gets an economist's blood boiling more quickly than a challenge to the doctrine of free trade: 的确,迄今为止,再也没有比对自由贸易主义的挑战更令经济学家怒火中烧的事了。

3. MRI data can be sent over the Internet to Asian radiologists capable of diagnosing the problem at a small fraction of the cost: 磁共振成像数据可以通过英特网传送给亚洲的放射学家,他们有能力作出诊断,收费也很低。

4. These anecdotes suggest a seismic shift in the world economy brought on by three major developments: 这些趣闻表明三大发展使世界经济发生了重大变化。

5. inexpensive, high-bandwidth communications make it feasible for large work forces to be located and effectively managed anywhere: 收费不高,传输迅捷的宽带通讯使得大批劳动力得到及时配置,而且无论在哪里都能得到有效管理。

6. Any worker whose job does not require daily face-to-face interaction is now in jeopardy of being replaced by a lower-paid worker: 现在,任何一位其工作不需天天与同事交往的人员,时刻都有被一位低工资的人员替代的危险。

7. Most economists want to view these changes through the classic prism of "free trade": 绝大多数经济学家想从自由贸易的这个棱镜中观察这些变化。

8. Comparative advantage is undermined if the factors of production can relocate to wherever they are most productive: 如果这些生产要素能够配置到最能发挥它们效能的地方,那么比较优势就得到了削弱。

9. In the past, we have supported free trade policies. But if the case for free trade is undermined by changes in the global economy, American policies should reflect the new reality: 我们一直支持自由贸易政策。但是,如果全球经济的变化削弱了自由贸易,美国的政策就应该反映这种新的现实。

Section III Speaking Up

Try to answer the following questions after you have read/heard the above passage.

1. Why do the authors quote Keynes at the beginning of their article?
2. What has made shifting jobs to the developing world possible?
3. What are some of the characteristics of the new economic era described by the authors?

4. How is today's world different from that of Ricardo's in terms of production?
5. What are some of the proposed solutions for the jobless problem? Do the authors think these measures are adequate?
6. What are these authors arguing against: free flow of goods or free flow of factors of production?

Section IV Summary Writing

Write a short summary of the passage you have just read/heard.

Unit 9
Speaking in Quotes

Section I Listening Comprehension

I. Listen to the following passages and then decide whether the following statements are true or false.

1. The American model is regarded as the best model of capitalism so far.
   ○ True
   ○ False

2. Fisheries can make great benefits from catching seabirds.
   ○ True
   ○ False

3. Gordon Brown, the newly elected Prime Minister is working hard to promote Britain as world-class in education.
   ○ True
   ○ False

4. Paul Bremer is certain that American-style democracy will come to rule Iraq but there will be many difficulties to overcome on road to the democratic rule.
   ○ True
   ○ False

5. Bremer is concerned about the violence against and the public opposition to American occupation in Iraq.
   ○ True
   ○ False

6. More and more people are suffering from atherosclerosis usually named hardening of the arteries, but there is hardly anything one can do about it.
   ○ True
   ○ False

7. An unhealthy lifestyle, which may lead to disorders of the blood fats, development of diabetes or pre-diabetes, and the onset or aggravation of high blood pressure, can increase the chances of atherosclerosis.

○ True

○ False

8. Foreign policy analysts advocate increasing imports of oil from the politically unstable oil-producing regions.

○ True

○ False

9. The U. S. forces will stay in Iraq whether the Iraqis ask them to leave the country or not.

○ True

○ False

10. Violence over the next six months will increase despite the successful military operations that had been achieved so far, according to Bremer.

○ True

○ False

II. Choose the one answer that best fits the meaning of the statement you have heard.

1. What happened at around 1:30 p. m. ?

   a. A furniture truck caught fire and exploded.

   b. The airborne division bombed a furniture truck near its headquarters.

   c. A suicide bomber was found driving a truck in the vicinity of Ramadi.

   d. A bomb from a truck went off.

2. The report on the explosion _____.

   a. confirmed the death of three people in the explosion

   b. described who the bombers might be

   c. stated tentatively that three bombers were killed

   d. was not quite sure how many people there were in the truck

3. The state news media _____.

   a. appealed for calm after the incident

   b. appealed for blood donations

   c. appealed for help to dig up the wounded

   d. declared that many people died in the explosion

4. The proportion of under-fives who were underweight in 2005 was _____.

   a. 46%   b. 41%   c. 33%   d. 29%

5. Which statement is true about Malta's immigrant population?

   a. It has a large immigrant population.

   b. Its immigrant population is more than 3,000.

   c. Its immigrant population totals 7,000.

   d. Its immigrant population comes to less than 1% of the island's 400,000 population.

6. China's demand for more energy _____.
   a. will exacerbate the shortage of supply worldwide
   b. will make it difficult for oil-exporting countries to cope with
   c. will yield more profits for oil exporters
   d. will create more jobs in the developing countries
7. European heads of governments declared _____.
   a. to improve their social welfare
   b. to boost R&D
   c. to make more investment in hi-tech industries
   d. to upgrade their age-old industries
8. According to economists, _____.
   a. Japan's pension system is in bad shape
   b. Japanese people are spending less than they used to
   c. Japanese economy is in a glut, which hurts consumer spending
   d. Japan's GDP growth is about half the pace of that five years ago
9. Japan's economy _____.
   a. has experienced a series of recesses in a decade
   b. has been expanding for the past six months
   c. is growing at a rate of 0.1 percent in recent months
   d. is continuing to decline
10. What does the report say about the job market in Japan?
    a. Sales growth in the overseas market has helped to stop job cuts in big companies like Sony.
    b. Japan lost 210,000 jobs in November.
    c. The unemployment rate at the moment of speaking is close to its record high.
    d. 190,000 people gave up hope of finding a new job.

Section II Reading

Light heavy lifters

Prompt: Nanotechnology is one of the frontiers of contemporary science and progress is being made almost daily. The text reports on the latest development of research in this fascinating area. It describes how scientists have found ways to manipulate the movements of tiny matters and make them do useful work. The way the author presents these findings also shows that hi-tech need not be unfathomably difficult to understand. Science can be fun and with a touch of humor.

Nanotubes of various sorts may provide the building blocks of the brave new world of nanotechnology that the field's true believers envisage developing over the next few years.[1] Such believers think that it will be possible to build complicated "nanoscale" devices (ie, mechanisms whose components have dimensions measured in nanometers, or billionths of a meter). But if such machines are to be built, something will be needed to put those components together. Fortunately, the believers have an answer to this puzzle. They envisage the heavy lifting (or rather the light lifting) being done by modified versions of natural molecules called motor proteins. These proteins are what give muscles their pulling power, make sperm strong swimmers and even drag the chromosomes in a dividing cell out of each other's way.

Motor proteins work by pairing up with other tiny structures called microtubules, just as the teeth of a gear fit into a bicycle chain[2]. By fixing tubules to a glass sheet, or similar substrate, it is possible to get the motors to "walk" along them. Alternatively, fixing the motors to the substrate causes them to pass the tubules overhead, rather like a conveyor belt.

This sounds promising, but until recently there was no way to vary the direction of movement, or to load and unload the stuff being transported. However, work published over the past few months show that progress toward a nanoscale construction site is slowly being made.

The first breakthrough was by Richard Superfine, of the University of North Carolina at Chapel Hill, and his colleagues. They have devised a way to direct the flow of microtubules. The motor proteins and tubules are deposited on to a glass substrate which has two wires on it. Arranged as a cross. When the electricity is passed through the wires, the motors pile the tubules up wherever the electric field is strongest. The tubules also align themselves with the direction of the filed. This suggests it will be possible to move and direct tubules using a mesh of wires. By switching the current in different wires on and off to produce stronger and weaker electric fields in particular places.

Natural motor proteins, unfortunately, are often temperamental. In particular, they dislike excessive heat. That problem has been overcome by Bruce Bunker, at Sandia National Laboratories in Albuquerque, New Mexico. Dr. Bunker and his colleagues have extracted a heat-tolerant motor protein from fungus which lives in high-temperature environments. Indeed, this protein not merely tolerates high temperatures, but positively thrives in them. It passes microtubules along almost ten times faster at 45℃ than it does at 20℃. That provides a means of controlling the speed of motor-protein conveyor belts, simply by varying the temperature.

But being able to direct the flow of microtubules is not much use unless they can deliver a useful payload[3]. To this end, Jonathon Howard and his colleagues at the Max Planck Institute of Molecular Cell Biology and Genetics in Dresden, Germany, have worked out how tubules can be used to transport, position and stretch strands of DNA. Tubules and DNA strands are mixed together in solution, and biochemical processes are then used to attach one end of each DNA strand to a tubule, and the other end to a class sheet[4]. By positioning the tubules in particular ways, it is possible to arrange the DNA strands precisely. These strands can be used as templates to lay down other materials or can be chemically modified to give them useful electrical properties.

Finally, there is the question of fixing nanoscale components together so that they can form actual machines. Dr. Howard, together with Henry Hess, of the University of Washington, in Seattle, has devised a way to transfer tiny plastic beads from a moving microtubule to a fixed one. He does this by crashing the first tubule into the second, bending the latter double, and causing it to bond with the bead. The first tubule then continues on its way. Plastic beads are commonly used in nanotechnology research to carry substances around on their surfaces, so this approach could be employed to deliver specific materials to particular places when needed.[5]

Collectively, these results demonstrate that researchers are inching (or, perhaps nanometering) towards general-purpose nanoscale construction techniques.[6] Nanotechnology, after all, is a field where progress is measured in tiny steps.

Words and Expressions

nanotube 纳米管
building block 砌块
nanoscale 纳米秤
nanometer 毫微米
motor protein 运动蛋白
chromosome 染色体
microtubule 微管
gear 齿轮

a conveyor belt 传送带
deposite 放置
align 对准；使成一直线
temperamental 性能不稳定的
fungus 真菌
payload 载荷
strand 纤维；丝状体
template 模板

Notes

1. Nanotubes of various sorts may provide the building blocks of the brave new world of nanotechnology that the field's true believers envisage developing over the next few years: 相信纳米技术的人预计，在随后的几年中，随着纳米技术的发展，各种纳米管将可能为建筑业提供纳米建筑材料。
2. Motor proteins work by pairing up with other tiny structures called microtubules, just as the teeth of a gear fit into a bicycle chain: 运动蛋白与叫做微管的微小结构协调工作，就如同自行车的轮齿与链条咬合在一起工作一样。
3. But being able to direct the flow of microtubules is not much use unless they can deliver a useful payload: 但是能够引导微管的流动并无太大的意义，他们必须还能运载有效载荷。
4. Tubules and DNA strands are mixed together in solution, and biochemical processes are then used to attach one end of each DNA strand to a tubule, and the other end to a class sheet: 将纳米管和DNA束一同放到溶液里，然后采用生化工艺将每束DNA的一端同纳米管相联

接，将另一端连接到一玻璃片上。

5. Plastic beads are commonly used in nanotechnology research to carry substances around on their surfaces, so this approach could be employed to deliver specific materials to particular places when needed: 纳米技术研究中，通常使用塑料珠，通过其表面来运送物料。因此，可以用这种方法将所需要的材料运送到指定的地点去。

6. Collectively, these results demonstrate that researchers are inching towards general-purpose nanoscale construction techniques: 总的来说，这些结果表明研究人员正在朝着建造多用途纳米秤的技术缓慢地逼近。

Section III Speaking Up

Try to answer the following questions after you have read/heard the above passage.

1. What will be needed to put those components together if the complicated "nanoscale" devices are to be built?
2. How do motor proteins work?
3. How was the first breakthrough made by Richard Superfine, of the University of North Carolina at Chapel Hill, and his colleagues?
4. Do natural proteins like excessive heat?
5. What was the way devised by scientists to direct the flow of microtubules?
6. Is nanotechnology a field where progress is measured in great steps?

Section IV Summary Writing

Write a short summary of the passage you have just read/heard.

Unit 10

Speech Acts

Section I Listening Comprehension

I. Listen to the following passages and then decide whether the following statements are true or false.

1. European and Japanese regulators do not wish to tell the public about their fast screening methods for sick animals.
   ○ True
   ○ False

2. Homeland Security required all passengers boarding civilian planes be questioned for possible terrorist acts.
   ○ True
   ○ False

3. It is suggested that people who gives up firing missiles at civilian airplanes should be awarded.
   ○ True
   ○ False

4. In the aftermath of the earthquake, international aid soon came to the rescue at Tehran's request.
   ○ True
   ○ False

5. Only by using a large amount of medications prescribed by doctors can one avoid the risk of atherosclerosis and its complications.
   ○ True
   ○ False

6. Britons believe that higher education is a human right and governments should not charge higher fees.
   ○ True
   ○ False

7. In UK, a college graduate earns an average of 25,000 to 30,000 pounds a year.
   ○ True

○ False

8. Scientists now have a better knowledge of learning complex skills.
   ○ True
   ○ False

9. It is more interesting to study the learning behavior of young children than those of adults.
   ○ True
   ○ False

10. The voluntary fund is likely to go busted.
    ○ True
    ○ False

II. Choose the one answer that best fits the meaning of the statement you have heard.

1. How did Iran respond to the proposed U. S. aid?
   a. It was accepted with doubts.
   b. It arose mixed feelings in some.
   c. It triggered off more debate inside the country.
   d. It fell on deaf ears.

2. Was there a unanimous opinion on the U. S. aid?
   a. Hard-liners made a turn in their hostile attitude toward the U. S. .
   b. Public opinion remained divided over the issue.
   c. The reformists are more worried this time around.
   d. It is widely held that the aid offers a chance for ending Iran's international isolation.

3. How was George Bush viewed by the Iranians?
   a. The hard-liners wanted to wage a war against him.
   b. The reform-minded Iranians expressed appreciation of his generous act.
   c. There was across-the-board antagonism towards the president's demand.
   d. He was a controversial topic for the upcoming election.

4. Iran rejected an offer from Washington _____.
   a. to inspect its human rights violation
   b. to inspect its nuclear facilities
   c. to assess the environmental impact of the earthquake
   d. to assess the need for more humanitarian aid

5. Washington confirmed _____.
   a. that it would send a team out to Iran to assess the conditions in Bam
   b. that Iran declined the offer of a U. S. visit to Bam
   c. that Tehran closed the door in the U. S. face
   d. that there is hope for a U. S. team to visit the quake-hit areas in the future

6. Which of the following would the U. S. aid include?

    a. Aid workers to staff a hospital in Bam and more private donations.

    b. Surveying the quake's damage to the ancient city.

    c. Continued economic sanctions.

    d. All of the above except (c).

7. Japan and South Korea _____.

    a. export beef to the United States and other countries in the world

    b. stopped importing beef from the United States this year

    c. were the only countries that imported beef from the U. S. in the past

    d. accounted for most of the beef imported from Australia

8. The Recording Industry Association of America _____.

    a. persuaded people to download its music from the Internet

    b. is trying to stop people steeling their music stored in the computer

    c. started suing people playing their music to the public

    d. has taken effective measures to dissuade people downloading music from the Internet

9. The percentage of people downloading music _____.

    a. has dropped dramatically over a period of six months, the survey found

    b. has increased between May and November

    c. has remained the same for the two surveys

    d. is difficult to know after law suits against allegations of file trading

10. The legal actions have _____.

    a. created more downloaders of music from home computers

    b. changed people's attitude toward intellectual property rights

    c. been effective in curbing legal downloading and trading of music

    d. no effect whatsoever

Section II Reading

Justice Takes its time for an Innocent Man

Bob Herbert

Prompt: It is said that there are two things that can help understand how people act in a modern society: economics and law. We have read about economics and now we turn to legal matters in this text. It is about how justice, or rather injustice, was done in the United States. It is sad that the black young man Darryl Hunt was wrongly charged and had to spend nineteen years before he was acquitted. The story brings us into the process of U.S. legal system and offers a number of legal terms frequently used.

Darryl Hunt heard the door to his prison cell open. He looked up and saw a warden. "You need to pack your stuff," the warden said. "You're being released in a few minutes." It was Christmas Eve. After 19 years, two murder convictions, a number of attempts on his life, and some of the deepest disappointments he could ever have imagined, Hunt, once a free-spirited youngster and now a soft-spoken, deeply religious man, was finally being allowed to walk out of prison.[1] DNA had come to his rescue.[2]

Nearly two decades ago, on the morning of August 10, 1984, a 25-year-old white woman named Deborah Sykes was attacked on her way to work in downtown Winston-Salem of North Carolina. The assailant was a black man, and the crime was incredibly violent. Sykes was beaten, raped, sodomized and stabbed 16 times. Her body was found sprawled on the grass in a small, rundown park.

It was a sensational local story, and the racial angle was pushed to the max.[3] A great deal was made of the fact that Sykes was not just white, but tall and good-looking as well. A former Ku Klux Klansman reported seeing her with a black man in the moments before the attack, but said he hadn't realized the woman was in trouble. When he learned what had happened, he wept. Winston-Salem was in an uproar. A black man had to be found.

The first candidate was named Terry Thomas. He was identified by an alleged eyewitness. A murder warrant was ordered and a celebratory press announcement was readied. The authorities had their man. Except for one thing. Terry Thomas couldn't have done it. He was in jail when Deborah Sykes was murdered. So the search resumed. And the events that followed were clear manifestations of the cancers that have been allowed to spread throughout the criminal justice system in the United States.[4] The Hunt case is a tragic, two-decade study of incompetence, misconduct and racism by law enforcement officials at every level, up to and including the judiciary.[5]

After Terry Thomas, Darryl Hunt became a suspect. He didn't fit the initial descriptions given to the police or look like the composite drawings being circulated. But he was 19 and black, which was enough. The former Klansman — who was mentally disturbed and was paid a reward for his information — said yes, indeed, Hunt was the man he had seen with Sykes. And the alleged eyewitness who had fingered Terry Thomas with such certainty now claimed to be equally certain about Darryl Hunt.

Hunt said he was innocent. There was no physical evidence of any kind linking him to the crime. And there were no reliable witnesses. But Hunt was charged, and the state sought the death penalty. Prosecutors told the jury that Hunt, and Hunt alone, had attacked, raped and killed Sykes. He was convicted in June 1985. But the jury, unsure of what had really happened, refused to impose the death penalty. Hunt was sentenced to life in prison. Errors by the prosecution led to a new trial in 1990. This time the prosecution's story changed. Hunt had accomplices, prosecutors said — at least one, maybe two. (The alleged accomplices were never tried.) Hunt was convicted again, and again sentenced to life.

By the early 1990's it had become possible to do reliable DNA tests on the semen collected from Sykes's body. Hunt was eager to have the semen analyzed. The state was not. A judge ordered the tests, which showed that the semen could not have come from Hunt — or from the two alleged accomplices. Incredibly, that didn't matter. The judge refused to order a new trial. There was obviously a fourth man, the judge said, and he may have been an accomplice of Hunt's as well. The state liked that idea, and adopted it as its own. Another, even weirder idea was advanced by a federal magistrate who reviewed the case.[6] He said he couldn't exclude the possibility that "an alleged sexual pervert" had deposited the sperm after Sykes had been killed.

Finally, last year, an extraordinary sequence of events forced the truth into the open.[7] In response to motions by Hunt's lawyers, a judge ordered the state to compare the DNA evidence with genetic profiles of state prisoners compiled in a DNA database. In November, the Winston-Salem Journal started an eight-part series that detailed the mistakes, the unreliable witnesses, the official misconduct, the DNA evidence and many other aspects of the case. With pressure growing, a new generation of investigators ran a broad check of the DNA. Lo and behold, the check led them to a man named Willard Brown whose DNA matched that of semen taken from Sykes. On Dec. 23, Brown was arrested and charged with kidnapping, rape, armed robbery and murder.

Words and Expressions

warden 监狱长
assailant 袭击者
sodomize 鸡奸
sprawl 四肢伸开躺着
rundown 破败的；失修的
warrant 逮捕令
misconduct 滥用职权
composite drawing 综合画像（根据见证

人的描述而绘成）
accomplice 共犯；共同犯罪者
semen 精液；精子
magistrate 执法官
pervert 性变态者
genetic profile 基因图
Lo and behold 你瞧；真怪

Notes

1. … Hunt, once a free-spirited youngster and now a soft-spoken, deeply religious man, was finally being allowed to walk out of prison: Hunt，一位从前无拘无束而今却说话温和，虔诚十足的人，最终获准走出了监狱。
2. DNA had come to his rescue: DNA 是 "deoxyribonucleic acid" 的缩写，脱氧核糖核酸-基因讯息的载体。to sb.'s rescue 意思是 "营救某人"。文中指 DNA 帮他洗脱了罪名。
3. It was a sensational local story, and the racial angle was pushed to the max: to the max 指最大程度的。文中指这件轰动一时的惨案激起了人们的种族情绪。
4. And the events that followed were clear manifestations of the cancers that have been allowed to

spread throughout the criminal justice system in the United States: 美国刑事司法体制中普遍存在的弊端在随后发生的事件中暴露无疑。

5. The Hunt case is a tragic, two-decade study of incompetence, misconduct and racism by law enforcement officials at every level, up to and including the judiciary: 亨特一案是地地道道的悲剧，调查耗时20年，期间充斥着下至警察上至法官各级执法人员的无能、滥用职权、和种族歧视。

6. Another, even weirder idea was advanced by a federal magistrate who reviewed the case: 复审这一案件的联邦执法官提出了一个更加荒诞的假设。

7. Finally, last year, an extraordinary sequence of events forced the truth into the open: force... into the open 意思是"揭露；把……公开"。本文指一连串的惊人事件终于使事实真相大白于天下。

Section III Speaking Up

Try to answer the following question after you have read/heard the above passage.

1. What had come to Hunt's rescue?
2. Why couldn't Terry Thomas have done the murder?
3. What made Darryl Hunt become a suspect?
4. Why was Hunt eager to have the semen analyzed?
5. Do you think the Hunt case is tragic? And why or why not?

Section IV Summary Writing

Write a short summary of the passage you have just read/heard.

Unit 11
Traveling to Other Lands

Section I Listening Comprehension

I. Listen to the following passages and then decide whether the following statements are true or false.

1. According to the "road map" peace plan, the formation of an independent Palestinian state should happen by the end of next year.
   ○ True
   ○ False
2. Natural systems can reduce the amount of carbon dioxide in the atmosphere caused by carbon emissions.
   ○ True
   ○ False
3. According to Mr. Trichet, a translator writing in the *Financial Times*, the word "brutal" means "sudden", not "cruel" or "vicious".
   ○ True
   ○ False
4. The French economy was quite strong and the French were even outpacing their American rivals for a time in the spring.
   ○ True
   ○ False
5. The euro area's finance ministers have called on the ECB to do something about the euro's rise.
   ○ True
   ○ False
6. Interest rates are currently rising in America.
   ○ True
   ○ False
7. The European Parliament is considering the easing of rules for innovations incorporated in software which might have some bad effects as business-method patents.
   ○ True
   ○ False

8. The new generation of drugs stop tumours and kill all rapidly proliferating cells, but they also cause side effects.
   ○ True
   ○ False

9. One reason for this process of diminution is the restriction of food supply caused by large predators.
   ○ True
   ○ False

10. A number of 6 million people around the planet died from cancer in 2000.
    ○ True
    ○ False

II. Choose the one answer that best fits the meaning of the statement you have heard.

1. Porsena's was _____.
   a. one of the biggest tombs of the lot
   b. a big tomb consisting of ten pyramids
   c. a monument with a square base whose sides were 19 metres long and 15 metres high
   d. a monument of rectangular masonry

2. Which of the following statements is closest in meaning to what was said above?
   a. Evolutionary biologists believe that boys are more likely to die at a given age than their female contemporaries.
   b. It is believed that the sex ratio is unbalanced at the age when people are reproducing.
   c. In Britain, as well as in the United States and Canada, the proportion of boys being born is growing.
   d. All over the world, more boys are born than girls, which is due to chemical pollutants that are mimicking the effects of sex hormones.

3. Which of the following statements is closest in meaning to what was said above?
   a. Counterfeiting has led to the drop of the price of desktop-publishing systems.
   b. Counterfeiting has gone mainstream since the price of desktop-publishing systems has dropped.
   c. Skilled crooks have led to the drop of the price of desktop-publishing systems.
   d. 14% of the counterfeits seized this year were digitally produced, compared with 1% a decade ago.

4. Which of the following statements is NOT true?
   a. In some countries patent applications are public after 18 months.
   b. In the United States, patent applications are normally kept from the public.
   c. Patent offices need to collect and publish data about what happens once patents are granted.
   d. More openness would help to measure the quality of the patent system.

5. The video security systems _____.
   a. play an important role in arresting terrorists before they take action
   b. have cost the U. S. Department of Homeland Security more than $40 million so far
   c. are mainly deployed near Washington
   d. work better than they have been expected to
6. What concerns have been raised along with the use of modern biotechnology in agriculture?
   a. The environmental and human health consequences of transgenic products.
   b. The price potentials of transgenic products in agriculture.
   c. The medical costs of the people consuming transgenic products.
   d. The risks involved in the distribution of transgenic products in agriculture.
7. Why did Federal agents arrest a Florida man?
   a. Because he registered an illegal Internet domain name.
   b. Because he registered a pornographic website.
   c. Because he lured kids to web porn.
   d. Because the Internet domain names are misspelled.
8. Which of the following statements is closest in meaning to what was said above?
   a. NASA launched Compton Gammaray Observatory early Monday.
   b. NASA has launched three observatories so far.
   c. The space-based observatory will see objects that previously have been undetectable.
   d. The observatory's mission is expected to last four to five years.
9. According to a report in the online version of the journal *Science*, _____.
   a. coral reefs in the Caribbean have declined by 80 percent in the last ten years
   b. coral cover in the region has fallen by 40 percent
   c. coral reefs in the Caribbean have declined to 30 percent
   d. the decline rate of coral cover equals rates of tropical forest loss
10. Which of the following statements is true according to what was said above?
    a. The dollar rose to a new high against the euro.
    b. The American economy has rebounded.
    c. Japan's economy has not bottomed out yet.
    d. The performance of many economies in Latin America is less than expected.

Section II Reading

Budapest's Pride of Palace[1]

Prompt: This is a report on the newly renovated Gresham Palace in Budapest, which has stood by the side of the Danube for nearly a hundred years and has witnessed social changes of the last century. The rebirth of this marvelous piece of architecture is not without diffculty but, in spite of that, its completion serves as a model for the restoration of other historic cites in Eastern Europe.

It was a fixer-upper, to put it mildly. The 1907 Gresham Palace, one of the most treasured landmarks in Hungary, has reopened as a luxury hotel after severe construction delays and cost overruns. It stands as a model, of sorts, for the restoration of other historic properties in Eastern Europe, from the palaces of Prague to those in St. Petersburg[2].

With its peacock-adorned iron gate, a façade flecked with Venetian glass mosaics, textured tiles and stunning views of the Danube, the Art Nouveu hotel, which began receiving guests in June, is an example of what perseverance and deep pockets can achieve. It is also a monument to the difficulty of breathing life into the half-ruined historic properties dotting the landscape of Eastern Europe[3].

When it opened nearly 100 years ago, six stories high and stretching over an entire city block, the Gresham's amenities included electric lights, mahogany elevators and a central vacuuming system. Its electric iron gates sank into the ground when carriages pulled into the Gresham's interior arcade, discharging visitors onto a new type of pavement called asphalt.

The city was booming then, serving alongside Vienna as a capital of the Austro-Hungarian Empire.[4] The palace was built for the Gresham Life Assurance Society, a British company bent on conquering a new market and leaving no doubt about its cash reserves. A Hungarian architect, Zsigmond Quittner, pulled out all the stops, incorporating offices, a coffeehouse and 18 sprawling apartments with high ceilings, silk wallpaper, parquet floors and servants' quarters. The vaulted arcade — lined with shops and capped with a dome — was covered with 20,000 grooved glass tiles based on a design by Frank Lloyd Wright.

"The Gresham is a symbol of gone-by splendor," said Andras Torok, an authority on Budapest's culture and history. "It always reminded us of what a wonderful place this city really is."

The vaulted arcade — lined with shops and capped with a dome — was covered with 20,000 grooved glass tiles based on a design by Frank Lloyd Wright[5].

By the late 1940s the Gresham was a hodgepodge of offices and dreary communal apartments. And though named a national landmark in 1976, it kept crumbling. Soon many of the mosaics dropped off the façade, gathering in clumps on drooping balconies, some of which were sprouting trees. The arcade, dark, filthy and reeking of urine, was being used as a backdrop for music videos.

Turning all this into a historically correct contemporary hotel proved a challenge for Bela Fejer, the man credited with the Gresham's renaissance[6]. Fejer, a lawyer and developer whose company, Gresco, paid about $20 million for the property at the end of 1999, then struck a deal with investors and the Four Seasons hotel chain to bring the palace back to life[7].

Fejer escaped Budapest in 1956, when he was 12, to settle in Toronto, and returned in 1989 as a developer of office buildings. His son, Patrick, an architect who helped build the Staples Center in Los Angeles, signed on as head of design for the Gresham, overseeing a team of architects. The original budget was about $120 million, and when work began in late 2000, completion was expected within two years.

The project had already experienced delays, including a three-year standoff with the tenants of the upstairs apartments, who did not want to move. In the somewhat murky and perpetually shifting business climate of the post-Soviet era, there were protests that a national landmark was being sold to Westerners, and charges that the prime minister, Petere Medgyessay, a former banker and a paid consultant on the project, had benefited personally from the sale.

Nevertheless, the developers moved forward with an ambitious plan. Along with restoring the building to its original grandeur, it called for 179 guest rooms (including a $3,000-a-night suite), 14 elevators, two restaurants, a spa and an air-conditioning system that circulates only fresh air. Then there was the heavy lifting: workers had to replace the back wall and raise the roof.

All this came at a price. Logistical problems and squabbles among the various players and subcontractors pushed the completion date back — and back again. Though precise figures are hard to come by, last October the developers said the bottom line land climbed to more than $140 million. And that was before four more months of unanticipated work. The entire project took close to six years.

The timing of the opening could be better for the owners. The city has a glut of luxury hotels in historic buildings. Workers are finishing up the renovation of another early-20th-century confection, the New York Palace, which is famous for its ornate coffee-house and will open as a Boscolo hotel next year. Another five-star hotel is planned in the former Ballet Institute.

Julian Carminero, a former manager of the George V in Paris and now the general manager of the Gresham, is confident that "the charisma and flow of history" in his hotel is unrivaled[8], "I don't want to be unfair to the competition," he added, "but rarely do hotels offer this".

Words and Expressions

fixer-upper 年久失修的建筑
facade （尤指宏伟建筑的）正面
flecked with 点缀着
Venetian glass 威尼斯玻璃
Art Noveau 新艺术派风格
Danube 多瑙河
amenities 便利设施
mahogany 红木
parquet floor 镶木地板
grooved glass tiles 沟槽状的玻璃瓦

hodgepodge 混杂；拼凑
crumble 破碎；瓦解
reek 发臭
murky 黑暗；阴沉
grandeur 富丽堂皇
subcontractor 分包商
a glut of 大量的；许多的
ornate 装饰华丽的
charisma 魅力

Notes

1. Budapest's pride of palace: 布达佩斯的骄傲——格雷舍姆宫，这篇文章题目借用了一个英语中的成语 pride of place, 意思是"值得骄傲的地方"。作者将 place 换成了 palace。

2. It stands as a model, of sorts, for the restoration of other historic properties in Eastern Europe, from the palaces of Prague to those in St. Petersburg: 格雷舍姆宫的修复堪称为修葺从布拉格的宫殿到圣彼得堡王宫等东欧历史建筑做出了榜样。

3. It is also a monument to the difficulty of breathing life into the half-ruined historic properties dotting the landscape of Deastern Europe: 格雷舍姆宫的修复也彰显出恢复那些凋敝的著名历史建筑物生机之难，这样的建筑遍布东欧，构成了那里一道道的风景。

4. The city was booming then, serving alongside Vienna as a capital of the Austro-Hungarian Empire: 那时，布达佩斯这座城市与维也纳一样也是奥匈帝国的首都，十分繁荣。

5. The vaulted arcade — lined with shops and capped with a dome — was covered with 20,000 grooved glass tiles based on a design by Frank Lloyd Wright: 这一拱廊是按照美国的建筑师弗兰克·劳埃德·怀特的方案建造的，两旁商店林立，顶部建有一个穹顶，上面覆盖着两万片带有沟槽的琉璃瓦。

6. Turning all this into a historically correct contemporary hotel proved a challenge for Bela Fejer, the man credited with the Gresham's renaissance: 对于承担修复格雷舍姆宫工程的贝洛·费耶尔来说，要把这个宫殿建成既符合历史又富有时代气息的宾馆的确是一大挑战。

7. Fejer, a lawyer and developer whose company, Gresco, paid about $20 million for the property at the end of 1999, then struck a deal with investors and the Four Seasons hotel chain to bring the palace back to life: 费耶尔是一名律师兼开发商，他的格雷斯科公司1999年底花了2000万美元将格雷舍姆宫买下，然后同四季饭店连锁签下合同，使其恢复原貌。

8. Julian Carminero, a former manager of the George V in Paris and now the general manager of the Gresham, is confident that "the charisma and flow of history" in his hotel is unrivaled: 朱利安·卡尔米内洛这位巴黎乔治五世酒店的前任经理，现任格雷舍姆宫酒店总经理，为酒店无与伦比的妩媚动人与源远流长而踌躇满志。

Section III Speaking Up

Try to answer the following questions after you have read/heard the above passage.

1. What is the name of the building that has reopened as a luxury hotel in Budapest?
2. When did the Art Nouveu hotel begin receiving guests?
3. Why is the Gresham Palace regarded as a symbol of gone-by splendor by experts?
4. What did Bela Fejer do before he returned to Budapest for the renovation of the palace?
5. What was the original budget for the restoration of the Gresham?

6. How long did it take to finish the entire project of the Gresham?
7. Why is Julian Carminero, the general manager of the Gresham, so proud of his hotel?

Section IV Summary Writing

Write a short summary of the passage you have just read/heard.

Unit 12

The Flowers

Section I Listening Comprehension

I. Listen to the following passages and then decide whether the following statements are true or false.

1. It is dangerous for people to live on the Earth if CO_2 concentrations continue to rise.
   - ○ True
   - ○ False

2. The collection industry is losing money because of stricter federal and state regulations on their practices.
   - ○ True
   - ○ False

3. According to figures released on Friday, the 12-nation block grew at an annual pace of just 1.2% in the first quarter.
   - ○ True
   - ○ False

4. The uninsured in inner and suburbia don't need to pay for the treatment of their illnesses.
   - ○ True
   - ○ False

5. Europe and Japan have both developed a sustainable economy.
   - ○ True
   - ○ False

6. American households saved very little of their income because they are not making enough money.
   - ○ True
   - ○ False

7. About 85,000 patents are granted to foreign applicants each year in America.
   - ○ True
   - ○ False

8. A new idea is that researchers need to combine several drugs into a therapy so that several mutations can be treated simultaneously.
   ○ True
   ○ False
9. The government program aims to provide low-cost health care to the Americans who don't have insurance.
   ○ True
   ○ False
10. Our gestures are always in line with what we say when we communicate with other people.
    ○ True
    ○ False

II. Choose the one answer that best fits the meaning of the statement you have heard.

1. What is the above passage mainly about?
   a. Archaeological excavation.
   b. A wealthy settlement near the Bisenzio river.
   c. Artifacts unearthed at a site known as Gonfienti.
   d. Gabriella Poggesi, the archaeologist.
2. The three researchers _____.
   a. have spent several years devising the printers that leave no traces
   b. can detect and analyze the invisible patterns
   c. have developed computer programs that can tell reliably which printer was used to create a document
   d. can trace individual printers with their naked eyes
3. The Standing Committee _____.
   a. will review and discuss scientific guidance for food and fiber production
   b. will respond to all kinds of concerns about the environment
   c. will help identify emerging issues in the broad areas of agricultural biotechnology
   d. will focus on the applications of biotechnology to food and fiber production
4. The new undergraduate admissions policy _____.
   a. does not include race as a factor
   b. awards minority applicants an extra 20 points
   c. quantifies the contribution of race to admission decisions
   d. gives highest priority to academic performance
5. Which of the following statement is true, according to the above message?
   a. Singapore has lost 28 percent of its native forest habitat since 1819.
   b. Singapore has lost nearly 95 percent of its overall biodiversity since 1819.

c. All of Singapore's surviving species are concentrated in one-quarter of the country's total area.

d. Most of Singapore's surviving species are concentrated in land designated as forest reserves.

6. In which year the highest number of HIV infection among drug users was reported?

 a. 2000.   b. 2001.   c. 1999.   d. 1994.

7. Which of the following is NOT true?

 a. Trans fatty acids increase the risk of heart disease.

 b. Trans fatty acids increase levels of "good" cholesterol.

 c. Trans fatty acids can be found in cookies, crackers and dairy products.

 d. Trans fatty acids can be found in meats and fast food.

8. Which is not the symptom of the infection of the mentioned disease?

 a. Swollen lymph nodes.   b. Headaches.

 c. Vaccination.   d. Severe sweating.

9. Which is NOT the reason related to the shrinking of the world's freshwater reserves?

 a. Climate change.   b. Poor sanitation.

 c. Pollution.   d. Population growth.

10. Which statement is true according to the above passage?

 a. More exhibitors attended the Comdex this year.

 b. Fewer attendees attended the Comdex this year.

 c. Comdex has surpassed the Consumer Electronics Show lately.

 d. The technology industry's centre of gravity has shifted away from sexier consumer-electronics devices towards PCs.

Section II Reading

Poppy Glut Brings Crash in Opium Prices

So many farmers grew opium in Afghanistan this spring that the country's opium market is now flooded, causing prices for this illegal drug to drop by an average of 65 percent across the country, according to Afghan government officials, Western diplomats and opium farmers.

While an overabundance of opium is a setback for the country in the short term, Afghan and Western officials say this year's drop in prices may actually prove to be a boon in the effort to slow the explosive spread of opium across the country.

Afghanistan produces two-thirds of the world's opium, but comparatively little of it is consumed domestically. Before being shipped to Europe and other destinations, the raw opium is processed into heroin in remote border areas and in neighboring Pakistan.

Experts say the high price farmers receive for opium is by far the largest incentive they have to grow the illegal crop. If prices tumble far enough and the government mounts a credible crackdown, farmers may decide that growing opium is no longer worth the risk, they say.

Afghan and Western officials consider the drug to be one of the gravest threats to Afghanistan's stability. Proceeds from the trade function as a powerful force pulling the country apart by corrupting local government officials, strengthening regional warlords who defy the central government and funding an increasingly violent Taliban insurgency[1].

These officials say they must speed up efforts to introduce alternative crops in the areas where farmers who grew opium this year fared poorly. They say a brief window exists to legitimately argue to impoverished Afghans that opium will no longer enrich them.

Even with the drop in prices, the scope of the country's opium trade remains staggering[2]. It appears that a record number of farmers, including vast numbers of Afghans who live in areas where opium has not been grown before, chose to sow it this year.

Last year, an estimated 1.7 million Afghans, 7 percent of the country's population, grew opium in 28 of the country's 31 provinces.

Opium generated an estimated $1 billion in 2003, roughly one-quarter of Afghanistan's gross domestic product[3]. Limited efforts by the Afghan government, the United States and Britain to use eradication and alternative crops to slow the production of opium have failed[4].

U.S. and Afghan officials say the boom in production was fueled by a surge in prices, creating an almost insurmountable temptation for farmers in one of the world's poorest countries[5]. For decades, opium prices remained comparatively low in the country, at roughly $30 a kilogram, or 2.2 pounds, according to the United Nations Office on Drugs and Crime. But after the Taliban enacted a brief ban on opium production in 2001, the prices soared 20-fold to $750 a kilogram[6].

Eager to get in on this bonanza, farmers planted more and more opium in 2002 and 2003, according to the United Nations[7]. Higher production brought prices down to roughly $350 a kilogram in 2002 and $283 in 2003.

This spring an oversupply of opium has driven the prices down to roughly $100 per kilogram on average across the country, according to Western diplomats. In the southern province of Helmand, long a center of opium cultivation, tomatoes are selling for more than opium, according to farmers and shopkeepers.

One Western diplomat said that strong crops in northern Afghanistan flooded the opium market there. A handful of government raids on processing labs also appears to have made dealers nervous about buying large amounts of opium, he said. Dealers are shying a way from buying and stockpiling large stashes of opium, fearing they could be destroyed in a raid, and that too, has driven down demand and prices[8].

In the south, the same thing appears to be happening. A trip last weekend to Helmand and neighboring Kandahar Province, another bastion of opium cultivation, confirmed a sharp drop in prices. Whether this will convince more farmers not to grow opium next year is unclear.

The vast majority of the profits from the opium trade is believed to go to middlemen, processors and smugglers. Many impoverished Afghans grow opium as sharecroppers — borrowing land, seeds or cash from wealthy Afghans for the chance to grow the lucrative crop. Lower prices this year may increase their indebtedness.

Words and Expressions

poppy 罂粟
glut 过剩；过量
overabundance 过剩；过量
setback 倒退；失败
boon 裨益；非常有用的东西
tumble 暴跌
mount 发动；开展
crackdown 制裁；镇压
defy 违抗；蔑视

insurgency 叛乱
impoverished 赤贫的；贫困的
staggering 巨大的；大得惊人的
bonanza 宝藏
stash 藏匿物；贮藏物
bastion 堡垒
sharecroppers 佃农
lucrative 赚钱的

Notes

1. Proceeds from the trade function as a powerful force pulling the country apart by corrupting local government officials, strengthening regional warlords who defy the central government and funding an increasingly violent Taliban insurgency: 来自鸦片交易的收益成为一股强大的力量，通过腐蚀地方政府官员，使国家分裂。同时，这也加剧了地方军阀与中央政府的对抗，并助长了塔利班的叛乱。

2. Even with the drop in prices, the scope of the country's opium trade remains staggering: 即使鸦片价格不断下跌，阿富汗的鸦片交易量仍然大得惊人。

3. Opium generated an estimated $1 billion in 2003, roughly one-quarter of Afghanistan's gross domestic product: 据估计2003年鸦片交易收入达到10亿美元，约占阿富汗国内生产总值的四分之一。

4. Limited efforts by the Afghan government, the United States and Britain to use eradication and alternative crops to slow the production of opium have failed: 由阿富汗政府、美国和英国采取的用以根除鸦片和替代鸦片种植努力均告失败。

5. U.S. and Afghan officials say the boom in production was fueled by a surge in prices, creating an almost insurmountable temptation for farmers in one of the world's poorest countries: 美国和阿富汗的官员说鸦片交易价格的上涨刺激了产量的扩大，而这对于世界上最贫穷国家

之列的阿富汗的农民产生了一种几乎无法抵御的诱惑。

6. But after the Taliban enacted a brief ban on opium production in 2001, the prices soared 20-fold to $750 a kilogram: 然而,在2001年塔利班对鸦片种植实行短暂的取缔之后,鸦片价格飞涨20倍,达到每千克750美元。

7. Eager to get in on this bonanza, farmers planted more and more opium in 2002 and 2003, according to the United Nations: 根据联合国的报告,渴望据此发财的农民们,在2002年和2003年种植了更多的鸦片。get in 参与(某活动)。

8. Dealers are shying a way from buying and stockpiling large stashes of opium, fearing they could be destroyed in a raid, and that, too, has driven down demand and prices: 由于害怕遭遇突然搜查,经销商们不敢大量收买和储藏鸦片,这也使鸦片的需求和价格大为下跌。shy away from 避开;退缩。

Section III Speaking Up

Try to answer the following questions after you have read/heard the above passage.

1. What caused the opium prices' drop in Afghanistan according to Afghan government officials, Western diplomats and opium farmers?
2. Why may this year's drop in opium prices actually prove to be a boon in the effort to slow the explosive spread of opium across the country?
3. What is considered one of the gravest threats to Afghanistan's stability according to Afghan and Western officials?
4. How much did the price reach after the Taliban enacted a brief ban on opium production in 2001?
5. Have the efforts to slow the production of opium succeeded or not? And why?
6. The vast majority of the profits from the opium trade is believed to go to sharecroppers, isn't it?

Section IV Summary Writing

Write a short summary of the passage you have just read/heard.

_____
_____
_____
_____
_____
_____

Unit 13
In Search of Life's Origin

Section I Listening Comprehension

I. Listen to the following passages and then decide whether the following statements are true or false.

1. Recently, people have more and more confidence in the government because of its works.
   ○ True
   ○ False

2. Opium business can bring one fifth of $320 for Afghanistan every year.
   ○ True
   ○ False

3. The figures show a good sign for Europe's economies.
   ○ True
   ○ False

4. The competitiveness of Germany's exports will be weakened if the euro causes the dollar price of oil to rise.
   ○ True
   ○ False

5. America's call-centre business faces the problem of hiring.
   ○ True
   ○ False

6. Patents are now a public embarrassment since patent offices around the world are being flooded with applications.
   ○ True
   ○ False

7. Mortality rates from heart disease and strokes in the United States have fallen in the last three decades.
   ○ True
   ○ False

8. Gene chips can help treat cancer patients.
   ○ True
   ○ False

9. The theory of "Machiavellian mind" is that human intelligence is in a behavioural equivalent of the peacock's tail.
   ○ True
   ○ False

10. Mark used to be treated badly by people who think of gays as something nasty.
    ○ True
    ○ False

II. Choose the one answer that best fits the meaning of the statement you have heard.

1. According to Karen Norberg, _____.
   a. among children born out of wedlock there were more girls than boys
   b. the chance of a woman giving birth to a girl is higher if she has been living with a man before the child was conceived
   c. for parents who were not cohabiting, boys were born 51.5% of the time
   d. women who have not been living with a man are more likely to have daughters

2. Which of the following statements is NOT true, according to the passage?
   a. In ancient times, forgers would be put to death.
   b. In Dante's "Inferno", forgers were placed in one of the lowest circles of hell.
   c. Today, desktop counterfeiters worry a lot because the systems they use are everywhere.
   d. Counterfeiting may soon be prevented from happening thanks to the newly developed technologies of anti-counterfeiting.

3. According to the UN, there are _____ Africans under 14 nowadays in Africa.
   a. 237 million   b. 348 million   c. 400 million   d. 120 million

4. The power failure _____.
   a. might have been caused by terrorist attacks
   b. affected more than 120 million people
   c. stranded travelers at airports and train stations
   d. hampered cash machines but not cellular telephone service

5. Which of the following statements is NOT true, according to the passage?
   a. Researchers said estimates of atomic bomb survivors' radiation doses are accurate.
   b. Doubts about the accuracy of methods used to collect exposure data in 1945 prompted the review.
   c. The earlier methods were unable to detect radioactive fallout because the researchers could not get close to the bomb site.

d. The amount of nickel in each copper sample can be correlated to the intensity of radiation exposure at the site.
6. Which of the following statements is NOT mentioned as serious consequences of coral loss?
   a. A reduction in tourism.
   b. Increased coastal damage from hurricanes.
   c. The extinction of the estimated 1 million species of fish.
   d. The collapse of reef fisheries.
7. Which of the following statements is closest in meaning to what was said above?
   a. The number of Americans who die from AIDS each year has dropped dramatically.
   b. 40,000 Americans are diagnosed as HIV carriers each year.
   c. Nearly a third of the 85,000 to 950,000 U. S. residents living with HIV/AIDS are aware they carry the virus.
   d. From 1981 to 2001, nearly one-third of all HIV infections are drug users and their sex partners.
8. Which of the following is true according to what you heard?
   a. Dennis Collins' retirement compensation package has been questioned by the press recently.
   b. The bill before the U. S. House of Representatives would not limit the amount of money to be given to charity every year.
   c. The bill has met great opposition from the pensioners.
   d. Dennis Collins was the founder of the James Irvine Foundation.
9. Which of the following statements is NOT mentioned in this passage?
   a. Microsoft's gradual establishment of its dominance in PC software owes much to its ability to outlast its competitors.
   b. Microsoft's gradual establishment of its dominance in PC software owes much to its anti-competitive behaviour.
   c. Microsoft's gradual establishment of its dominance in PC software owes much to its customer service strategies.
   d. Microsoft's gradual establishment of its dominance in PC software owes much to its experience to avoid traps and pitfalls.
10. According to the passage, _____.
    a. more money is going to be used to build houses in risky places
    b. Ashford is a safe place for building houses
    c. Thames Gateway is a safe place to build houses
    d. there are 151,000 houses being built in risky places now

Section II Reading

The Case for[1] a "Grand Bargain"

Prompts: One of the hotspots on the world scene today is the confrontation between the United States and Iran. With the U.S. changing its high command in the military and Iran showing no sign of compliance, the potentially dangerous situation there can spiral into a war at any moment. The article discusses ways of deflating the tensions by engaging Iran.

If a military attack looks too dangerous and sanctions will not bring Iran to its knees[2], must the world accept that the Islamic Republic will soon have a bomb? Maybe. Plenty of governments in the Middle East[3] are already working out how best to prepare for life alongside a nuclear-armed Iran. But what if sanctions and the threat of force were combined with more positive incentives for Iran, such as security guarantees and normal relations with the United States? Might not a beleaguered regime that was offered some such "grand bargain" see it as an honorable way to give up its nuclear plans?

That is the thinking of those who say the mistake of the Bush administration has been to confront Iran instead of engaging it[4]. Four years ago Iran gave tantalizing signs of wanting to end the long confrontation[5]. The superpower's rapid disposal of the Taliban regime[6] in Afghanistan after September 11th, 2001 and its preparations to invade Iraq had made it look like a formidable enemy. In 2003 Iran is reported quietly to have offered to open broad negotiations with America on all outstanding issues, including nuclear weapons and Israel. But for various reasons — mainly, say some, the hubris of America's own neo-conservatives — this opportunity was missed. And by the time America had run into serious trouble inside Iraq two years later, Iran's mood had changed.

Since President Ahmadinejad's election, Iran has come to be less scared of America. The superpower's overstretched armies in Afghanistan and Iraq now look more like hostages than menacing invaders[7]. Although the Bush administration already blames Iran for many of its woes in Iraq[8], it knows the Iranians would and could inflict even more damage on American forces[9] there if America were to bomb Iran. Other American reverses elsewhere in the region have no doubt added to Iran's self-confidence. The regime portrays Israel's war against Hizbullah in Lebanon last summer — and Hamas' success last month in wresting the Gaza Strip from Fatah — as a victory for its own proxies and a defeat for America's[10].

Here, though, is a puzzle. If an Iran brimming with self-confidence[11] is no longer afraid of America, why did it decide to take part at the end of May in the first formal high-level talks it has held with the United States since the American embassy hostages left Tehran in January 1981? To judge from the defensiveness on display at Tehran's Friday prayers before the meeting, this about-turn[12] was a highly sensitive one, controversial with the regime's hard-liners and difficult to explain to its supporters after all the years spitting defiance at the Great Satan.

The explanation favored by Western diplomats is that the Iranians feel more vulnerable than they admit. Though buoyed up after last summer's Lebanon war, the regime's fortunes have since declined[13]. There was that blow to President Ahmadinejad's supporters in last December's municipal elections. President Bush, contrary to expectations, reinforced American forces in Iraq and the Persian Gulf instead of reducing them. American forces in Iraq have arrested five Revolutionary Guards there (the Iranians say they were diplomats). Russia and China surprised Iran by withdrawing their protection in the Security Council and agreeing to sanctions[14].

In short, say Western diplomats, the pressure is working. Yet it may be working in both directions: the Bush administration, after all, has simultaneously performed a U-turn of its own by talking to Iran after a long period of refusing contact. At present both sides are saving face by stressing that Iraq is the only subject on the table. America's official line is that there will be no widening of the discussion unless Iran suspends uranium enrichment and complies with the Security Council's other demands. However, many loud voices in Washington D.C., and a few softer ones in Tehran, see this as an opportunity to move to a broader negotiation that could culminate in an historic reconciliation between the old enemies[15].

Could it happen? America and Iran have some common interests. Both claim to want a stable and united Iraq and both support its present government. Neither wants the Taliban back in charge of Afghanistan (though Iran is reported to be arming some Taliban fighters). As Shias, the Iranians are as hostile as America is to al-Qaeda, whose jihadists in Iraq have murdered thousands of Shias and bombed their holiest shrines. But on the other side of the ledger are areas where the interests of the two countries collide[16].

Words and Expressions

beleaguer 围困；包围
tantalizing 引诱人的
formidable 可怕的
hubris 傲慢；自大
overstretch 勉强维持的，不堪重负的
menacing 威胁的；险恶的

wrest 攫取，抢夺
proxy 代理人，代表
defiance 违抗；藐视
buoy 鼓舞，鼓励
ledger 收支总帐

Notes

1. the case for: 表示理由。这里的 the case for the "grand bargain"，就是要来讲一讲 "讨价还

价"的理由。

2. to bring someone to his knees: 使某人屈服，让他就范。例如：It is the failure in the war that brings the dictator to his knees. 正是由于战争的失败才使独裁者屈服。

3. the Middle East: 中东，一般泛指西亚，北非地区，约 24 个国家，1500 余万平方公里，3.6 亿人口。

4. That is the thinking of those who say the mistake of the Bush administration has been to confront Iran instead of engaging it: 抱有这种想法的人认为布什当局的错误就在于与伊朗对峙而不是约束它。

5. ... gave tantalizing signs of wanting to end the long confrontation: giving sings of 发出……信号要做某件事情，这里说当时伊朗发出过诱人的信号似乎想要结束长期的对抗。tantalizing 引诱人的。例如：A high salary is usually a tantalizing promise for the newly employed. 对于新员工来说，高薪往往是诱人的承诺。

6. Taliban regime: 阿富汗的塔利班政权。塔利班在波斯语中是学生的意思，它的大部分成员是阿富汗难民营伊斯兰学校的学生，故又称伊斯兰学生军。它是阿富汗一个重要派别，领导人是穆尔维·奥马尔，该派别于 1995 年在阿富汗执掌政权，"9·11"事件后，在美军事打击下，塔利班政权垮台。

7. The superpower's overstretched armies in Afghanistan and Iraq now look more like hostages than menacing invaders: 现在看来，美国驻扎在阿富汗和伊拉克不堪重负的军队不像令人恐惧的入侵者，更像是人质。2001 年 9 月 11 日恐怖袭击之后，美国于 2001 年和 2003 年分别发动了对阿富汗和伊拉克的战争，并且成功地推翻了塔利班和萨达姆政权，美国似乎取得了辉煌的胜利，但至今美国军队仍然无法从两国脱身，他们天天面临死亡的威胁，美国似乎陷入了阿富汗和伊拉克泥沼。

8. ... blames Iran for many of its woes in Iraq: 把其在伊拉克遇到的诸多问题都归咎于伊朗。blame... for: 把……归咎于，指责。例如：
A dropped cigarette is blamed for the fire in the factory. 一根乱扔的烟被指为引起工厂火灾的罪魁祸首。

9. ... inflict even more damage on American forces: 让那里的美军招致更大的损失。inflict... on（upon）sb.（sth.）使遭受打击，使吃苦头。例如：We inflicted a humiliating defeat on the home team. 我们让主队吃了一场很没面子的败仗。
Chinese parents tend to inflict supplement classes on their children. 中国的家长往往会逼孩子们上辅导班。

10. 这一段里提到了中东地区的一些重要组织，如黎巴嫩的 Hizbullah（真主党），巴解组织领导的 Fatah（法塔赫），以及主张暴力更为激进的组织 Hamas（哈马斯），后面还提到 jihadist（圣战者）；中东地区的穆斯林主要分为两大教派，Shia 什叶派和 Sunny 逊尼派。策划 9·11 事件的基地恐怖主义组织，英文是 al-Qaeda。

11. brimming with confidence: 形容一副踌躇满志的样子。brim with 盛满，（使）满。例如：
The girl is brimmed with confidence before the examination. 女孩在考前信心百倍。
Hearing the exciting news, the middle-aged man's eyes brimmed with tears. 听到那个令人兴奋的消息，中年人热泪盈眶。

12. about-turn: 180 度的大转弯，下文用的 U-turn，意思相同。

13. Though buoyed up after last summer's Lebanon war, the regime's fortunes have since declined: 尽管去年夏天黎巴嫩战争的胜利使伊朗深受鼓舞，但此后它的运气却一直不佳。buoye up 鼓舞，鼓励。buoy 原是指放在水中的浮子，这里是说伊朗曾因为去年夏天的黎巴嫩战争而一时受到鼓舞。

14. Russia and China surprised Iran by withdrawing their protection in the Security Council and agreeing to sanctions: 俄罗斯和中国在安理会不再保护伊朗并且同意对它进行制裁，这让伊朗大为震惊。
the Security Council 安理会，它是联合国重要机构，负责维护世界和平与安全，中国和俄罗斯都是安理会五大常任理事国成员。

15. However, many loud voices in Washington D. C., and a few softer ones in Tehran, see this as an opportunity to move to a broader negotiation that could culminate in an historic reconciliation between the old enemies: 然而，许多美国强硬派人士以及伊朗一些温和派人物都把这一切视为双方开展更为广泛谈判的契机，这可能会为这对宿敌带来历史性的和解。
culminate in (with) 最终将成为……，（以某种结果）告终。再例如：It is said that the marriage between the president and his wife culminated in divorce. 据说，总统与夫人的婚姻以离婚而告终。

16. But on the other side of the ledger are areas where the interests of the two countries collide: 另一方面，两国的确存在利益冲突。这是一个倒装句，其中 on the other side of the ledger 是另一方面的意思，相当于 on the other hand 的意思。

Section III Speaking Up

Try to answer the following questions after you have read/heard the above passage.

1. What do you know about the confrontations and conflicts in the Middle East?
2. Can nuclear weapons protect or destroy the world? Try to give an example to explain it.
3. What are your suggestions to eradicate war all over the world?
4. The United States has long claimed to be the guardian for world safety. Would you like to comment on its role in the world?

Section IV Summary Writing

Write a short summary of the passage you have just read/heard.

Unit 14
The Little Guy

Section I Listening Comprehension

I. Listen to the following passages and then decide whether the following statements are true or false.

1. The station streamed its broadcasts over the Internet in order to get more money from its advertisers.
   ○ True
   ○ False

2. Many American people are better off these days as they don't have to pay their hospital bill.
   ○ True
   ○ False

3. Both France and Germany performed satisfactorily in the first half of the year.
   ○ True
   ○ False

4. The collapse of the index was in part attributable to the further integration of the euro zone.
   ○ True
   ○ False

5. The police officers failed to rip up the poppy in Helmand because it was too dangerous for them to.
   ○ True
   ○ False

6. In 1998 America introduced so-called "business-method" patents, which have greatly encouraged commercial innovation.
   ○ True
   ○ False

7. In a competition between regulated and unregulated cells, the regulated ones will always win.
   ○ True
   ○ False

8. Dwarfism is one frequent trend observed in many island species.
   ○ True
   ○ False

9. The instructor might catch more of the students' attention in the appearance-based class.
   ○ True
   ○ False

10. The number of children a woman has is limited compared with the most successful male in the society.
    ○ True
    ○ False

II. Choose the one answer that best fits the meaning of the statement you have heard.

1. Which of the following statements is true, according to the passage?
   a. The approaches of the three researchers are quite different.
   b. The three researchers' approaches are all based on detecting imperfections in the print quality of documents.
   c. Old-school forensic scientists were unable to trace documents to particular typewriters based on quirks of the individual keys.
   d. The researchers from Purdue believe the perfect pieces of engineering leave unique patterns of banding in their products.

2. Which one of the following statements is false?
   a. The study will focus on biological methods for confining transgenic crop plants, grasses, trees, fish and shellfish.
   b. The study will consider methods used for other categories of transgenic organisms.
   c. The committee will not discuss other available or possible biological confinement methods.
   d. Methods resulting in significant reductions in the risk of escape into the environment will be identified.

3. Which of the following is NOT a fact according to what you have heard?
   a. Although similar in many ways to smallpox, monkeypox is less infectious than smallpox.
   b. Although similar in many ways to smallpox, monkeypox is less deadly than smallpox.
   c. The disease occurs primarily in Central and West Africa.
   d. State and federal officials know no patients had direct contact with infected prairie dogs kept as pets.

4. Which of the following is NOT mentioned?
   a. Three New England states filed suits which aims to reclassify carbon dioxide as a "criteria pollutant".
   b. Three New England states filed suits which aims to cite the chemical's contribution to global

warming.

    c. Three New England states filed suits which aims to force the government to regulate carbon dioxide emissions.

    d. Three New England states filed suits which aims to require the government set and enforce standards for allowable atmospheric levels of these pollutants.

5. Which of the following is NOT mentioned in the treaty against smoking?

    a. The treaty calls for new labeling for tobacco products.

    b. The treaty calls for an advertising ban.

    c. The treaty calls for outdoor air controls to reduce second-hand smoking.

    d. The treaty calls for stronger legislation against tobacco smuggling.

6. Which of the following is correct according to the passage?

    a. Microsoft has been through a bruising battle with antitrust regulators.

    b. Mr. Gates's position as the industry's figurehead has been challenged.

    c. The computer industry is currently having a hard time.

    d. Mr. Gates has earned 870 billion U. S. dollars over the last two decades.

7. Smugglers' Gulch _____.

    a. is a ravine which is watched 24 hours a day

    b. is a place where many illegal immigrants would get help from America

    c. is a place where Rafael is trying to cross the fence into Mexico

    d. is one of the places of Mexico

8. According to the Economist Intelligence Unit, it will take the new members _____.

    a. more than half of the century to catch up if they grow by about 4%

    b. more than a decade years to catch up if they grow by 3%

    c. 19 years to catch up if they grow by 3%

    d. 90 years to catch up if they grow by about 4%

9. The advantage of the new system is that _____.

    a. it improves its efficiency in identification

    b. the scope of the system is increased

    c. provides more protection against terrorism

    d. protects privacy for individuals

10. If the U. S. dollar falls too fast, what will be the risk?

    a. It will help to enlarge America's external deficit.

    b. It will prevent the U. S. economy from recovering.

    c. It will reduce bond yields.

    d. It will bring more investment risks.

Section II Reading

A New Biofuel from Fruit Sugars

Prompts: With oil price skyrocketing and growing environmental concerns, people are turning to alternative resources that provide the power to drive their cars. This article reports the latest endeavor by scientists in search of a new generation of biofuel as substitute for fossil fuel.

Replacing carbon-rich[1] fossil fuels with more environmentally friendly alternatives should slow global warming. As part of that drive, both America and Europe have embraced biofuels — liquids derived from plants that can be used to power cars and other vehicles. By their very nature, biofuels cannot be carbon-free because carbon is essential to life on Earth. Burning biofuels does indeed release carbon dioxide, a greenhouse gas. The attraction is that the volume of gas released exactly matches that taken up by the plant when it was growing. So overall (and with the huge proviso that[2] you do not count the fossil fuel used to farm the stuff) biofuels are carbon-neutral.

In America, the Department of Energy has set a target for 30% of the 2004 gasoline demand for vehicles to be met by biofuels by 2030. The European Union wants 25% of transport fuels to be derived from biofuels by the same date. At present, the most widely used substance is ethanol, which can be made from sugar cane, sugar beet and maize (or corn, as it is called in America). But ethanol does not pack a particularly powerful punch[3]. It is also susceptible to absorbing water, further diluting its oomph. It takes days to ferment the stuff. A biofuel that did not suffer from these limitations would be welcome.

That is what a team led by James Dumesic of the University of Wisconsin-Madison claims to have developed. The researchers think they have devised a biofuel that has a 40% higher energy density than ethanol, that repels water and that can be made relatively speedily.

One of the most frustrating aspects of biofuels is the stark contrast between what exists in nature and what you can put in the tank[4]. Plants are rich in carbohydrates, a group of organic compounds based on carbon and water, itself a combination of hydrogen and oxygen. These carbohydrates take the form of chains of thousands of sugar units[5]; each unit contains six carbon atoms and a similar number of oxygen atoms. An ideal fuel, on the other hand, should lack oxygen. Its molecules should also be small, that is, they should contain few carbon atoms. Creating an efficient fuel from plants thus presents a headache.

To date, scientists have approached the problem by taking one of two routes. The chemists have tinkered with heat and metal catalysts to refine their materials. Biologists, meanwhile, have recruited enzymes and microbes to do the job[6].

The team led by Dr. Dumesic combined the two methods. It was thus able to break down long carbohydrate chains to form small, useable molecules while simultaneously removing the oxygen and maintaining the energy content of the biofuel. The researchers began by using enzymes to snip the carbohydrates into fragments that were then rearranged to form a sugar called fructose, which is found in fruits.

They doused the fructose in acid, which catalysed a chemical reaction expelling oxygen atoms as water molecules. The researchers immediately added a second catalyst and some hydrogen, which eliminated more oxygen. The result was a fuel called "2.5-dimethylfuran".

The new biofuel can be made directly from fructose, which is present in fruits such as apples, pears, berries and melons as well as some root vegetables. It can also be manufactured from the large polymer chains found in cereals, grasses and trees. Perhaps the most promising method, from a biochemical point of view, would be to use glucose, a sugar common in food[7].

The resulting biofuel is not only energy-rich and water-repellent but it also has a higher boiling point than ethanol[8]. Keeping it liquid in a vehicle's fuel tank should therefore be straightforward.

But this biofuel shares a disadvantage with ethanol: its raw material is food. Ideally, biofuels would be made from waste farm products rather than crops. That way, the chaff could be used to produce biofuel for transport and the wheat could be used for people.

Unfortunately for science, nature conspires against this[9]. Plants have evolved chemical and structural properties that make it difficult to them to break down. One possibility would be to use genetic modification to create plants that are more amenable to[10] such manipulation. Another is to use existing chemical or biological techniques, or to combine the approaches, rather as Dr. Dumesic and his colleagues have done. Whichever works best, the second generation of biofuels is coming down the pipeline[11].

Words and Expressions

biofuel 生物燃料（指曾经为活质的燃料）
fossil fuel 矿物燃料（如煤或石油）
embrace 欣然接受
proviso 条件，限制条款
transport fuels 运输用燃料
ethanol 乙醇
sugar cane [植] 甘蔗
sugar beet 甜菜
be susceptible to 对……敏感
dilute 削弱，降低
oomph 活力
ferment （使）发酵

repel 抵制，排斥
stark 明显的
carbohydrate [化] 碳水化合物
organic compound 有机化合物
microbe 微生物
fructose 果糖
2.5-dimethylfuran 2.5-二甲基呋喃
polymer chain 聚合物链
glucose 葡萄糖
repellent 防……的，隔绝……的
chaff 谷壳，糠
amenable 可用某种方式处理的

Notes

1. carbon-rich: 复合形容词，含碳量高的，类似的结构还有 carbon-free（不含碳的）、carbon-neutral（碳中和性的）、energy-rich（能量高的）和 water-repellent（无水的）等。

2. with the proviso that: 在……前提条件下，正式用语，常见于法律、科技等文体。

3. But ethanol does not pack a particularly powerful punch: 但是乙醇不具备很强劲的推力。

4. One of the most frustrating aspects of biofuels is the stark contrast between what exists in nature and what you can put in the tank: 生物燃料最令人望而却步的问题之一，就是自然界存在什么物质，而我们又能把什么东西加到油箱里的这种明显的矛盾。

5. take the form of: 以……形式出现。这句话的意思是：这些碳水化合物以数以千计的链状糖单位形式而存在。

6. … scientists have approached the problem by taking one of two routes. The chemists have tinkered with… Biologists have recruited… to do the job. 科学家们分别采用了两种不同的方法来解决这一问题——化学家利用加温和催化剂提炼这些物质，生物学家则利用酶和微生物来达到同样的目的。在这一小段里，作者用了一连串的几个动词短语来叙述，连贯、简洁、地道，值得学习。

7. Perhaps the most promising method, from a biochemical point of view, would be to use glucose, a sugar common in food. 从生物化学的角度来看，最有效的方法也许是使用食物中普遍存在的一种糖分——果糖来生产生物燃料。a sugar common in food 是一个带后置定语的名词短语。

8. The resulting biofuel is not only energy-rich and water-repellent but it also has a higher boiling point than ethanol: 最终制成的生物燃料不但能量高，不含水分，而且它比乙醇的沸点更高。

9. Unfortunately for science, nature conspires against this: 遗憾的是对于科学来讲，老天似乎有意和人们作对。conspire 是搞阴谋诡计，常用的名词形式是 conspiracy。

10. more amenable to: 更加易于……该句的意思是：一种可能的方法就是通过转基因种植便于人们使用的植物。

11. Whichever works best, the second generation of biofuels is coming down the pipeline: 不管哪种方法最有效，值得肯定的是第二代生物燃料必将走进人们的生活。

Section III Speaking Up

Try to answer the following questions after you have read/heard the above passage.

1. Why are scientists busily exploring biofuels to take the place of fossil fuels?
2. According to the text, what's the problem with the biofuels?
3. Do you think that biofuels can come into wide use one day in the future? Why or why not?

4. What are your suggestions for the increasingly severe energy shortage?
5. Would you like to say something about genetic modification technology?

Section IV Summary Writing

Write a short summary of the passage you have just read/heard.

Unit 15
Stretching the Limits

Section I Listening Comprehension

Listen to the following passages and then choose the best answers to the five questions for each passage.

Exercise I

1. The passage is mainly about the problem of _____.
    a. safe drinking water
    b. poverty
    c. sustainable development
    d. global warming
2. Which of the following is NOT mentioned as uses of water?
    a. Life necessity.
    b. Source of energy.
    c. Environmental protection.
    d. Medical care.
3. All of the following is related to the water problem EXCEPT _____.
    a. rapid consumption
    b. increasing pollution
    c. lack of access
    d. racial discrimination
4. How many people are expected to benefit from the MDGs with respect to water supply every day?
    a. 200,000.
    b. 400,000.
    c. 600,000.
    d. 800,000.
5. The speech is most probably made on such an occasion as _____.
    a. the International Day for the Eradication of Poverty 2001
    b. the World Environmental Day 2003
    c. the Rewarding Ceremony of the Equator Prize 2004
    d. the UN General Assembly 2002

Exercise II

6. What is the most appropriate title for the passage?
    a. The Origin of the Universe
    b. The Hubble's Discovery
    c. The Big Bang Hypothesis
    d. The Formation of the Milky Way

7. Hubble's discovery implies _____.
   a. that distant stars and galaxies are receding from the earth
   b. that the speed of recession is proportionate to distance
   c. that the universe is expanding
   d. the universe was previously in infinitely small mass
8. Which of the following is NOT mentioned as relevant to the formation of galaxies and stars?
   a. Explosion.   b. Rotation.   c. Fission.   d. Radiation.
9. Which of the following is NOT mentioned as being testable?
   a. Speed of star recession.
   b. The temperature at deep space.
   c. The background radiation spectrum.
   d. Gravitational pull.
10. What is the speaker trying to do in the passage?
    a. Telling a legend of outer space.
    b. Reporting scientific findings.
    c. Debating over an academic issue.
    d. Describing the universe.

Exercise III

11. The passage is mainly about international cooperation _____.
    a. in poverty reduction   b. in economic growth
    c. in debt relief   d. in cultural exchange
12. Which of the following is NOT mentioned as benefits of international aid?
    a. It promotes globalization in economic growth.
    b. It creates a more equitable world community.
    c. It improves foreign relations.
    d. It contributes to national integrity.
13. Which of the following is NOT a concern of parties involved in international relief?
    a. The contributions are not given to the targeted beneficiaries.
    b. The aided nation is not fully authorized to dispose the relief resources.
    c. The donors are asked to provide an unfair share of donation.
    d. The recipient is forced to accept some unpleasant terms.
14. The speaker of the passage believes that _____.
    a. international development efforts need a written contract
    b. international aid depends on mutual trust and understanding
    c. world economic growth rests on a mutually beneficial contract
    d. world cultural exchange contributes to political reforms

15. The speaker of the passage implies that _____.
    a. tension between donors and recipients are inevitable
    b. performance monitoring should be strengthened
    c. performance regulations requirements should be alleviated
    d. differences between donors and recipients can be dissolved

Exercise IV

16. Which of the following makes the most appropriate title for the passage?
    a. Reading Books   b. Handling Books
    c. Owning Books   d. Buying Books

17. According to the speaker it is better _____.
    a. to have books of your own
    b. to borrow books from friends
    c. to inherit books from ancestors
    d. to have no books of others

18. Which of the followings is NOT mentioned as an advantage of marking books?
    a. It highlights the reader's personal interests.
    b. It helps the reader identify the wanted lines.
    c. It reminds the reader of his past experiences.
    d. It signifies the reader's private ownership.

19. The speaker argues for his point by _____.
    a. comparison and contrast   b. cause and effect
    c. exemplification   d. definition

20. What will the speaker most probably talk about next?
    a. How to make evaluation of books.
    b. How to take care of books.
    c. How to build up collection of books.
    d. How to keep record of books.

Section II Reading

The Child is Father to the Patient

Prompt: The controversy over "nature or nurture" can be traced back to the times of Plato. New findings in scientific research today, especially in the area of genetics, seems to add new dimensions to this. We may feel that, to a large extent, our way of life determines our weight, our state of health and our thriftiness; however, scientists are telling us that much of these has to do with decisions made early in life, indeed, very early in life, when one is still in its mother's womb.

About 15 years ago, David Barker, of Southampton University, in England, wondered if some adult diseases had their roots at the beginning of life, in developmental "decisions" taken by fetuses.[1] Sometimes there decisions might be forced on a fetus by less than ideal circumstances. Sometimes they would be guesses about the future that turned out to be wrong. But the result in all cases would be misery in later life. Heart disease, obesity and late-onset diabetes frequently seem to trace their origins back to conditions in the womb, or in the first few weeks of infancy.[2] So do cognitive ability, earning power, and even greed and sloth.

Dr. Barker's initial observation, based on several thousand people born in Hertfordshire before the second world war, was that babies who are particularly small grow into adults with a high risk of heart disease. Since then, low birth-weight has been associated with a collection of symptoms linked together in 1988 known as "syndrome X". The features of this syndrome are high blood pressure, disturbed fat metabolism and obesity. These, in turn, are indicators of somebody who is likely to develop heart disease and late-onset diabetes.[3]

The small, food-deprived fetuses give rise to unhealthy adults is not exactly a surprise.[4] What is surprising, though, is Dr. Barker's idea that the pattern of their disease might be shaped by natural selection — in other words that it is programmed into a developing fetus.

There are two prongs to this hypothesis. The first is that a fetus has to cut its coat according to its cloth.[5] Faced with a limited amount of food, it has choices about how to use it. Dr. Baker's suggestion is that food will be allocated in ways that give an individual the best chance in early life, at the expenses of later years when he will have had children and might, indeed, have died of something else. Above all, the growth of the brain is protected.

The second prong is that a fetus takes its cue about what it will eat after it is waned from its mother's physiology, and adapts accordingly.[6] In this case, disease is caused when the prediction is wrong. In particular, individuals adapted for a low-calorie, low-fat environment who find themselves, through improved circumstances, in a high-calorie, high-fat environment, might be expected to have problems.

Dr. Barker's idea is that a fetus faced with a lack of nutrients develops thrifty habits. Developmental pathways are controlled by genes, but those genes are subject to regulation.[7] Exactly what changes in genetic regulation are involved in the programming of thrift is unclear, although a few of the genes involved have been identified. However, the result, according to Dr. Barker, is twofold. First, the fetus's tissues become more resistant to insulin — a molecule that opens the door for glucose to enter cells so that it can be burned to release energy, or used as feed-stock to make other molecules. Second, the fetus becomes better able to lay down fat deposits in later life.

The advantage of laying down fat when food is plentiful is more obvious. It helps mature animals to get through lean times.[8] Some scientist even goes so far as to describe the human "beer" belly as the equivalent of a camel's hump. These days, however, there are no lean times. Diets are calorie-rich, and getting more so. As a result, both mechanisms are going horribly wrong. Even in the West, people conceived a decade or two ago are eating far more sugar and fat than their mothers did. The shift is greater still in many poor and middle-income countries. The result is epidemics of obesity, diabetes due to too much blood sugar and heart disease due to high blood pressure and disturbed fat metabolism associated with changes in the body's fat-storing cells.

Words and Expressions

fetus 胎儿
diabetes 糖尿病
cognitive ability 认知能力
sloth 懒惰
metabolism 新陈代谢
prong 分支；分岔
hypothesis 假说；前提
allocate 分配；分派

low-calorie 低热量的
nutrient 营养品；食物
regulation 调节机制
insulin 胰岛素
molecule 分子；摩尔
glucose 葡萄糖
lean times 营养缺乏期
hump 驼峰

Notes

1. About 15 years ago, David Barker, of Southampton University, in England, wondered if some adult diseases had their roots at the beginning of life, in developmental "decisions" taken by fetuses: 约15年前，英国南安普敦大学的 David Barker 博士就想搞清楚是否成年人的疾病植根于生命的起始阶段，在胎儿的发育期就已确定。

2. Heart disease, obesity and late-onset diabetes frequently seem to trace their origins back to conditions in the womb, or in the first few weeks of infancy: 心脏病，肥胖病和后来得的糖尿病常常可以追根朔源到当时在子宫里的状况，或婴儿期最初几周的状况。

3. These, in turn, are indicators of somebody who is likely to develop heart disease and late-onset diabetes: 这些就预示着某人可能患上心脏病和晚期发病的糖尿病。

4. The small, food-deprived fetuses give rise to unhealthy adults is not exactly a surprise: 幼小而营养匮乏的胎儿导致成年后体弱多病就不足为奇。文中 give rise to 意思是"引起；导致"。

5. The first is that a fetus has to cut its coat according to its cloth: 第一种说法是胎儿必须"量力而为"。to cut one's coat according to its cloth 直接译过来是"有多大的布料，裁出多大的衣衫"，意思是说做事要"量入为出"、"量力而为"。

6. The second prong is that a fetus takes its cue about what it will eat after it is waned from its mother's physiology, and adapts accordingly: 第二种说法是胎儿从母体身体状况中能了解到将来断奶以后有什么样的食物可以吃到，并做出相应的调整。

7. Developmental pathways are controlled by genes, but those genes are subject to regulation: 发育的途径由基因决定，但那些基因取决于胚胎发育的调节机制。be subject to 意思是"取决于……的；由……决定的"。

8. The advantage of laying down fat when food is plentiful is more obvious. It helps mature animals to get through lean times: 当食物充足时储存脂肪的优势是显而易见的。这有助于成年动物度过营养匮乏期。

Section III Speaking Up

Try to answer the following question after you have read/heard the above passage.

1. What does the author tell about the origin of heart disease, obesity and late-onset diabetes?
2. What implications does low birth-weight have for one's life later on?
3. What choice does a fetus have when it faces a limited amount of food?
4. How can a fetus make a wrong prediction about its life in the future?
5. What changes will occur when a fetus is faced with a lack of nutrition?
6. Why do scientists compare the human "beer" belly to a camel's hump?

Section IV Summary Writing

Write a short summary of the passage you have just read/heard.

_____
_____
_____
_____
_____
_____
_____
_____
_____

Unit 16
Getting the Gist

Section I Listening Comprehension

I. Listen to the following passage about coping with climate change and then write a short summary of around 150-200 words of what you have heard.

II. Listen to the following passage about Jefferson and Hamilton and their roles in the American history and then write a short summary of around 150-200 words of what you have heard.

Section II Reading

I Google, Therefore I Am[1]

Prompts: The development in the IT industry has brought cyberspace into parallel existence with human living, something that we have to face up whether we like it or not. That seems to be the philosophical message behind this report of scientific progress currently being made with Robots, who are going online to escape the narrow confines of their programming and learning about the world.

Shut your eyes and picture a Buddha's hand citron[2]. Chances are you can't, unless you happen to know it's an exotic yellow, tentacled fruit that looks a bit like a small bunch of bananas[3].

The exercise gives a taste of what it's like[4] for robots, which struggle to "picture" almost every word or phrase they come across. That's because until they are switched on, they have never seen anything in the real world.

Now that looks set to change[5]. Just as you might run a Google image search to see what a Buddha's hand citron looks like, so robots, and computer programs, are starting to take advantage of the wealth of images posted online to find out about everyday objects[6].

When presented with a new word, instead of using the limited index it has been programmed with, which is the conventional method, this new breed of automatons goes online and enters the word into Google. The robot or software uses the resulting range of images to recognize the object in the real world.

It's easy to program a robot to recognize specific objects. For instance, when given a picture of a chair, a robot can usually find that same chair in the real world using the colors, textures and angles of the image.

This system breaks down, though, when you ask a robot to identify a chair it has never seen before[7]. The great variation in size, color, shape and sometimes number of legs a chair might have makes it unlikely that the robot can identify any chair based on just the images it has been shown. And the difference between, say, a small table and a chair can be very slight, making things even more confusing.

Humans don't have this problem because they tend to lump visual information into groups based not on how many legs a chair has, or its exact dimensions, but whether or not we recognize it as being built to sit on[8]. Such an idea is extremely difficult for robots to grasp because they don't interact with the world in the same way. To get round this, researchers are focusing on building software that extracts images from the web[9].

This ability could allow robots to retrieve household objects for visually impaired people or those who have trouble walking[10]. It could also mean robots become capable of teaching themselves about the world. To test the idea, scientists organized the first Semantic Robot Vision Challenge at the annual conference of the American Association for Artificial Intelligence in Vancouver. Four teams took part, entering one robot each.

The robots were given a list of 20 objects, including a DVD, a CD case, a banana and a calculator, that would be strewn across tables and chairs in a 6-metre-square area. The robots were allowed one hour to search the Internet for images that were relevant to the words on the list and to analyze them. After that, they had to set out in search of the items.

The first stage of the challenge involved turning the hundreds of images that you get in response to a Google search for, say, "red bell pepper" into a description that could be used to recognize that object in the real world.

To do this, the teams equipped their robots with software that analyzes the shading patterns in all of the images brought up by the search and picks out telltale features within them. A large proportion of the images will be of red bell peppers, but there will be plenty of others of, for example, dishes containing them or pictures of cookbooks. Assuming that the largest single group of images will be of peppers themselves, the software takes these images as the standard to form a kind of fingerprint. It then compares all the images with this standard. Those that have very different shading and won't help the robot understand what the object looks like are discarded and those that are similar are kept.

Once armed with this knowledge of what their target objects look like, the robots then struck out into the real world[11]. The robots used stereo cameras to identify shapes that stood out from the tables or floor where they were strewn. The robots then snapped pictures of these objects and compared them to their index of fingerprints. If they discovered a match, that object was declared "found".

Although it is likely to be at least a few years before these robots find their way into the home as domestic assistants, the type of software they run on has a more imminent application: improving web image searches[12]. For example, a Google image search of "banana" returns mostly pictures of the familiar fruit, but within the top 20 results it also returns a man sitting on a banana-shaped chair and banana spiders on their web.

This is because the search engine uses the text attached to the pictures to decide which ones are relevant. Programs that understand what objects actually look like, based on analyzing characteristics of the images they find online, could better decide whether they were relevant to a particular word. Researchers say this would likely result in more relevant search results[13].

>> **Words and Expressions**

tentacled 似触手的，触角的
conventional 普通的，常见的

automaton 自动装置，机器人
lump 把……归并在一起

retrieve 检索
impaired 受损的，能力受影响的
strew 撒，使散落
telltale 能说明问题的
snap 给……拍快照；快摄照片
imminent 临近的；即将发生的

Notes

1. I Google, Therefore I Am: 这一题目是从笛卡尔的 I think, therefore I am（我思故我在）那句名言改编过来的，使互联网的存在已经上升到本体论的哲学高度，不禁让人对互联网之强大产生了些许敬畏。

2. a Buddha's hand citron: 一种热带水果，因其形状像是双手合十的佛手，因此而得名佛手。

3. Chances are you can't, unless you happen to know it's an exotic yellow, tentacled fruit that looks a bit like a small bunch of bananas: 除非你刚好知道那是一种黄色的带触手的奇异水果，就像一小把香蕉一样，否则，你可能无法想象。chances are (that) … 可能…… Chances are that he on't have to pay. 他可能不用付钱。

4. … gives a taste of what it's like: 让人尝到做……的滋味。再例如 This video gives a taste of what it's like to be a programmer and the effects the high demands can have on family life.

5. Now that looks set to change: 现在这注定是要改变的了。这一句引入转折，本段的作用就是承上启下。

6. so robots, and computer programs, are starting to take advantage of the wealth of images posted online to find out about everyday objects: 于是，机器人以及电脑程序就开始利用网上大量的图像来搜寻日常用品。take advantage of 利用；the wealth of 大量，众多

7. This system breaks down, though, when you ask a robot to identify a chair it has never seen before: 然而，当你要机器人识别它以前从未见过的椅子时，该系统就不能正常运行了。break down 在本句是"出故障，不能正常运行"的意思，该短语其他的意思还有"失败，垮掉，划分"等。

8. Humans don't have this problem because they tend to lump visual information into groups based not on how many legs a chair has, or its exact dimensions, but whether or not we recognize it as being built to sit on: 人类就不会出现这样的问题，因为他们往往不会根据椅子有几条腿或椅子的确切尺寸来分组视觉信息，而是看它是否能坐。tend to 往往会，常常就。例如：Women tend to live longer than man. 女人往往比男人长寿。People tend to think that this problem will never affect them. 人们往往认为这个问题绝不会影响到他们。

9. To get round this, researchers are focusing on building software that extracts images from the web: 为了克服这一困难，研究人员正全力以赴开发能够从网上筛选图像的软件。get round sth. 意思是绕过，此处为克服困难。

10. This ability could allow robots to retrieve household objects for visually impaired people or those who have trouble walking: 这使得机器人能够帮助盲人或行走困难的人检索家用物品。

11. ... the robots struck out into the real world: 这句话形容智能机器人就像初出茅庐的年轻人那样到外面去闯世界。用动词短语 strike out 表示"谋生"。例如 Twenty years later, with two pieces of paper that said I had mechanical engineering degrees from Cornell University, I struck out into the real world.

12. Although it is likely to be at least a few years before these robots find their way into the home as domestic assistants, the type of software they run on has a more imminent application: improving web image searches: 尽管至少要在多年之后，机器人才有可能走进千家万户去做家庭助手，但是他们使用的软件将马上用来改进网上图像的搜索。注意该句的翻译，a few years before 多年之后。

13. Researchers say this would likely result in more relevant search results. 研究人员表示，这很可能会找到更多相关的搜索结果。注意 result in 与 result from 的区别。result in 是导致，引起；而 result from 是由……导致，由……引起。例如：The failure in the experiment resulted in withdrawal of investment by many joint-ventures. 实验的失败导致许多合资企业收回投资。

This chronic disease is resulted from bad dieting habit in young ages. 这种慢性病是由儿时不良饮食习惯引起的。

Section III Speaking Up

Try to answer the following question after you have read/heard the above passage.

1. Some people say that the robots are so wisely designed that some day in the future they will take the place of human beings. What's your opinion about it?
2. Do you think that researchers are able to develop a robot that is completely the same to a man? Why or why not?
3. What are the advantages and disadvantages of the widely used Internet?
4. Currently, too many people, especially the young, are addicted to Internet games. Please comment on it.
5. What do you usually use a computer for?

Section IV Summary Writing

Write a short summary of the passage you have just read/heard.

Unit 16 Getting the Gist

Practice Tests

Sample Test One

Part I

Listen to the following short passages and then decide whether the corresponding statements are true or false. There are 10 statements in this part of the test, 2 points for each statement.

1. On a global scale people killed or injured by violent acts come close to 1.6 million.
   ○ True
   ○ False

2. The report present information on a variety of areas of personal and social conflict including violence against women in the family.
   ○ True
   ○ False

3. Violence within the family should not be dealt with by the police or the justice departments.
   ○ True
   ○ False

4. Fish is the least energy-efficient because most fossil fuel is required in order to catch some fishes.
   ○ True
   ○ False

5. People should not be alarmed by the deaths caused by violence because they are only a very small part of the problem of violence.
   ○ True
   ○ False

6. There were more people killed in road accidents than those dying of HIV/AIDS worldwide in 2000.
   ○ True
   ○ False

7. Violence brought about by large groups of people or the state is more serious than violence by individuals.
   ○ True
   ○ False

8. Reducing social inequalities is likely to help to reduce the number of violent crimes.
   ○ True
   ○ False

9. The victims of violence are not the only ones who suffer the consequence of such behavior.
   - ○ True
   - ○ False
10. The media often exaggerate the number of people killed in war.
    - ○ True
    - ○ False

Part II

Listen to the following short passages and then choose one of the answers that best fits the meaning of each passage. There are ten passages in this part of the test, each with 1 question, which carries 2 points.

11. France and Italy increased their wine exports to the U. S. because _____.
    a. consumption in their home markets has doubled
    b. consumption in their home markets has tripled
    c. price of wine in the U. S. has risen sharply in the last 10 years
    d. their home markets have reduced

12. Which of the following statement is true?
    a. The U. S. has boycott the import of wine from Australia.
    b. The U. S. economy is in a boom.
    c. The U. S. dollar has reduced in value by 26% against the Australian dollar.
    d. Australian wine makers decided to raise the price of their products.

13. Which of the following statements is true according to the passage?
    a. Peugeot Citroen is the second largest carmaker in the world.
    b. Peugeot Citroen is the second largest joint-venture in China.
    c. Dongfeng Motor is second only to Citroen in their carmaking venture.
    d. Peugeot Citroen decided to expand their Chinese factory with their local partner.

14. What is the current capacity of the joint-venture?
    a. 300,000.   b. 600,000.   c. 150,000.   d. 307,000.

15. Which of the following statements is true of Aluminum Corp. of China?
    a. It is the biggest maker of the metal in the world.
    b. It wanted to increase its production.
    c. It wanted to break the world record.
    d. It was sold to Alcoa and institutional investors to survive.

16. Which of the following ways can make you an American citizen?
    a. To be born in America.
    b. To secure the right to work in America.
    c. To continuously live in America for 5 years with no criminal record.

d. Either of the above.

17. How much of the company's profits will be used to increase its working capital?

   a. One third.

   b. Two thirds.

   c. More than half.

   d. The exact number or proportion is unknown.

18. How much aluminum does China consume on a yearly basis?

   a. 120 million tons.   b. 12 million tons.

   c. Half a million tons.   d. 700,000 tons.

19. Foot-and-mouth _____.

   a. is quite unfamiliar to Britons because they don't raise livestock

   b. can be contagious among animals

   c. has cost Britons around $8 billion to slaughter the affected animals

   d. spread in 2001 because the government knew nothing about the disease

20. According to the international carbon-trading system, _____.

   a. countries where there is no deforestation might get paid

   b. deforestation has nothing to do with the increasing amount of carbon emissions in the atmosphere

   c. countries that release less carbon into the atmosphere can buy "credits" from those releasing more

   d. the more carbon a country releases into the atmosphere, the more credits it could get

Part III

Listen to the following longer passages and then choose the best answer to each of the questions. You may need to scribble a few notes in order to answer the questions. There are four passages in this part, each with 5 questions. And each question carries 2 points.

Passage One

21. What did Henry Ford do a hundred years ago?

   a. He fell in love with an American girl.

   b. He disgraced Jay Gatsby.

   c. He started his carmaking business.

   d. He staged a party at his home.

22. The sales volume of cars in America today is _____.

   a. over 16 million   b. 20 million

   c. 26 million   d. not known from this passage

23. The American carmaking industry _____.

   a. is riding smoothly

    b. is preparing to celebrate Ford's 100th birth party this year
    c. is in need of change to get out of the bottom
    d. is doomed to failure during competition from abroad
24. What happened to Chrysler in the 1990s?
    a. It nearly went bankrupt.　　　　b. It merged with Daimler-Benz.
    c. It was bailed out by the government.　d. It was beaten by Japanese carmakers.
25. What did GM do in 1992?
    a. It was pushed over edge.　　　　b. It downgraded it credit-rating.
    c. It survived another crisis.　　　d. Its CEO fell ill.

Passage Two

26. When did Mulick began treat autism?
    a. In the 1970s.　b. In the 1960s.　c. 166 years ago.　d. 1,000 years ago.
27. The current number of children subject to autism is _____.
    a. 1/16　　　b. 1/60　　　c. 1/166　　　d. 1/6
28. What are the popular treatments used by parents to cure autism?
    a. Dairy or wheat products.　　　b. National supplements.
    c. Special diets.　　　　　　　　d. Vitamin C.
29. Why are the fad treatments discussed in the media and on the Internet?
    a. Because they are effective.
    b. Because they are quite popular.
    c. Because many parents can have access to them.
    d. Because they have been adequately studied.
30. Which of the following statements about Chelation therapy is NOT true?
    a. It involves taking medicines to remove the heavy metal mercury from the body.
    b. It is used years ago as a new treatment against cancer.
    c. It has been proven effective.
    d. It is dangerous.

Passage Three

31. What did scientists learn about CFCs in the early 1970s?
    a. It was a health hazard.
    b. It causes damage to the skins of humans and animals.
    c. It is an ozone-depleting substance.
    d. It caused climate changes.
32. How did governments of countries react to this?
    a. They took immediate steps to curb the development.
    b. They simply dismissed it off as whimsical thinking of the academics.

c. It took a long time for them to come to an agreement to resolve the issue.

d. They refuse to sign the agreement.

33. The Montreal Protocol declared _____.

    a. that the use of ozone-depleting substances shall be banned entirely in the developed countries

    b. the production of such substances shall be phased out in both the developed and the developing countries

    c. the production of such substances shall be transferred to the developing countries

    d. it will take 50 years before a complete ban will take effect

34. Without the Protocol, the levels of ozone-depleting substances _____.

    a. would have been increased more dramatically today

    b. would have subsided gradually

    c. would have maintained the level of the 1980s

    d. would be hardly noticeable to the world

35. What led to the signing of the Protocol?

    a. Wide-spread disease of humans and animals.

    b. Scientific evidence and public opinions.

    c. Intensive negotiations.

    d. The resolve of political leaders of different countries.

Passage Four

36. Which of the statements best describes a cataract?

    a. It is a normal part of an eye.

    b. It can spread from one eye to another.

    c. It has no effect on any normal eye.

    d. It blurs vision and prevents the lens from focusing an image on the retina.

37. The only effective treatment for a cataract is _____.

    a. to remove the eye

    b. to replace the eye with an artificial one

    c. to remove the clouded lens

    d. to wear sun glasses

38. Which is the best time to take out a cataract?

    a. After it turns white.

    b. No set recommendations.

    c. Before it turns white.

    d. To have both cataracts removed at the same time.

39. How long does complete healing generally take?

    a. Four to six weeks.   b. Half a year.

    c. At least four to six weeks.   d. Four to six days.

40. For people over 64, how often should they take an eye exam?

    a. Every two years.   b. Every half a year.

    c. Every six weeks.   d. every other year.

Part IV

Write a summary of approximately 200-250 words of a passage you are going to hear. The passage is around 500 words in length.

Sample Test Two

Part I

Listen to the short passages and then decide whether the corresponding statements below are true or false. There are ten questions in this part of the test, 2 points for each question.

1. We would not have been able to visit many places 100 years ago because they were uninhabited by people.
   ○ True
   ○ False

2. Most of traffic accidents happen in the poorer countries today.
   ○ True
   ○ False

3. What cause the reductions in the incidence and impart of road traffic injuries in the developed countries is their high-income per capita.
   ○ True
   ○ False

4. France tackled the problem of road accidents by cutting 20% of traffic on the road.
   ○ True
   ○ False

5. In Africa and South America, public transportation is a main cause of road accidents.
   ○ True
   ○ False

6. Past experience show that it is impossible to improve road safety in lower-income countries.
   ○ True
   ○ False

7. Setting and enforcing laws on seat-belts, child restraints, helmets and drink driving are some of the measures that have proved effective in preventing road accidents.
   ○ True
   ○ False

8. A successful program for preventing road accidents would require the coordination of many different groups from government and civil society.
   ○ True
   ○ False

9. The public health community can increase its contribution by simply ringing the alarm bell.
   ○ True
   ○ False

10. Road accidents are preventable if everyone of us acts up to give up private cars in favor of using the public transport system.
    ○ True
    ○ False

Part II

Listen to the following short passages and then choose one of the answers that best fits the meaning of each passage. There are ten questions in this part of the test, 2 points for each question.

11. Which of the following is NOT mentioned as a factor fueling urbanization?
    a. Cars coming into possession of families.
    b. Mechanization of agriculture.
    c. Service industry.
    d. Jobs in manufacturing.

12. It's _____ in June according to the passage.
    a. rainy   b. unusually cold   c. unusually hot   d. unusually cool

13. In the richer countries, _____.
    a. the process of urbanization has been reversed
    b. citizens from poorer countries pour into large cities
    c. the poor people could not afford phones, faxes or the Internet to relocate to the suburbs
    d. the rich people don't like city life

14. Businesses are also leaving the central cities in the rich countries because _____.
    a. they cannot cope with the regulations on environment protection
    b. they look for cheaper sources of labor in the third world
    c. they want to help the developing countries
    d. they want to sell their products to the people in the developing countries

15. According to the above passage, how many people visited the United States in 1989?
    a. 30 million.   b. 40 million.   c. 38 million.   d. 43 million.

16. Transportation for almost all citizens of the world has been affected by _____.
    a. airplane and jet
    b. private cars and buses, trucks and railways
    c. satellites and GPS systems
    d. all of the above except (c)

17. Which of the following is NOT mentioned as change effected by air-conditioning?
    a. Standard of comfort.
    b. Immigration to warmer places.
    c. Development in the southern United States.

d. Distribution of electricity to the warmer locations.

18. Which of the following is NOT mentioned as a possibility enabled by the advent of computer technology?

   a. New ways of data processing.

   b. Development of large-scale organizations and of science.

   c. Shopping, banking and communicating the Internet.

   d. Participating in warfare through computer programmed pilotless airplanes.

19. What has changed our conception and mode of creativity?

   a. Science research institutions created by private and public investment.

   b. The automated assembly line production of Henry Ford's automobile factories.

   c. The management techniques of Frederick Taylor.

   d. The national government of countries.

20. Which of the following is considered as a synthetic substance we find in use in our daily life?

   a. Petroleum.   b. Rubber.   c. Glass.   d. Plastic.

Part III

Listen to the following longer passages and then choose the best answers to the questions. You may need to scribble a few notes in order to answer the questions satisfactorily. There are four passages in this part, each with 5 questions. And each question carries 2 points.

Passage One

21. When have annual carbon emissions quadrupled?

   a. Since the late 18th century.   b. Since the mid-20th century.

   c. Since the 1950s.   d. In a recent 12-month.

22. Where do one-fourth of global carbon emissions largely come from?

   a. Burning fossil fuels.   b. Electricity generation.

   c. Deforestation.   d. Residential and commercial buildings.

23. Which of the four major sectors contributing to carbon emissions accounts for the largest share?

   a. Industrial processes.   b. Residential and commercial buildings.

   c. Transportation.   d. Electricity generation.

24. Which nation is the largest polluter in the world?

   a. USA.   b. China.   c. Russia.   d. Japan.

25. Which statement about China is NOT true?

   a. It comes the second among nations in carbon emissions.

   b. It has five percent of the world's population.

   c. It accounted for nearly half of the global increase in emissions in the last decade.

   d. Its carbon emissions have jumped 47% since 1990.

Passage Two

26. After World War II, Southeast Asian countries _____.
    a. were continued to be ruled by the colonial powers
    b. changed their attitudes to the colonialist rule
    c. refused to teach English at school
    d. made Malay their national language

27. Singapore become fully independent _____.
    a. in 1959   b. in 1960   c. in 1965   d. in 1970

28. Singapore decided to keep English as its working language, because _____.
    a. it offers better access to the international community
    b. it is a language that belongs to no particular social group in Singapore
    c. it allows Singapore to stay in good term with UK
    d. it was the only language used in school in the past

29. Out of the 4 million people that make up the Singaporian population, _____.
    a. 77 percent of them are ethnic Chinese that speak Mandarin
    b. nearly half of them are descents of Chinese from different parts of China
    c. no social group speak a native language that is shared by all others
    d. only a small proportion speak English as their native language

30. What is the best title for this passage?
    a. Independence from the Colonial Rule in Southeast Asia
    b. English as a Legacy of Colonial Power
    c. English as a Bridge in Singapore
    d. English, the Language of the Colonial Power

Passage Three

31. What has happened in the past half-century?
    a. The population of 15 countries has reduced by more than half.
    b. Many countries have made unprecedented economic progress.
    c. Many countries are still struggling with underdevelopment.
    d. Urbanization has been taking place at a fast pace.

32. The financial crisis of 1997—1998 _____.
    a. has made many people in the poorer countries homeless
    b. has stayed on for many years
    c. has a lasting impact on the poorer countries
    d. is a thing of the past

33. Which of the following is NOT mentioned as a success in the latter half of the 20th Century?
    a. The increase of life expectancy in developing countries.
    b. The lowing of infant mortality rates.

c. The increase of university enrolment by 80%.

   d. The increased access to safe drinking water and basic sanitation.

34. Nearly half the world's population _____.

   a. still lives in the developing countries

   b. earns less than $1 a day

   c. has no access to safe drinking water

   d. lives on less than $2 a day

35. Which of the following could be an appropriate title?

   a. Economic Gains and the Poorer Countries' Woes

   b. Economic Accomplishment of the Past Century

   c. Economic Deprivation in the Developing Countries

   d. A Polarized World

Passage Four

36. What could be an appropriate title for the passage?

   a. Identity Crisis for Women

   b. Role Changes of Genders and the Industrial Revolution

   c. Sex and Work

   d. The Struggle Towards Equality of Men and Women

37. What changes did the emergence of factories have on the family?

   a. It separated men from women in the family.

   b. Women had to work alongside their husbands in factories.

   c. Women had to leave home to work in factories.

   d. Men had lost their dominating role in the family.

38. The industrial brought with it _____.

   a. political struggle by the working classes

   b. shifting roles for the female in the family

   c. more wealth for the women who worked in factories

   d. confusion of cultural identity for women

39. Which of the following is NOT a cause for men to replace women in the workplace?

   a. Higher wages.   b. Heavier workload.

   c. Economic hardship.   d. Immigration.

40. The male workers in the factories demanded _____.

   a. higher pay

   b. better working conditions

   c. better family care

   d. women be paid differently with men

Part IV

Write a summary of approximately 200-250 words of a passage you are going to hear. The passage is around 500 words in length.

_____
_____
_____
_____
_____
_____
_____
_____
_____
_____

Sample Test Three

Part I

Listen to the short passages and then decide whether the corresponding statements below are true or false. There are ten questions in this part of the test, 2 points for each question.

1. The Bush administration has done little in terms of investment in agriculture in the United States, making its farm products difficult to compete with imports from Latin America.
   ○ True
   ○ False

2. Global warming has raised the sea water levels and caused flooding of farmland in Canada.
   ○ True
   ○ False

3. The speaker believes that English literature should be taught to English learners throughout the world so that this literary tradition can live on.
   ○ True
   ○ False

4. Brazilians account for more than 3% of the world's population.
   ○ True
   ○ False

5. It is expected that Canon's profits will reach $1.4 billion for the last quarter of the year.
   ○ True
   ○ False

6. The French and the Germans have in recent years had a number of disputes over farm reforms and the costs of financing EU enlargement.
   ○ True
   ○ False

7. Amino acids are combined differently according the DNA blueprint to form chemically more complex proteins.
   ○ True
   ○ False

8. Jury trial is a symbol of American freedom and popular justice because it was invented by the Americans in the British colonies before the War of Independence.
   ○ True
   ○ False

9. National or regional news agencies were established to make the voices of the Third World countries heard.

- ○ True
- ○ False

10. Nuclear weapons are dangerous, but fusion hydrogen bombs are far more powerful than fission bombs.
    - ○ True
    - ○ False

Part II

Listen to the following short passages and then choose one of the answers that best fits the meaning of each passage. There are ten questions in this part of the test, 2 points for each question.

11. Which of the following was NOT mentioned as a feature of 18th century France?
    a. A magnet for researchers and the general reader.
    b. The center of intellectual seedbed of revolution.
    c. A superpower with global influence.
    d. A motor of economic globalisation.

12. The speaker of this passage believes that _____.
    a. the current view of evolution is that progress occurs randomly
    b. mutations on which evolution is based is pre-determined
    c. it is possible to repeat the process of evolution in nature
    d. survivors in the process of evolution are those with superior characters

13. What does the speaker say about "the state"?
    a. Europe is a nation of many states.
    b. The expansion of European power created many nation states.
    c. The notion of nation state had never existed before the expansion of European power.
    d. When the word "state" is used, it usually refers to both nations and states.

14. What challenging task does the Canadian government face now?
    a. To start talks with local official on reducing emissions.
    b. To reduce emissions by 6% in two years in order to meet the Kyoto target.
    c. To reduce emissions by 20% of its current level in 2012.
    d. To ratify the Kyoto Protocol, which requires emissions reduction of 6% below 1990 levels.

15. Which of the following aspects is NOT mentioned in the above statement as a function of the discovery phase in the civil procedure?
    a. To help clearing up the issues.
    b. To reveal facts.
    c. To freeze testimony.
    d. To promote settlement.

16. The number of people who speak English as a foreign language today amounts to _____.

a. thirty-four million b. three or four billion
c. three or four hundred million d. three or four million

17. If Kobe Bryant is found guilty of these criminal charges, he will face a punishment of _____.
    a. life in prison
    b. fines of at least 25,000 dollars
    c. fines ranging from 3,000 to 750,000 dollars
    d. at least fines of 3,000 dollars and probation

18. Which of the following statements is closest in meaning to what was said above?
    a. There is a great need that SIM cards replace the current credit cards now.
    b. People can use mobile phones to transfer money nowadays.
    c. Sooner or later, the bank branches developed by banks will be replaced with the cash machines.
    d. There are other barriers other than the infrastructure that prevents the switch to mobile cash.

19. What do we know about the situations in Liberia from this news report?
    a. It continued to rain in the capital Monrovia, which caused a number of casualties.
    b. Failure of a rocket launch killed at least 11 people in the Liberian capital Monrovia.
    c. Rocket attacks have caused more casualties among thousands of displaced people in Monrovia.
    d. The victims include children studying in the Newport High School.

20. What does the UN report say about the food needs in Angola?
    a. The Angolans will need food aid due to their unimproved crop production.
    b. The Angolans will require thousands of tonnes of cereal to be delivered before the next harvest.
    c. The food needs remain high because of the increase in the number of refugees and combatant soldiers.
    d. To alleviate the food needs in Angola, the report suggests that thousands of soldiers must be demobilized.

Part III

Listen to the following longer passages and then choose the best answers to the questions. You may need to scribble a few notes in order to answer the questions satisfactorily. There are four passages in this part, each with 5 questions. And each question carries 2 points.

Passage One

21. This passage is about _____.
    a. globalization of trade and capital
    b. illegal immigration to the industrialized countries

c. tightening control of immigration in the fight against terror

d. international immigration in the context of globalisation

22. How does this passage describe the immigration issue in the developed countries?

   a. Only political leaders are concerned.

   b. The United States has banned all students from Muslim countries from entering its territory.

   c. Australia remains a safe haven for asylum seekers.

   d. More Europeans have turned against immigrants from poorer countries.

23. Which of the following statement is true?

   a. The people are more worried about illegal immigrants that arrive hidden in trucks and boats.

   b. Illegal immigrants far outnumber those arrive legally.

   c. Immigrants continue to move to the richer countries despite tightened measures.

   d. Tightening the immigration measures will help to alleviate the problem.

24. The problem of immigration is attributable to _____.

   a. the fact that it is backed by economically powerful people

   b. leaking of the border

   c. human smuggling as an organized crime

   d. increased international trade and economic activities

25. The speaker of this passage is of the opinion that _____.

   a. more strict measures are needed to tighten the control of immigration

   b. immigration is a fact of life that the developed countries have to put up with

   c. EU should not accept the new member countries to lessen the burden of immigration

   d. the policies of the liberal democracies are the root cause of the problem

Passage Two

26. How many individuals annually become legal immigrants in America in recent years?

   a. About 7 million.   b. More than 3 million.

   c. Around 1 million.   d. About 9 million.

27. Which nation has the most to get into USA?

   a. India.   b. China.   c. Japan.   d. Mexico.

28. Which state is the most popular for immigrants to get in?

   a. California.   b. Texas.   c. Florida.   d. New York.

29. Which operation was the first to deter illegal immigration?

   a. Operation Hold the Line in El Paso.

   b. Operation Gatekeeper in San Diego.

   c. Operation Safeguard in Tucson.

   d. Operation Rio Grande in McAllen.

30. When was the controversial Operation Safeguard was first launched?

   a. In 1993.　　　b. In 1990.　　　c. In 1995.　　　d. In 1996.

Passage Three

31. Which one of the following is most appropriate as the title of the passage?

   a. Elephants and Mice　　　　　b. Man and Beast

   c. Elephant and Bees　　　　　 d. Wild Life Protection

32. Which one listed below is most dangerous to elephants?

   a. A disgruntled farmer with a rifle.　　　b. Poachers.

   c. Mice.　　　　　　　　　　　　　　　　d. Bees.

33. Elephants are afraid of bees because _____.

   a. they are too small to catch

   b. there are too many of them in the forest

   c. bees can attach certain parts of the elephant's body

   d. bees can kill elephants

34. What is an effective way of keeping the elephants away from farmland?

   a. Placing hives full of bees on the farmland that elephants frequent.

   b. Placing empty bee hives on the farmland.

   c. Placing either occupied bee hives or empty ones on the farmland.

   d. Releasing the bees in the face of an approaching elephants.

35. The speaker of the passage is of the opinion that _____.

   a. protecting the farmland is more important than protecting wild animal

   b. protecting endangered species is more important than protecting the interests of the farmers

   c. protecting the farmland and the wild animals are equally important

   d. one can rely more on bees than mice to frighten beasts off the farm

Passage Four

36. What would be an appropriate title for the passage?

   a. Supporting Tobacco is Bad Economics

   b. Tobacco Industry and Its Economic Profits

   c. Smoking and Health

   d. The Cost of Smoking

37. Which of the following statements is true of the tobacco industry?

   a. Tobacco is bad for people's health but good for the national economy.

   b. Tobacco has had a favourable economic impact in many countries in recent years.

   c. Developed countries such as UK and the U. S. should transfer their technology in the tobacco industry to the developing countries.

   d. Tobacco industry is bad for the economy for rich and poor countries alike.

38. What do most studies show?
    a. A decline in the tobacco industry would lead to more unemployment.
    b. The rate of employment has nothing to do with the tobacco industry.
    c. Increase in tobacco production will result in the decline of employment.
    d. The workforce may be better off with a reduced tobacco industry.
39. What does the world bank study show?
    a. The use of tobacco results in a global net loss of US $ 200 billion per year in the developing world.
    b. Economic loss caused by tobacco in the developing countries equals that of the developed countries.
    c. Huge amount of economic loss has been incurred by closing down tobacco factories in the developing countries.
    d. The use of tobacco results in a global net loss of US $ 200 billion per year, but it does not affect the quality of life of smokers or their families.
40. The best cure for smoking-related diseases is _____.
    a. to refuse to smoke
    b. to improve environmental protection
    c. to stop the selling of cigarettes in shops
    d. to increase taxation on tobacco

Part IV

Listen to the following passage about humanitarian aid to the Iraqi people in war. Write a short summary of around 150-200 words of what you have heard. This part of the test carries 20 points.

Sample Test Four

Part I

Listen to the short passages and then decide whether the corresponding statements below are true or false. There are ten questions in this part of the test, 2 points for each question.

1. There is not much evidence to indicate the impending decline in global rates of oil production.
   ○ True
   ○ False

2. According to the speaker, employers have been increasing their payment of medical insurance for their staff.
   ○ True
   ○ False

3. "Atmospheric inversion" refers to the phenomenon that temperatures decrease as latitude increases.
   ○ True
   ○ False

4. The military people are beginning to use more of lightweight materials that are popular with the commercial sector.
   ○ True
   ○ False

5. According to the speaker, it is more difficult to measure the velocities of distant galaxies than the distance between them.
   ○ True
   ○ False

6. The Millennium Summit set forth the Millennium Development Goals are represented as a list of 8 quantifiable, time-bound targets.
   ○ True
   ○ False

7. This technological revolution makes it difficult for people to protect their privacy.
   ○ True
   ○ False

8. UV-B radiation, which is harmful to human health, is due to the damage of the ozone layer caused by CFCs.
   ○ True
   ○ False

9. China and USA rank the first in Group A and Group D respectively during the semifinals.

○ True
○ False

10. The emergency planners and homeland security officials stay on duty all days and nights for fear of terrorist attacks.

○ True
○ False

Part II

Listen to the following short passages and then choose one of the answers that best fits the meaning of each passage. There are ten questions in this part of the test, 2 points for each question.

11. How many Taliban militants were arrested for the attack on UN aid workers?
    a. One.　　　　b. Two.　　　　c. Three.　　　　d. More than three.
12. Which of the following countries is NOT mentioned in the passage?
    a. USA.　　　　b. UK.　　　　c. France.　　　　d. Germany.
13. How many brothers did Edward M. Kennedy lose during 1960s?
    a. Four.　　　　b. Three.　　　　c. Two.　　　　d. One.
14. According to the passage, a jet engine uses all of the following to generate power EXCEPT _____.
    a. air　　　　b. oil　　　　c. electricity　　　　d. fire
15. Which of the following does capillaries do?
    a. Carry blood to the heart.　　　　b. Carry blood from the heart.
    c. Connect arteries and veins.　　　　d. Remove waste.
16. According to the passage, David Beckham and his wife are likely to do all the following EXCEPT _____.
    a. to consult their agent　　　　b. to live separately
    c. to get divorced　　　　d. to sue the Sunday Mirror
17. Which of the following is a more accurate figure of urban population according to the passage?
    a. 350 million.　　b. 329 million.　　c. 219 million.　　d. 207 million.
18. Which of the following can be inferred from the passage?
    a. The Food Guide is very helpful to the American people.
    b. The Food Guide has been successfully implemented.
    c. The Food Guide does not give detailed information.
    d. The Food Guide offers a proper diet for average Americans.
19. Which of the following statements is NOT true of the passage?
    a. The employers and employees may be conflicted in medical insurance.

b. The government wants to cut down costs in medical insurance.

c. Medical insurance excludes many new medical technologies.

d. Medical insurance promotes development of new medicines.

20. The general public is doing all the following to work for the Millennium Development Goals EXCEPT _____.

   a. to offer suggestions and proposals

   b. to take part in publicity and promotion campaign

   c. to assist in implementation work

   d. to help with the evaluation of outputs

Part III

Listen to the following longer passages and then choose the best answers to the questions. You may need to scribble a few notes in order to answer the questions satisfactorily. There are twenty questions in this part of the test, 2 points for each question.

21. Which of the following makes the most appropriate title for the passage?

   a. Global Warming   b. Globalization

   c. International Terrorism. d. World Economics

22. According to the passage, the world is becoming interdependent in all the following aspects EXCEPT _____.

   a. politics   b. economics   c. environment   d. culture

23. The speaker of the passage implies that protectionism might work against _____.

   a. economic integration   b. environmental upgrading

   c. spread of AIDS   d. cultural exchange

24. Which of the following is NOT true of market economy?

   a. It increases inequality.   b. It decreases inequality.

   c. It increases poverty.   d. It reduces poverty.

25. What is the speaker of the passage trying to say about globalization?

   a. It is more negative than positive in terms of its impact.

   b. It is significant both economically and politically.

   c. It is an irresistible trend rather than a matter-of-fact.

   d. It is hard to say whether it is good or bad.

Passage Two

26. The passage is about how to deal with _____.

   a. irrational ideas   b. gender differences

   c. ethnic groups   d. national integrity

27. Which of the following is true according to the passage?

   a. Men consider themselves inferior to women.

b. Women consider themselves superior to men.

c. Scientists consider themselves superior to poets.

d. Human beings consider themselves inferior to non-humans.

28. Which of the following is NOT cited as an example of male superiority or inferiority?

    a. Most poets are male.　　　　b. Most politicians are male.

    c. Most scientists are male.　　d. Most criminals are male.

29. The speaker of the passage suggests that _____.

    a. there might be other beings superior to mankind in universe

    b. human beings are not necessarily superior to jelly fish

    c. some nations are undoubted inferior to others

    d. males are evidently superior to females

30. The speaker of the passage is trying to _____.

    a. describe an event　　　　b. telling a story

    c. making an argument　　　d. making an explanation

Passage Three

31. What did the astronauts clear out of the International Space Station on Monday?

    a. A refrigerator.　　　　b. Cargo bay.

    c. A camera.　　　　　　d. An ammonia tank and a camera mounting.

32. Which statement about the debris is wrong?

    a. They may tumble from space and burn up in Earth's atmosphere.

    b. There is a little chance that they can hit the earth.

    c. The camera mounting may disintegrate completely before it arrives at the Earth.

    d. They can be carried back to the Earth.

33. How long can the ammonia tank remain in orbit before it falls on Earth?

    a. 300 days.　　b. 30 days.　　c. 96 days.　　d. 17 days.

34. How many missions can be carried out before the retirement of the space shuttles?

    a. 40.　　b. 14.　　c. 17.　　d. 70.

35. When will the space shuttles retire?

    a. 2020.　　b. 2010.　　c. 2005.　　d. 2050.

Passage Four

36. The passage is about the use of energy from _____.

    a. the sun　　b. the wind　　c. the water　　d. the oil

37. Which of the following statements is true according to the passage?

    a. Oil energy has been popular with the manufacturing industry.

    b. Solar energy is too expensive for family use at present.

    c. Wind energy is much used in plateaus.

d. Water energy is widely used in costal regions.
38. How much of the solar radiation can be converted into usable energy?
   a. 5%-10%.   b. 10%-15%.   c. 30%-45%.   d. 40%-55%.
39. Which of the following photovoltaic material is more expensive according to the passage?
   a. Nano-based.   b. Carbon-based.   c. Crystal-based.   d. Silicon-based.
40. It can be concluded from the passage that _____.
   a. it is hopeful to bring solar energy into average households
   b. it is feasible to use nuclear energy to run home appliances
   c. it is economical to use water to heat houses
   d. it is possible to use wind to power machines

Part IV

Listen to the following speech about September 11th attack by the American President George Bush. Write a short summary of around 150-200 words of what you have heard. This part of the test carries 20 points.

Sample Test Five

Part I

Listen to the short passages and then decide whether the corresponding statements below are true or false. There are ten questions in this part of the test, 2 points for each question.

1. The growth rate of the human population reached its peak, of less than 2% a year, in the early 1960s.
   ○ True
   ○ False

2. The truth turns out that almost one-fifth of the world's forests lost forever.
   ○ True
   ○ False

3. The limit to the amount of fossil fuels and metal ores that can be extracted from the earth is far greater than many environmentalists would have people believe.
   ○ True
   ○ False

4. Known reserves of all fossil fuels, and of most commercially important metals, are now as large as they were.
   ○ True
   ○ False

5. Energy shortages do look like a serious threat both to the economy and to the environment.
   ○ True
   ○ False

6. Cement, aluminium, iron, copper, gold, nitrogen and zinc account for 75% of global expenditure on raw materials.
   ○ True
   ○ False

7. In the course of the 1970s the world will experience starvation of tragic proportions — hundreds of millions of people will starve to death.
   ○ True
   ○ False

8. The daily food intake in poor countries is enough for survival.
   ○ True
   ○ False

9. The total impact of the release of greenhouse gases is likely to pose a devastating problem for the future of humanity.

○ True
○ False

10. More than 190 nations adopted the treaty against smoking after six years and three rounds of negotiations.

○ True
○ False

Part II

Listen to the following short passages and then choose one of the answers that best fits the meaning of each passage. There are ten questions in this part of the test, 2 points for each question.

11. Which of the following was NOT mentioned as one of the environmental fears?

    a. The population is ever growing, leaving less and less to eat.

    b. Natural resources are running out.

    c. Forests are disappearing and fish stocks are increasing.

    d. The planet's air and water are becoming even more polluted.

12. According to the passage, the bald eagle _____.

    a. used to be the endangered bird in the U.S.

    b. is fat and can not fly

    c. used to be courageous than the turkey

    d. will lose protection from being hunted after June 28th

13. What do we learn from this passage about America's unemployment?

    a. Unemployment rose to 0.1%.   b. Unemployment rose to 5.7%.

    c. Unemployment rose to 5.6%.   d. Unemployment rose to 5.3%.

14. Which of the following is NOT true according to the passage?

    a. There is the "Free Trade but Unfair Trade" crowd.

    b. There is the "America First" crowd.

    c. There is the "Level Playing Field" crowd.

    d. There is the "Free Trade but Fair Trade" crowd.

15. New York City _____.

    a. suffered more loss of jobs than San Jose

    b. suffered less loss of jobs than San Jose

    c. was scarcely wounded by terrorism

    d. was wounded by terrorism as much as San Jose

16. Which of the following statements is true according to the above passage?

    a. San Jose was not the center of the 1996—2000 tech boom.

    b. San Jose was the center of subsequent shake-out.

c. A few places experienced greater increases in jobs and incomes in the boom era as San Jose.

d. A few places suffered as great a hangover as San Jose.

17. How many jobs did Sacramento add in the same two years?
    a. 120,000.   b. 34,700.   c. 69,300.   d. 33,900.
18. Which of the following statements is true of monkeypox?
    a. Monkeypox occurs mainly in Central and East Africa.
    b. Smallpox is more deadly than Monkeypox.
    c. Smallpox is less infectious than Monkeypox.
    d. Monkeypox is quite different from Smallpox.
19. Which is NOT included in the questionnaire?
    a. Backaches.   b. Dizziness.   c. Cough.   d. Rashes.
20. What will be the death toll by 2020 projected by the agency?
    a. 5,000,000.   b. 35,000,000.   c. 70,000,000.   d. 10,000,000.

Part III

Listen to the following longer passages and then choose the best answers to the questions. You may need to scribble a few notes in order to answer the questions satisfactorily. There are four passages in this part, each with 5 questions. And each question carries 2 points.

Passage One

21. The main idea of this passage is _____.
    a. the population of the world will bomb
    b. the battle to feed humanity is over
    c. the population explosion is turning out to be a bugaboo
    d. hundreds of millions of people will starve to death
22. Which of the following statements is true about "The Population Bomb"?
    a. It sold very well.
    b. It was written by Dr. Ehrlich in 1978.
    c. The prediction in this book came true.
    d. According to the book, the battle to feed humanity isn't over.
23. According to the United Nations, agricultural production in the developing world has increased by _____.
    a. 6% per person since 1968   b. 45% per person since 1998
    c. 18% per person since 1949   d. 52% per person since 1961
24. The daily food intake in poor countries _____.
    a. has increased to 1,942 calories in 1961
    b. has increased to 2,615 calories in 1968

c. has increased to 2,650 calories in 1998

d. is expected to rise to 3,020 by 2030

25. The proportion of people in developing countries who are starving _____.

a. was 45% in 1949

b. has declined to 28% today

c. is expected to decline to 20% in 2010

d. is expected to decline to 16% in 2030

Passage Two

26. The passage is mainly about _____.

a. gay marriage

b. gay divorce

c. human rights

d. the infamous crime against nature

27. Which description is NOT mentioned by Blackstone about homosex?

a. An infamous crime against nature.

b. An offence that is as malignant as rape.

c. A heinous act.

d. A crime not fit to be named.

28. America's sodomy laws was struck down by the Supreme Court in _____.

    a. 1986   b. 1996   c. 2002   d. 2003

29. The first state court to rule that gays had a constitutional right to wed was _____.

a. the Maryland's Supreme Court

b. the Massachusetts' Supreme Court

c. the New Mexico's Supreme Court

d. the New Jersey's Supreme Court

30. How many American states have forbidden same-sex marriage clearly?

    a. Three.   b. Four.   c. Five.   d. Six.

Passage Three

31. The passage is about _____.

a. the nation's health care system

b. automobile accidents, breast cancer and AIDS

c. the investigation of the transplant error

d. organs transplant

32. Which of the following statements is true?

a. A seventeen-year-old girl underwent a heart-lung transplant.

b. The girl received type-O organs.

c. Her own blood is O-positive.

d. Her surgeons corrected their mistake almost immediately.

33. Which is NOT mentioned as one of the symptoms she had?

    a. Swelling.
    b. Fever.
    c. Stroke.
    d. Bleeding in her brain.

34. The serious problems highlighted by the incident are _____.

    a. medical mistakes kill more than 98,000 people each year
    b. medical mistakes kill more people than automobile accidents each year
    c. medical mistakes kill less people than breast cancer each year
    d. medical mistakes kill as many people as AIDS each year

35. What did Congress do in response to the report?

    a. To require other medical facilities to make serious changes.
    b. To require hospitals to report errors resulting in serious harm or death.
    c. To require hospitals to reduce the number of errors by 50% over five years.
    d. To allocate $50 million in researching the causes and prevention of medical mistakes.

Passage Four

36. In this passage, "that homophobia has receded" implies that _____.

    a. more Americans have become homosexual
    b. less Americans have become homosexual
    c. homosexuality should not be accepted
    d. America is becoming more tolerant

37. What is the attitude of half of those over 55 toward homosexuality?

    a. They can't accept it.
    b. They can tolerate it.
    c. They consider it natural.
    d. They don't think it morally wrong.

38. When was a total ban on gays working for the federal government repealed?

    a. In 1982.
    b. In 1975.
    c. In 2000.
    d. In 2005.

39. How many same-sex couples were there in America in the year 2005?

    a. 600,000.
    b. 1.4 million.
    c. 777,000.
    d. 30% of the whole population.

40. What results in the rapid increase in the number of same-sex couples?

    a. Americans' moral level has receded.
    b. The American government has left it uncontrolled.
    c. Americans are becoming more liberal.
    d. As people are more tolerant, more gay couples are willing to be counted.

Part IV

Write a summary of approximately 200-250 words of a passage you are going to hear. The *passage is around 500 words in length.*

Answer Key

Unit 1
I.
1. F 2. F 3. T 4. F 5. T 6. F 7. F 8. T 9. T 10. T

II.
1. d 2. d 3. b 4. b 5. b 6. a 7. b 8. c 9. d 10. b

Unit 2
I.
1. F 2. T 3. T 4. F 5. F 6. T 7. F 8. F 9. F 10. F

II.
1. b 2. c 3. b 4. c 5. c 6. d 7. c 8. b 9. b 10. b

Unit 3
I.
1. F 2. F 3. F 4. F 5. F 6. T 7. F 8. F 9. T 10. F

II.
1. d 2. c 3. b 4. d 5. d 6. d 7. b 8. d 9. a 10. d

Unit 4
I.
1. F 2. T 3. T 4. F 5. F 6. F 7. F 8. F 9. T 10. T

II.
1. b 2. d 3. c 4. b 5. d 6. b 7. d 8. b 9. a 10. b

Unit 5
I.
1. T 2. T 3. F 4. T 5. T 6. F 7. F 8. T 9. F 10. F

II.
1. d 2. c 3. c 4. d 5. a 6. a 7. c 8. b 9. c 10. b

Unit 6
I.
1. T 2. F 3. F 4. F 5. F 6. F 7. F 8. T 9. F 10. F

II.

1. a 2. d 3. a 4. c 5. c 6. d 7. b 8. d 9. d 10. a

Unit 7

I.

1. F 2. T 3. T 4. F 5. F 6. F 7. F 8. F 9. F 10. F

II.

1. b 2. b 3. a 4. a 5. c 6. d 7. a 8. b 9. d 10. c

Unit 8

I.

1. F 2. F 3. F 4. F 5. T 6. F 7. F 8. T 9. F 10. T

II.

1. d 2. d 3. d 4. a 5. c 6. c 7. b 8. b 9. d 10. b

Unit 9

I.

1. F 2. F 3. F 4. T 5. F 6. F 7. T 8. F 9. F 10. T

II.

1. c 2. b 3. b 4. d 5. d 6. c 7. b 8. d 9. a 10. c

Unit 10

I.

1. F 2. F 3. F 4. T 5. F 6. F 7. T 8. T 9. F 10. T

II.

1. c 2. b 3. d 4. d 5. b 6. d 7. b 8. d 9. a 10. c

Unit 11

I.

1. T 2. T 3. F 4. F 5. F 6. F 7. T 8. F 9. F 10. T

II.

1. d 2. a 3. b 4. b 5. b 6. a 7. c 8. c 9. b 10. b

Unit 12

I.

1. T 2. F 3. F 4. F 5. F 6. F 7. T 8. F 9. T 10. F

II.

1. a 2. c 3. c 4. d 5. d 6. d 7. b 8. c 9. b 10. b

Unit 13
I.

1. F 2. F 3. F 4. T 5. T 6. F 7. T 8. T 9. F 10. F

II.

1. d 2. c 3. b 4. c 5. c 6. c 7. d 8. a 9. c 10. c

Unit 14
I.

1. F 2. F 3. T 4. F 5. T 6. F 7. F 8. T 9. F 10. T

II.

1. b 2. c 3. d 4. b 5. c 6. a 7. a 8. a 9. d 10. b

Unit 15
I.   1. a   2. d   3. d   4. c   5. b
II. 6. b   7. c   8. c   9. a   10. b
III. 11. a   12. d   13. b   14. b   15. a
IV. 16. c   17. a   18. d   19. a   20. c

Sample Test One
Part I

1. F 2. T 3. F 4. T 5. F 6. F 7. F 8. T 9. T 10. F

Part II

11. d 12. c 13. d 14. c 15. b 16. d 17. a 18. b 19. b 20. a

Part III

21. c   22. a   23. c   24. b   25. c
26. a   27. c   28. c   29. c   30. c
31. c   32. c   33. b   34. a   35. b
36. d   37. c   38. b   39. a   40. d

Sample Test Two
Part I

1. F 2. T 3. F 4. F 5. T 6. F 7. T 8. T 9. F 10. F

Part II

11. a 12. a 13. a 14. b 15. c 16. d 17. d 18. d 19. a 20. d

Part III

21. b 22. c 23. d 24. a 25. b
26. b 27. c 28. a 29. c 30. c
31. b 32. c 33. c 34. d 35. a
36. b 37. c 38. b 39. a 40. a

Sample Test Three
Part I

1. F 2. F 3. F 4. F 5. F 6. T 7. T 8. F 9. T 10. F

Part II

11. b 12. d 13. c 14. c 15. d 16. c 17. d 18. d 19. c 20. b

Part III

21. d 22. d 23. c 24. d 25. b
26. c 27. d 28. a 29. b 30. c
31. c 32. b 33. c 34. c 35. c
36. a 37. d 38. d 39. b 40. a

Sample Test Four
Part I

1. T 2. F 3. F 4. T 5. F 6. T 7. T 8. T 9. F 10. F

Part II

11. b 12. d 13. b 14. d 15. c 16. c 17. c 18. d 19. d 20. d

Part III

21. b 22. d 23. a 24. c 25. b
26. a 27. b 28. b 29. a 30. c
31. d 32. d 33. a 34. b 35. b
36. a 37. b 38. b 39. d 40. a

Sample Test Five
Part I

1. F 2. T 3. T 4. F 5. F 6. F 7. F 8. T 9. F 10. F

Part II

11. c 12. a 13. b 14. a 15. a 16. b 17. d 18. b 19. a 20. d

Part III

21. c 22. a 23. d 24. c 25. a
26. a 27. b 28. d 29. b 30. c
31. a 32. c 33. b 34. b 35. d
36. d 37. a 38. b 39. c 40. d

Transcripts

Unit 1 A World in Action

Section I Listening Comprehension

I. Listen to the following passages and then decide whether the following statements are true or false.

1. In an age where there is more information available than ever before, we may end up being one of the least informed people in recent history — content with sitting by a computer or cell phone texting some inane personal comment about a nonexistent story while the world goes up in flames around us.

2. Russia grabbed the headlines last month by planting a flag on the ocean bed to dramatize its claim under the UN Law of the Sea to oil and mineral rights beneath a large part of the ocean. Other nations surrounding the ocean are equally determined to grab a slice of the action.

3. Although people cannot choose their parents or slow down the march of years, they can do a great deal to reduce their risk of atherosclerosis, first and foremost by adopting a healthy lifestyle. Avoid being overweight; follow a prudent diet; and incorporate physical activity into your daily life, as this helps you avoid disorders of the blood fats, development of diabetes or pre-diabetes, and the onset or aggravation of high blood pressure. Moreover, do not smoke, or stop if you do.

4. The U.S. Department of Agriculture banned Canadian beef in May after mad-cow disease turned up in a single calf there. Now it is America's turn. More than 30 countries have banned U.S. beef imports since the disease was detected in a slaughtered 6-year-old in Washington State on Dec. 23.

5. Gordon Brown has not been short of crises since becoming prime minister, with everything from incompetent terrorist plots to record-breaking floods to contend with. The most recent began on August 3rd, when cows at a farm near Guildford, in southern England, tested positive for foot-and-mouth disease, a contagious and debilitating sickness that mainly affects cloven-hoofed animals.

6. The old Utopian dream that the Internet would undermine the very notion of the nation state belongs in the dustbin of history. The reality is rather more mundane: the sorts of disagreements that characterize other global issues such as trade, the environment and human rights, are now migrating to the net work, as the Internet becomes part of the fabric of everyday life.

7. Today's vehicles bear little resemblance to the shaky craft flown at Kitty Hawk on December 17th, 1903, by Wilbur and Orville Wright. New craft have broken the sound barrier, mastered vertical take-off and landing, and visited the moon.

8. The dollar has been weakening even as America's economy has been picking up sharply. At the start of this week it fell after an upbeat assessment by the Federal Reserve. The Fed said that it would keep interest rates unchanged and that they would not rise for a "considerable" period.

9. The fear of currency crises and the subsequent unemployment, bankruptcies and stalling of economic growth have made many developing countries' government even more wary about the free flow of capital than they are about free trade. Freely flowing capital can indeed be destabilizing. So called "hot money" — portfolio flows that can reverse direction at lightning speed — can send currencies spiraling up or down and play havoc with economic management.

10. Important shifts in public values have progressively broadened the scope of agricultural research to include goals related to the environment, human health, and communities. Changing public values and needs will create new market opportunities and will alter agriculture's relationship to the food and fiber system, the environment, and the fabric of American society.

II. Choose the one answer that best fits the meaning of the statement you have heard.

1. Oil markets appear more mysterious than they are. The details of the oil business are very complex — the various grades of oil, the complicated contracts used to buy oil and hedge against volatility, and the benchmarks that are used to negotiate prices — but few of those details matter for a discussion of the links between oil and foreign policy. Oil companies care about those details because they are trying to earn a profit on each individual contract, but national policy depends only on the general availability and overall price of oil.

2. Some psychologists propose sending an all-female crew to Mars. Even if women become irritable, they are less likely to commit suicide or murder each other than men are. Others think a mixed team would support each other better. But that, as the European experiment may demonstrate, raises the possibility of the first human Martian. Perhaps it would be better to stick to more psychologically robust and less libidinous space explorers: robots.

3. Terrorists are less inclined to seek the newest or most sophisticated method of attack than to fall back on pragmatic solutions. The car bomb has been a part of British life longer than the Internet. Since 1970, terrorists of one stripe or another have deployed at least 756 vehicle bombs around the world, according to research conducted for Time by the U.S. National Consortium for the Study of Terrorism and Responses to Terrorism at the University of Maryland.

4. Since its publication in France in May, Douglas Kennedy's *The Woman in the Fifth* has sold more than 200,000 copies and dominated best-seller lists. The novel will enjoy similar success when it appears in a dozen other countries over the next few months. That's an easy prediction to make because a) like the American author's six previous novels, this one is brisk, brainy and enjoyable, and b) each of those titles has sold at least half a million copies worldwide.

5. These days, female sports are more competitive than they have ever been. And with higher stakes have come more hazardous consequences. Boys who play football are still more likely to

suffer concussions than any athletes, but in some sports played by both sexes, girls actually run a higher risk of getting hurt. According to a new study in the Journal of Athletic Training, U. S. female high school soccer athletes suffered almost 40% more concussions than males did. In high school basketball, female concussions were nearly 240% higher. Female college athletes who play soccer, basketball, softball and hockey also bear higher concussion risks than their male counterparts.

6. After two years of preparatory talks, this week's first round of the United Nation's World Summit on the Information Society, should not have been contentious. Rather than demonstrate a harmony of global interconnectedness, however, the conference revealed serious divisions in the way the governments of rich and poor nations think about the Internet.

7. During the mid-1990s, when coffee prices soared, Vietnamese farmers planted coffee bushes with abandon. In a decade, the country grew from the world's 16th-biggest exporter to the second, helping to create a worldwide coffee glut in the process.

8. Financial systems can be liberalized a lot without letting in hot money. If a government opens up to investment from abroad — allowing foreign banks to buy local institutions, say, or allowing domestic banks to raise money on international capital markets — local banks can lend more to businesses large and small. This matters, because bank credit is often the only source of finance for many firms. The downside is that banks may become over-eager and make loans on which the returns do not justify the risks. That can produce horrible busts.

9. The demands for research to support national needs in continued productivity gains, more and varied products, better human health in terms of nutritional outcomes and reductions in foodborne disease, enhanced biosecurity, animal welfare, environmental benefits, and viable rural communities are growing at the same time as scientific advances offer new opportunities for satisfaction of these demands.

10. The new vision promotes agriculture as a positive economic, social, and environmental force. It embraces further gains in food and fiber production — gains that will be crucial to meet the needs of an expanding U. S. and global population — but it also provides other benefits, such as enhanced public health, clean water, more diverse wildlife, rural amenities, and social well-being.

Unit 2 The Inner Self

Section I Listening Comprehension

I. Listen to the following passages and then decide whether the following statements are true or false.

1. I worry that, in our collective memory, the horrors of Hiroshima and Nagasaki have begun to fade. I worry about nuclear weapons falling into the hands of terrorists or ruthless dictators. I worry about nuclear weapons already in the arsenals of democracies — because as long as these weapons exist, there is no absolute guarantee against the disastrous consequences of their theft,

sabotage or accidental launch, and even democracies are not immune to radical shifts in their security anxieties and nuclear policies.

2. I hope that a side-effect of globalization will be an enduring realization that there is only one human race, to which we all belong. I hope that dynamic leaders within national governments, international institutions and civil society will step forward with the vision, the integrity and the will to reverse the inertia of fear and insecurity. I hope we can all agree to sit down together, and to start anew.

3. If the reforms succeed, and their economies pick up, France and Germany may yet surprise with a strong performance after years of relative weakness. If both countries would fully embrace labour and product market reforms, the International Monetary Fund has calculated that their GDP could be 10% higher than otherwise. There is, in other words, a high upside risk very much worth taking.

4. Cannes makes a fortune every year by hosting entertainment-industry events. The city takes so much money from the pockets of its visitors, indeed, that Hollywood studios periodically threaten to move the bash to Barcelona.

5. An Iranian earthquake specialist said in October that earthquake education in Iran was very poor, making people fatalistic about taking precautions. "Most people think what God wills, will happen. This is absolutely wrong. This thinking is poisonous," said Bahram Akasheh, professor of geophysics at Tehran University.

6. The 1982 Law of the Sea says that a country may claim rights to exploit any continental shelf extending from its territory to a depth of 2,500 meters. The deadline for nations to stake a claim under the treaty is 2009. Russia is claiming much of the Arctic Ocean because its Siberian shelf extends 2,000 kilometers along a thin promontory called the Lomonosov Ridge to the North Pole.

7. Europeans, led by Britain, are rethinking their long-held belief that university education should be financed almost entirely by the state.

8. Upon their return to Wisconsin, the family consigned the young Wright to a stay on an uncle's farm. The intimate involvement with nature he experienced on the farm made a lasting impression on Wright.

9. The belief that higher education is a citizen's right may have been reasonable when fewer Britons aspired to go to college, but it is quite different when 40 percent expect to go.

10. In France, where undergraduates pay between €280 and €350 a year, or about $350 to $435, to attend sprawling, chaotic universities, students recently took to the streets to protest against a number of proposed changes that, they feared, would lead to competition among universities and pave the way for increased privatization and higher tuition fees.

II. *Choose the one answer that best fits the meaning of the statement you have heard.*

1. Asian women and young girls have been brainwashed to disfigure themselves by undergoing

Frankenstein Surgery to meet these unreal Western standards of perfect beauty. I guess these young females have been poisoned by watching too many Hollywood movies and reading too many Western trash magazines; they follow these beauty standards blindly.

2. The scope of IT-enabled creative practices is suggested (but by no means exhausted) by a host of coinages that have recently entered common language — computer graphics, computer-aided design, computer music, computer games, digital photography, digital video, digital media, new media, hypertext, virtual environments, interaction design, and electronic publishing, to name just a few.

3. Although I don't expect there will be a change in this trend any time soon. We should all remember that there are people all over the world who lack basic health care: we should be using our money to help them instead of boosting our bosoms.

4. I was both interested and repulsed by your cover story on plastic surgery. It is said that so many people are so self-conscious that they would risk injury and spend their life savings on trying to alter their natural appearance. It does not surprise me, however, that many of the people getting this needless surgery are Asian.

5. I've read that the first breast implants were performed in Japan after World War II when barrels of industrial silicon were stolen from Japanese docks. This same silicon ended up in hundreds of Japanese prostitutes working the newly arrived invading forces. Of course, Westerners get their share of plastic surgery, too, but I think they have less of a cultural identity problem.

6. Imagine pulling into the nearest garage and filling up with whatever happens to be the cheapest fuel that day, be it petrol, ethanol (the active ingredient of booze) or any mixture of the two. Brazilian motorists now can, thanks to an innovation, put on the market a few weeks ago.

7. Many people dream of replacing petrol with ethanol. Because ethanol is made from plants, and plants draw their carbon from the atmosphere, burning it would eliminate a source of greenhouse gases and help to stem global warming. But the optimum conditions for burning petrol and ethanol are different, so a well-tuned engine needs to know what fuel it is being fed in order to adjust itself appropriately.

8. A reporter for Time magazine suffered severe shrapnel wounds and lost his hand when he tried to throw away a grenade that had been tossed into a Humvee he was riding in with a photographer and two U. S. soldiers.

9. Last week's bombings in Madrid have added a new dimension. If al-Qaeda were behind the attacks, the message may be that friends of America will be targeted. This interpretation has found credence in Australia, which has firmly aligned itself with Mr. Bush and has also been especially wary of terrorism since more than 100 of its citizens were killed in a Bali nightclub 18 months ago.

10. The last decade has been tough on travel agents. U. S. airlines at first halved and then largely eliminated commissions on domestic flights, forcing many agents to add fees to ticket prices.

That led many leisure travelers and business fliers to book their own tickets on the Internet. Then the stock market turned and the economy slowed, dragging travel down with it.

Unit 3 Well-Connected

Section I Listening Comprehension

I. Listen to the following passages and then decide whether the following statements are true or false.

1. Modern cyberspace is a deadly, festering swamp, teeming with dangerous programs such as "viruses", "worms", "Trojan horses" and "licensed Microsoft software" that can take over your computer and render it useless.

2. Cluster bombs are weapons that spread a large number of smaller bomblets over a broad area to halt troops or vehicles massing for attack.

3. Michael Weisskopf, who works for Time magazine, is an award-winning correspondent based in Washington. He covers national politics and investigations and was a finalist for the Pulitzer Prize in 1996 for national reporting.

4. Unlike their counterparts in Japan, most of whom are relatively isolated in Okinawa, most of the 37,000 American troops in South Korea are still stationed, half a century after the end of the Korean War in the country's two most high-profile locations: along the demilitarized zone with North Korea and in the heart of Seoul, the capital.

5. Like Sullivan, Wright had little patience with institutions. He left high school during his senior year, but was accepted at the University of Wisconsin as a special student in civil engineering. This too, proved a short tour, lasting less than two years.

6. Agricultural research will support agriculture as a positive economic, social, and environmental force and will help the sector to fulfill ever-evolving demands. These include further gains in food and fiber production and such other benefits as enhanced public health, environmental services, rural amenities, and community well-being.

7. The benefits of such practices have economic, social, political, and cultural components. IT-enabled creative practices have the potential to extend benefits broadly, not only to economic and cultural elites, where they are most immediately obvious, but also to the disadvantaged, and not only to the developed world but also to developing countries.

8. And their impacts extend in two directions: Just as the engagement of IT helps shape the development of inventive and creative practices, so also can inventive and creative practices positively influence the development of IT.

9. No intellectual domain of economic sector has monopoly on creativity; it manifests itself often unpredictably in multiple fields and contexts. But the manifestations vary in form and character, in associated terminology, and in the types of benefits that result.

10. In science and mathematics, the most fundamental outcome of creative intellectual effort is important new knowledge. Generally, scientists and mathematicians are clear on the difference

between such knowledge and that which results from incremental advances within established intellectual frameworks. Ground-breaking discovery is widely (though not universally) regarded as a product of great value in itself, but it is also valued more pragmatically — as an enabler of technological innovation.

II. *Choose the one answer that best fits the meaning of the statement you have heard.*
1. Accurate systems for monitoring fires would have enormous value. If such systems could predict how a wildfire was likely to behave, that would be even better. It would enable those in charge to decide which areas should be evacuated and how best to deploy fire-fighters and their equipment.
2. Fires depend on fuel, in the form of the plants they burn. Among the tasks of Earth-observation satellites currently in orbit are to assess how combustible that fuel is by measuring its moisture content, and to provide regular updates of conditions in areas that might be at risk from fire.
3. For a hundred years or so after his death the musical consensus in Europe was that Hector Berlioz was a crazy man who defied all the rules of composition. But the Frenchman's music obeyed its own rules and sounded like no one else's.
4. Learning is a basic, adaptive function of humans. More than any other species, people are designed to be flexible learners and active agents in acquiring knowledge and skills. Much of what people learn occurs without formal instruction, but highly systematic and organized information systems — reading, mathematics, the sciences, literature, and the history of a society — require formal training, usually in schools.
5. The development of creative methodologies for assessing infants' responses in controlled research settings has done much to illuminate early learning. Scientific studies of infants and young children have revealed the relationships between children's learning predispositions and their emergent abilities to organize and coordinate information, make inferences, and discover strategies for problem solving.
6. A fundamental tenet of modern learning theory is that different kinds of learning goals require different approaches to instruction; new goals for education require changes in opportunities to learn. The design of learning environments is linked to issues that are especially important in the processes of learning, transfer, and competent performance. Those processes, in turn, are affected by the degree to which learning environments are student centered, knowledge centered, assessment centered, and community centered.
7. Sheer shortages of freshwater are not the only problem. Fertilizer run-off and chemical pollution threaten both water quality and public health. More than one fifth of freshwater fish stocks are already vulnerable or endangered because of pollution or habitat modification.
8. The most serious immediate challenge is the fact that more than 1 billion people lack access to safe drinking water, while half of humanity lacks adequate sanitation. In many developing

countries, rivers downstream from large cities are little cleaner than open sewers. The health impact is devastating.

9. Some students of foreign policy like to categorize countries by the personality of their people. By that measure, Norsemen of a millennium ago were greedy psychopaths. Fierce warriors, pillagers and traders, the Vikings sacked Paris in 861, conquered much of England and northern France, settled Iceland and Greenland, discovered America and even helped to raid Baghdad.

10. The very existence of nuclear weapons gives rise to the pursuit of them. They are seen as a source of global influence, and are valued for their perceived deterrent effect. And as long as some countries possess them (or are protected by them in alliances) and others do not, this asymmetry breeds chronic global insecurity.

Unit 4 When, Where and How?

Section I Listening Comprehension

I. Listen to the following passages and then decide whether the following statements are true or false.

1. In late December, an advanced team of about 20 personnel from Japan's Air Self-Defense Force finally set foot in Kuwait and Qatar. Their work there is to prepare for the arrival of several hundred troops over the next few months to support reconstruction work in Iraq.

2. South Korea's economic ties with China, now its leading trading partner, are growing rapidly. As a budding rival to the United States for influence in Northeast Asia, China has assumed a new muscular diplomacy, most notably in the six-nation talks to resolve the North Korean crisis.

3. There must be a better way to respond to the opening up of new environments as the ice retreats. There is no need for a carve-up. No one can claim the Arctic as their god-given right, with the possible exception of the Inuit people, who lack the nationhood needed to stake a claim. And do we really have no better use for this near-pristine ecosystem than to plunge oil rigs down in the middle of it, especially when we know what climatic harm burning that oil will do?

4. China's $1.4 trillion economy, which has grown at twice the pace of India's during the past decade, could rival Japan's gross domestic product within the next six years.

5. India has more than its share of problems beyond shoddy roads and ports. This year, the economy is expected to grow about 8 percent, a rate that is catching investors' attention. But bureaucracy and profligate government borrowing may douse growth in the years ahead.

6. Earlier, Japanese ships were sent to the Indian Ocean to help U.S. action in Afghanistan, but only to provide logistical support. Then, parliament had to pass a special law allowing humanitarian missions in Iraq, but on condition that the troops are sent to areas away from combat.

7. Both the Tories and the Liberal Democrats cling to the idea of purely tax-funded higher education: the former intend to save money by cutting student numbers; the latter claim that extra money can be painlessly extracted from people earning more than £100,000 a year.
8. There is a precedent at the other end of the world. Nearly 50 years ago, at the height of the cold war, Russia, the U.S. and 10 other nations signed the Antarctic Treaty. They agreed to freeze their claims to the territory on the ice continent and to keep it a demilitarized, nuclear-free zone devoted to science. A decade ago, a supplementary agreement came into force banning any mineral exploitation on the continent. Has the world gone so far backwards since then that we cannot agree to something similar for the Arctic?
9. The good news for Europe is that there are a number of local companies that are as innovative as any. For instance AgustaWestland, a helicopter maker, is moving into what it dubs its "third era" of sustainable growth, following periods when it was classed as a "pioneer" and later as a "market leader". The company has launched two big research-based projects to achieve this.
10. Ever since the Industrial Revolution, British policymakers have been worrying that universities don't work better with businesses. In 1919 the economist Alfred Marshall bemoaned the fact that the fruits of "revolutionary discoveries" in science were reaped by businesses in Germany, "where industry and science have been in close touch".

II. Choose the one answer that best fits the meaning of the statement you have heard.
1. Resistance forces have assassinated a member of the Governing Council, the top Iraqi body appointed by the Americans, along with the deputy mayor of Baghdad, several judges, a top oil official and several senior policemen.
2. In a recent report, the European Commission said that European countries spend just 1.1 percent of their gross domestic product on higher education compared with 2.3 percent in the United States, with the difference coming from private financing including tuition.
3. Police are investigating whether four students, deported from Pakistan and now detained in Jakarta for suspected terrorism links, were involved in funding the bombing of the Marriott Hotel in Jakarta in August, which killed 12 people.
4. In the United States, the Federal budget is drifting into a future of unprecedented tax increases, huge deficits or both. This is no secret because the great driving force of change is the impending retirement of 77 million baby boomers and their heavy claims on federal retirement programs.
5. Because of the market's complexity, media accounts often suggest that oil markets move without a clear connection to economic fundamentals and that irrational fears or the actions of shadowy governments drive price and product availability. Although consumers' fears and suppliers' political decisions surely matter, their effects can be understood within a fairly traditional market framework. Two main processes determine oil prices: the forces of supply

and demand and constraints on those forces created by political risk and cartel behavior.

6. The American beef industry is facing a long road to recovering the world's trust, McDonald's issued a press release about its longstanding policy against using unhealthy cattle, like the one implicated in last month's recall. One of the biggest steps U. S. Secretary of Agriculture took last week was to ban the sale of meat from these animals.

7. In November, the American Heart Association said that it's better to eat fish than to avoid it, especially since there is still plenty of seafood like cod, farmed tilapia and shellfish that remain pure. And while the fish richest in omega — 3s often have the highest levels of contaminants, they are still safe, to a point. There's little solid evidence that low levels of contaminants like mercury in fish can harm healthy adults.

8. Because soot promotes the melting of snow and ice, it may exacerbate the problem of rising seas. The good news is that reducing the amount of soot in the air by installing exhaust filters on diesel trucks and buses and better managing forest fires is probably easier than getting Americans to give up SUVs. Fires are the source of about half the world's soot.

9. Federal prosecutors have begun a wide-ranging effort to curb the growing popularity of online gambling in the United States by quietly threatening legal action against American companies that do business with Internet casinos and sports betting operations based outside the country.

10. Several big media operations — including Infinity Broadcasting, Clear Channel and the Discovery Networks — stopped running advertisements for offshore Internet casinos last autumn in light of the threat of further scrutiny that might lead to prosecution.

Unit 5 Putting the Horse before the Cart

Section I Listening Comprehension

I. Listen to the following passages and then decide whether the following statements are true or false.

1. The British government and the universities say they have no choice but to raise tuition fees in the years to come. The universities, which are receiving $14.6 billion this year from the government, need $14 billion more over the next three years to maintain standards.

2. Belfast, a city of 277,000 best known for bombings and other acts of terror in the 1970's and 80's, now has a thriving nightlife. During the day the city resounds with work on new buildings and renovations of derelict warehouses. This activity is the result of the 1998 Good Friday peace agreement, which restored confidence in the future of the city.

3. The Paris opera was confused by the complexity of the orchestration and frightened by the scale of Berlioz's music. French audiences were largely indifferent or contemptuous. He died a prophet without honor in 1869, a lonely, near-tragic figure, embittered at the rejection by his countrymen.

4. Because many computer-based technologies are relatively new to classrooms, basic premises about learning with these tools need to be examined with respect to the principles of learning.

Transcripts

5. As the Swedish population becomes more heterogeneous, it may demand more choice within the welfare state and become more reluctant to pay exorbitant taxes.

6. Mr. Mubarak, Egypt's president, has never named a vice-president, nor even hinted at the possible identity of one. Coyly and repeatedly, he has said that it was hard to find anyone suitable.

7. Few real-estate speculators have over-borrowed from local banks. The government granted most of the land free; many firms are already cash rich; Dubai's building costs are low, thanks to those amenable Asians; and Standard Chartered thinks the Emirates' GDP will grow by 8% this year — as long as oil output grows and its price stays high.

8. Localizing software is a tedious job, but some people are passionate enough about it to resort to unusual measure. The Hungarian translation of Open Office was going too slowly for Janos Noll, founder of the Hungarian Foundation for Free Software. So he built some web-based tools to distribute the workload and threw a pizza party in the computer room at the Technical University of Budapest.

9. A useful BCI device, however, must be able to determine the subject's intention from a single brain-wave reading. For real-time applications, averaging hundreds of reading simply won't work. But the problem with such single-trial readings is that they are very difficult to interpret, because of the background noise produced both by the brain and by the EEG equipment.

10. Worldwide changes are transforming American agriculture into an endeavor focused not only on efficient food and fiber production but also on delivering improved public health, social well-being, and a sound environment. Recent scientific breakthroughs will make it easier for agriculture to achieve its potential for delivering a wide array of benefits to society.

II. Choose the one answer that best fits the meaning of the statement you have heard.

1. The changes now under way in agriculture's social and scientific context require a new vision of agricultural research — one that is grounded in lessons from the past, in changing American values, in a globalizing economy, and in scientific advances that have fundamentally altered the life, environmental, and social sciences.

2. In engineering, and in technology-based industry, creativity yields technological inventions. Such inventions can result in commercially successful products, in improvements to the quality of life, and in the generation of income streams through intellectual property licensing arrangements. Thus the social and economic benefits are often clearly identifiable and measurable.

3. Few technologies are currently as controversial as genetically modified (GM) crops. Critics, particularly in Europe, object to them on many grounds. A common objection is that they are unnatural, because they often involve the transplantation of genes from entirely different species.

4. Normally, maize, which is an important crop for livestock feed, has low levels of methionine.

Farmers typically have to add chemically synthesized methionine to their animal feed in order to keep their herds healthy.

5. Sony, the market leader, is changing the technological and business rules that have defined this cut-throat industry for two decades. By doing so, it hopes both to improve its fortunes — earlier this year the company admitted that its revenues and profits had unexpectedly plunged — and to fend off a challenge from Microsoft, which launched its first games console, the Xbox, in 2001.

6. What leads surprisingly large numbers of young people to follow the desperate course set for them by fanatics? A sense of oppression, of humiliation, of marginalization, can give rise to extremism. In 1962, the UN Secretary-General warned that an explosion of violence felt by those living in poverty and despair in a world of plenty.

7. We must press governments to ensure that in attacking terror, the cure does not become worse than the disease. The worry is that in many countries human rights have become the "collateral damage" of the war on terrorism — in particular the presumption of innocence, freedom from arbitrary detention, due process.

8. In farsighted decision, Microsoft says it will combat software piracy by allowing users to decide what price to pay for its new Microsoft Office suite. A spokesman says: "We recognize that some folk in some less advantaged countries can't afford the $3 million-per-box price-tag, so we'll let them pay what they think is right."

9. Apple released its first mobile phone in August. It's plain white, has no buttons and looks like an egg. All units of the first batch had to be recalled due to a design flaw: the surface cracks easily, and white and yellow goo leaks out. Long-term users complained of hearing clucking noises from inside.

10. Concerned about maintaining friendly ties with future growth markets on its eastern frontier, Germany realizes that its strategic and economic interests are best served by cooperative relations with Poland and other new members — who were outraged when Chirac bluntly told them they should have kept quiet rather than voicing their support for the United States during the war.

Unit 6 The Other Side of the Coin

Section I Listening Comprehension

I. Listen to the following passages and then decide whether the following statements are true or false.

1. Nigerians suspect the government's motives for taking away cheap petrol and doubt that the money saved will be put to good use.

2. The "war on terror" should provide an impetus to work towards a global security culture that will serve the interests of all countries equally, and will make reliance on nuclear weapons obsolete.

3. Alaska pollock — an inexpensive whitefish, used for processed seafood such as fish sticks and imitation crab meat — does not usually command the attention of the State Department. But a $9 million shipment of it, currently sitting on a dock in the Moroccan port of Agadir, has embroiled governments on both sides of the Atlantic, and underscores the risks of doing business at sea.

4. Still, during a visit in November by Defense Secretary Donald Rumsfeld, the two nations did not decide on a timetable and failed to agree on plans to relocate the Yongsan military garrison in Seoul. What is more, the important subject of reducing the force size was not raised, nor was the topic of what this all meant for the U.S.-South Korea security alliance.

5. In the aftermath of the success of Shenzhou 5 the question is, can the Chinese run a successful manned space program at less-than-exorbitant cost, when Russia and America failed?

6. Japan Tobacco's domestic market is now shrinking, not least thanks to successive tax hikes on cigarettes. In 1996-2001, the number of smokers in Japan — as a share of people aged 20 or over — fell from 27.1% to 24.4%. Japan Tobacco's domestic tobacco sales fell by 2.4% by volume in fiscal 2001, and by 3.5% last year. They will fall by a hefty 5.5% this year.

7. With the need to devise production methods, rewrite design and safety codes, encourage multiple sources of supply, and develop repair and maintenance procedures, it is no surprise that new materials such as engineering plastics, super-strength ceramics or carbon fiber generally take 30 years to go from invention to commercial use.

8. Memory has come to be understood as more than simple associations; evidence describes the structures that represent knowledge and meaning. Knowing how learners develop coherent structures of information has been particularly useful in understanding the nature of organized knowledge that underlies effective comprehension and thinking.

9. Key scientific findings have come from studies of people who have developed expertise in areas such as chess, physics, mathematics, electronics, and history. The examples are important not because all school children are expected to become experts in these or any other areas, but because the study of expertise shows what the results of successful learning look like.

10. Leaders of most of the Commonwealth's 54 countries gathered in Nigeria's capital Abuja, minus the uninvited Robert Mugabe, Zimbabwe's president. In his own annual state-of-the-nation speech Mr. Mugabe vowed to crack down on corruption and to curb inflation — currently officially 526% but estimated to be much higher — through price controls.

II. Choose the one answer that best fits the meaning of the statement you have heard.

1. European foreign ministers, meeting in Naples to thrash out the draft European Union constitution, settled few of the outstanding disputes. Joshka Fischer, Germany's foreign minister, declared that he was leaving Naples gloomier than he arrived.

2. China plans to more than double gas use by 2010 to cut pollution and the nation's $20 billion oil import bill. As world gasoline prices rise to records, suppliers are building CNG stations to

bolster sales.

3. China, where respiratory disease is the No. 1 killer, is turning to natural gas because it produces fewer harmful emissions. Chinese oil companies are spending more than $7 billion to tap the nation's gas fields and pipe the fuel to cities such as Beijing and Shanghai.

4. China's biggest oilfields such as Daqing, have been in production for half a century or more and their output is falling. By contrast, the country is just beginning to tap some of its largest gas reserves in Xinjiang in the far west and off the eastern and southern coasts.

5. Afghanistan has yet to resolve its power struggles, and the resulting insecurity means that large portions of the country are off-limits to aid workers. The country exports little but opiates, and a reconstructed Afghanistan — let alone a prosperous one — still seems a very long way off.

6. Japan has the highest life-expectancy in the world, one of the lowest birth rates and accepts few immigrants, leaving a diminishing workforce paying for a rising number of pensioners.

7. According to the Ministry of Health, Labour and Welfare in Japan, in 2000 the present value of the public pension system's liabilities exceeded its assets by 450 trillion *yen*, almost a year's GDP. The gap has since grown.

8. Poor investments have hobbled Japan's public pension funds, which may invest in shares and have often done so simply to prop up the stock market. The biggest state-run fund had a shortfall of 6 trillion *yen* at the end of March. The welfare ministry, disastrously, built holiday resorts with pension premiums. Now these must be sold. So far one has been sold, for 4% of what it cost to build.

9. Not surprisingly, public mistrust is growing, which makes the sums worse. In the national pension scheme covering the self-employed, farmers, fishermen and students, 37% of those supposed to contribute do not bother. Many fear the scheme will collapse before they retire.

10. A new generation of South Korean leaders, backed by young voters, is more independent-minded and less beholden to the United States. They regard the United States less as the country that fought in the Korean War than as the country that backed past military dictators.

Unit 7 Lending an Ear to Numbers

Section I Listening Comprehension

I. Listen to the following passages and then decide whether the following statements are true or false.

1. One of the many little annoyances of life in a crowded city such as London suburb of Haringey will be particularly unhappy. Those who own cars with high carbon-dioxide emissions will see their parking charges rise almost fourfold, from £25 a year to £90. A similar plan was enacted in Richmond, a wealthy western fringe of the city, in March. There, the price of parking a dirty car rose threefold, with even stiffer penalties for those who own more than one vehicle.

2. Both Germany and France are heading for budget deficits of nearly 4% of GDP. Social-security deficits are out of control. The shortfall is €10.6 billion in 2003 and 14.1 billion in 2004.

Unless changes are made, social-security payments could rise from over 45% of pay to 54% in 2030, by some estimates.

3. Today, only 35% of Germans believe that comprehensive social protection is possible without high contributions, down from 53% a decade ago, and as many as 70% agree that reforms are necessary. In France, a recent poll suggested that 51% of French people are in favor of the government continuing with reform.

4. Mobile telephony is finally taking off in India. Some 5 million new users have signed up since March; there are now over 17 million subscribers. Add to this around 3.5 million subscribers to a "limited" mobile service provided by fixed-line operators that works within a restricted area, usually a large city, and the total is even more impressive.

5. Price competition has also hurt profits. Mobile operators have made combined losses of 117 billion rupees ($2.6 billion) since the launch of limited mobile. Without this competition, they would have made a profit of 67 billion rupees.

6. U.S. inspectors have tested fewer than 30,000 of the roughly 300 million animals slaughtered in the past nine years and they get results days or weeks later. But the American system was never intended to keep sick animals from reaching the public.

7. On Thursday an American soldier died in a suicide truck bombing and mass resignations almost halved the first battalion of the new Iraqi Army.

8. About 350 passengers were screened for questioning Wednesday afternoon as they prepared to board Air France Flight 68, which had been scheduled to fly out at 7 p.m..

9. In June 2002, a quake measuring at 6.3 magnitude hit northern Iran, killing at least 229 people and injuring more than 1,000. About 35,000 people were killed in 1990 when earthquakes of up to 7.7 magnitude hit the northwest of Iran. Tehran was hit by a 7.0 magnitude quake in 1830.

10. Global freshwater consumption rose sixfold between 1900 and 1995 — more than twice the rate of population growth. About one third of the world's population already lives in countries considered to be "water stressed" — that is, where consumption exceeds 10 percent of total supply. If present trends continue, two out of every three people on Earth will live in that condition by 2025.

II. Choose the one answer that best fits the meaning of the statement you have heard.

1. Over the last century, the primary public need addressed by U.S. agriculture has been food and fiber production. The major focus of agricultural research, in turn, has been on enhancing agricultural productivity. The success of that endeavor has been substantial, as demonstrated by major productivity gains such as the tripling of corn yields over the last 50 years.

2. Jackson is one of many planners and development specialists working to further the revival of Belfast. The partnership is distributing $70 million in grants from the European Union. Their efforts are impressive, but the lingering effects of the old days of violence keep holding the city

back.

3. The European Union has also contributed a significant share of aid. Northern Ireland, even while it is enduring a loss of industrial jobs, enjoys a relatively low 5.6 percent unemployment rate. But now the first wave of aid reductions is coming. The European Union has been providing $1.6 billion for the 2001—2006 period, but after that, it warns, the money will be greatly reduced as the EU's attention shifts to new eastern members.

4. Europe is under-investing in R&D to the tune of €100 billion ($120 billion) per year compared with the United States. It is estimated that, between 1990 and 1996, American taxpayers forked out $140 billion on R&D compared with $70 billion coughed up in Europe. Half of the $140 billion of the public money spent on R&D in America was for defense research.

5. The Paris-based Lafarge group, the world leader in construction materials spends a paltry 1% of sales on corporate R&D. But with sales of €14.6 billion in 2002, that still means Lafarge has close on €150 million a year to spend on learning "how to crush stones and put them back together".

6. So far this year, some two and half million hectares (6 million acres) of North American forest have been consumed by fire. And several fires are still blazing in the west of the continent. The United States' Forest Service reckons it will spend around $900 million in 2003 on putting fires out, and the damage such fires have caused probably cost several times that figure.

7. A long drought, high winds and extraordinarily high temperatures have also created tinderbox conditions in Europe, where fires have destroyed at least 500,000 hectares of forest and killed more than 30 people.

8. Petrol burns best with an air-to-fuel ratio of around 14:1. This means that, for every kilogram of fuel burnt, all of the oxygen in 14 kilograms of air will be consumed. Ethanol, though, requires an air-to-fuel ratio of 9:1. The new technology works by "sniffing" the amount of oxygen in a car's exhaust. If too much or too little of the gas is sensed, it indicates that the fuel is burning in a less-than-optimal way, and thus that the air-to-fuel ratio is wrong. A signal is then sent to the engine to tweak the ratio appropriately.

9. Brazil has a history of promoting ethanol as a fuel. In the 1980s, the government encouraged it, in a misguided attempt to subsidize sugar farmers (since the main source of ethanol is fermented sugar) and cut oil imports. At the height of this policy, almost 80% of cars produced in Brazil ran on pure ethanol.

10. Maze-based E85 fuel (an 85% ethanol/petrol mixture) is already on sale in parts of America. In July, the National Ethanol Vehicle Coalition launched a project to promote greater use of E85 in Wisconsin, Missouri, Colorado, Minnesota, Michigan and Illinois. The coalition estimates that the market for E85 is now about 40 million liters a year. Better fermentation techniques, based on biotechnology, may multiply that many times.

Unit 8 Being Indirect and Probable

Section I Listening Comprehension

I. Listen to the following passages and then decide whether the following statements are true or false.

1. Still, one day, demand for fast long-haul flights could return. With only a modicum of technological progress, a quieter, more fuel-efficient supersonic passenger jet could be viable.

2. In hindsight, a number of the premises of the 1970 Treaty on the Non-Proliferation of Nuclear Weapons seem less than optimal. It temporarily legitimized the arsenals of the five countries that had already developed nuclear weapons.

3. A workable policy (on immigration) would be more selective, not more restrictive. Countries could, for instance, freely admit the citizens of any country with broadly the same income per head as theirs, letting them work or stay as long as they liked.

4. In the case of migrants from the poor world, countries should give preference to those who seem to integrate most readily. That would often mean favoring not just the skilled but those from culturally similar backgrounds. It might mean insisting that migrants learn the local language quickly; that they abide by local standards of tolerance and good behavior.

5. Race and religion must be a part of the public discussion of migration. To pretend that they do not affect attitudes makes policy more restrictive than it should be.

6. A decade-long surge in U.S. wine imports could come to an end this year with the decline of the dollar and a glut of Californian wine, crimping the sales of Australian vineyards.

7. In Norway, the centenary of independence from Sweden in 1905 makes that an inauspicious date for deciding on EU membership, but if pools show continued support for joining, a referendum will come soon after. If Norway joins, Iceland too will reconsider membership, in the hope of extracting a deal on fishing.

8. As more foreigners come in and settle in Sweden, they may in turn help to change their host country's values. Even neighboring Danes say they cannot understand why the Swedes have for so long put up with a nanny state that tries to run every aspect of their lives.

9. The new timetable for turning political control and sovereignty back to Iraqis will require some process to select a new Iraqi provisional legislature, possibly by people now serving as municipal and provincial council members.

10. Tomorrow's aircraft are likely to be still more marvelous, and perhaps even more different than today's are from the Wrights' pioneering effort. Predicting how different requires guess work, an open mind and even a dollop of science fiction.

II. Choose the one answer that best fits the meaning of the statement you have heard.

1. The C-17, built by Boeing, is one of the younger planes in the air force inventory, and would presumably have been equipped with a system that detects missiles and then either drops decoy

flares or deploys a laser to blind incoming missiles.
2. The American and British armies could have prevented hundreds of civilian injuries or deaths during the war in Iraq by eliminating the use of cluster munitions in populated areas, according to a study by a leading human rights group.
3. If the inventors of the first heavier-than-air machine capable of powered flight had been transported forward 100 years to the present day, they might be astounded at the way that those who followed in their wake have colonized the air.
4. Can plants hear? They all respond to light, which affects how they optimize growth and survival. Plants also have a sense of touch, allowing them to stiffen in response to wind, and a "taste" for nutrients. But whether they respond to sound is a mystery. Now Mi-Jeong Jeong of the National Institute of Agricultural Biotechnology in Suwon, South Korea, and colleagues claim to have identified two genes in rice that respond to sound waves. They also say that the promoter of one of the sound-sensitive genes could be attached to other genes to make them respond to sound, too.
5. In theory, the story that bones tell about the origins of the human race and the story that genes tell should be the same. In practice, they often start off different. Forty years ago, for example, palaeontologists thought that hominids, the group of primates that includes modern humans, had been distinct from other apes for some 25 million years. Molecular biologists, however, reckoned 5 million years a better estimate. With the discovery of more fossils, that has become the accepted number.
6. The IPCC says the Greenland ice sheet will take at least 1,000 years to melt. But Lenton's group — whose members include John Schellnhuber, the chief scientist on climate change at the recent G8 meeting in Germany — says the sheet could break up within 300 years, raising sea levels by 7 meters. This would flood hundreds of millions of people or more out of their homes. "We are close to being committed to a collapse of the Greenland ice sheet," Lenton says. "But we don't think we have passed the tipping point yet."
7. Mitochondria are often referred to as the power plants of the cell because they perform most of the chemical reactions that transform sugars into usable energy. However, mutations in the genes that control this process are common. Mitochondrial diseases affect at least 1 in 5,000 people and can lead to a variety of serious, incurable metabolic diseases, including disorders of the nervous system and blindness. The gradual accumulation of mutations in mitochondria over a lifetime could also be an important cause of ageing.
8. The limited impact of the diverse work of the Californians on the rest of the country should probably be attributed to the fact that the West Coast was still considered provincial by the Eastern architectural establishment.
9. Europe's industrial base certainly needs updating. It has more than its fair share of capital-intensive industries that have reached the end of their innovation cycles, and are unsure where

to go next. European industry is also investing too little in R&D, at least if it hopes to keep up in the knowledge-economy stakes. But increasing the amount that Europe spends on R&D is difficult when so much of its industrial bases is mature.

10. European industry faces a massive challenge if it is to meet the goal of spending 3% of GDP on R&D. Making a success of breakthrough research will mean more than spending money on laboratories and researchers. Fortunately, while many of Europe's ageing industrial firms may be slow to innovate, they are world-class when it comes to making and marketing products. That should hold them in good stead if they can make the shift to developing innovations from breakthrough research.

Unit 9 Speaking in Quotes

Section I Listening Comprehension

I. Listen to the following passages and then decide whether the following statements are true or false.

1. The fall of the Berlin Wall in 1989 did nothing to settle the debate about which model of social development is the best. Or, to be precise, the debate about whether the American model will continue to outdo all comers, or instead be replaced at the top of the economic heap by a rival.

2. You've heard of offsetting carbon. Well how about offsetting dead seabirds? Many seabird populations are threatened because the birds end up as by-catch in commercial fishing nets. If restricting fishing fails, the last resort is usually to close fisheries. Now two ecologists claim that a better way may be "biodiversity offsetting" — placing a levy on by-catch and using the money to pay for alternative conservation efforts.

3. In a speech to city grandees on June 20th, Gordon Brown who will be prime minister set out his plans for continuing the permanent revolution. He called for a national debate on how to make Britain world-class in education. And he promised to set up a new talking-shop: a "National Council for Educational Excellence", in which to have it.

4. "We're not going to have a Jeffersonian democracy here," he added. "The process will be bumpy. We'll have bad days and good days."

5. Bremer, appearing relaxed and in good humor, spoke in broad terms about the next phase of the U. S. occupation, a period that he predicted could bring a spike in violent attacks as well as a U. S. -nurtured public debate over the shape of the new Iraq.

6. Atherosclerosis, commonly called hardening of the arteries, causes heart attacks and strokes, as well as ravaging many other of the body's organs. It is on the rise worldwide and threatens to become a major cause of death, disability, and loss of useful life years not only in Western societies, but in the developing world. However, there is much that can be done to reduce the risk of suffering from this condition and its complications.

7. Although people cannot choose their parents or slow down the march of years, they can do a great deal to reduce their risk of atherosclerosis, first and foremost by adopting a healthy

lifestyle. Avoid being overweight; follow a prudent diet; and incorporate physical activity into your daily life, as this helps you avoid disorders of the blood fats, development of diabetes or pre-diabetes, and the onset or aggravation of high blood pressure. Moreover, do not smoke, or stop if you do.

8. Because the U.S. is a net oil importer, and a substantial one at that, concerns about energy security naturally raise foreign policy questions. One set of arguments is based on fears about dwindling global oil reserves and their increasing concentration in politically unstable regions. Those so-called peak oil worries have led some foreign policy analysts to call for increased U.S. efforts to stabilize — or, alternatively, democratize — the politically tumultuous oil-producing regions.

9. While it is too early to say how long U.S. forces might stay and under what conditions, Bremer said he believed Iraqis would ask for an agreement based on security conditions in the country.

10. "It's a question that really ought to be asked in six months, when we get through this very important crucial period and let's see where we are," he said. "My own guess is we're going to have an increase in violence over the next six months." "The violence will be precisely because of the fact that we're building momentum toward success," Bremer said.

II. Choose the one answer that best fits the meaning of the statement you have heard.

1. "A furniture truck was driven by a suicide bomber at approximately 1:30 p.m. at Champion Main, 82nd Airborne Division Headquarters, in the vicinity of Ramadi," a statement said.

2. "It is believed three Iraqis driving the vehicle were killed in the explosion," another statement said.

3. "Many people were believed to be trapped under debris," state news media said, "appealing for blood donations to help the wounded."

4. Although the extreme-poverty rate in Africa has fallen from an estimated 46% in 1999 to 41% in 2004, that is still way off the 2015 target of 22%. Hunger and malnutrition still gnaw at the region: the proportion of under-fives who are underweight has declined only marginally, from 33% in 1990 to 29% in 2005. Despite dramatic gains, Africa will not meet the goal of universal primary enrolment either; the rate is up from 57% in 1999 to 70% in 2005.

5. Malta may be densely populated (three times more than the Netherlands), but its immigrant population is still tiny. Officials say they have no precise total, but their estimate is below 3,000 — fewer than the commonly touted figure of 7,000 arrivals since 2002, and less than 1% of the island's 400,000 population. Malta's EU partners could be forgiven for feeling that, as in other respects, the union's southernmost member is just catching up with them.

6. China's demand for oil grew 10 percent in 2003, and it is expected to increase 6 percent this year, or the equivalent of 320,000 more barrels a day, according to the International Energy Agency. While the strain of coping with the growing thirst for oil may become evident in

China's energy infrastructure this year, oil exporters are toasting the emergence of an important market.

7. Late in 2002, in an initiative dubbed "more Research for Europe", European heads of government declared that the region should boost its industrial R&D to ensure future competitiveness and social well-being. The bureaucrats want to see Europe's R&D investment rise from its current 1.9% of GDP to 3% by 2010. And industry, they say, should provide most of that extra investment.

8. Concern about the pension system is one reason why consumer spending is not rising in Japan, hobbling the nation's economy, according to economists at J. P. Morgan securities Asia and Nomura research Institute. Since 1998, annual growth in consumer spending has slowed to half the pace of the preceding five years.

9. Consumers have so far been missing in Japan's recovery from its third recession since 1991. Japan's $4 trillion annual economy expanded for a sixth quarter in the three months to Sept. 30, growing 0.3 percent. Increased exports and capital spending by companies accounted for all the growth, countering a 0.1 percent decline in consumer spending.

10. Rising overseas sales are not stopping companies, including Sony, from cutting jobs to spur earnings, Japan's economy lost 190,000 jobs in November, a report said. The unemployment rate held steady at 5.2 percent close to a record 5.5 percent, because 210,000 people gave up looking for work.

Unit 10 Speech Acts

Section I Listening Comprehension

I. Listen to the following passages and then decide whether the following statements are true or false.

1. The officials declined to say exactly what they would recommend but acknowledged that European and Japanese regulators screen millions of animals using tests that take only three hours — fast enough to stop diseased carcasses from being cut up for food.

2. In response to the missile threat, in September the Department of Homeland Security asked contractors for proposals on how to equip civilian planes with military antimissile technologies.

3. Douglas Wills, a spokesman for the Air Transport Association, the trade group of the major airlines, said that there was no single solution, but that the government should be offering bounties for shoulder-fired missiles, to dry up the black market.

4. The government in Tehran quickly requested international aid to deal with the catastrophe, including sniffer dogs and equipment to search for bodies amid the rubble.

5. A healthy lifestyle by itself, however, often does not suffice to achieve optimum protection from atherosclerosis and its complications. Yet, there are a number of treatments that can reduce risk. Depending on the levels of cholesterol, the type of cholesterol carriers in the blood, blood pressure, blood sugar levels, etc., doctors can tailor a regimen of risk-reducing

medications. Even a baby aspirin a day in certain instances can lower the risk of cardiovascular events markedly.

6. The government argues that the move is essential if Britain's universities are to remain internationally competitive. But Blair is confronting formidable opposition inside and outside his party, as well as from student groups who say the plan would discourage would-be students and contradict the deeply held belief that higher education is a citizen's right.

7. Under the British plan, low-income students would have access to scholarships and grants to help with living costs, and no one would have to pay the tuition up front. Rather, the fees would be handled as loans, which students would be required to repay only after they have left school and begun earning about £25,000 or £30,000 a year.

8. Science now offers new conceptions of the learning process and the development of competent performance. Recent research provides a deep understanding of complex reasoning and performance on problem-solving tasks and how skill and understanding in key subjects are acquired.

9. While there are remarkable commonalities across learners of all ages, children differ from adult learners in many ways. Studies of young children offer a window into the development of learning, and they show a dynamic picture of learning as it unfolds over time. A fresh understanding of infant cognition and of how young children build on early learning predispositions also offers ideas on ways to ease their transition into formal school settings.

10. Some countries, notably in Africa, called for the creation of a special fund by western countries and technology firms to help subsidize hardware and software for poor countries. The idea got a frosty reception. The compromise reached is for a voluntary fund, if it goes forward at all.

II. Choose the one answer that best fits the meaning of the statement you have heard.

1. Iran's lukewarm response to overtures by the United States for American assistance for the Bam earthquake victims fueled a widening debate on the Islamic Republic's relations with its longtime nemesis.

2. Hard-liners who have always viewed adverse relations with Washington as a pillar of the Islamic revolution are dismissing the U. S. statements as just more "trickery from the Great Satan", while reformists fret aloud that Iran is about to miss yet another opportunity to end its international isolation.

3. Neither side appreciated President George W. Bush's repeating of U. S. demands on Iran in the same breath as his promise to amplify aid to quake victims, but the debate in Iran appears likely to become an important issue in parliamentary elections just six weeks away.

4. Iran rejected an offer from Washington to send a delegation to assess the need for further assistance and to help with the distribution of relief supplies in Bam, where 30,000 people were killed and tens of thousands were left homeless in an earthquake on Jan. 26.

5. Officials in Washington said Iran had cited the difficult conditions in Bam as the reason for not accepting the delegation, although Tehran did not close the door to a possible future visit.
6. Conservatives in Iran quickly condemned the U. S. offer and attacked Iranian officials who welcomed it. The U. S. measures included dispatching 81 aid workers to Bam to staff a hospital and to survey the damage, as well as the temporary suspension of some economic sanctions to allow private donations to Iran.
7. Japan and South Korea are among more than 30 countries that barred U. S. beef after a case of mad cow disease was confirmed in a Washington state herd. The two countries alone account for about two-thirds of U. S. beef exports that totaled as much as $3.8 billion in 2003.
8. The number of people swapping music files online has dropped by half, and the number of people downloading files on any given day has dropped 75 percent since the middle of last year, when the Recording Industry Association of America started suing people accused of making large numbers of songs available for downloading.
9. In a survey of 1,358 Internet users conducted last year from March to May, 29 percent said they had downloaded music. The percentage dropped to 14 percent when the question was asked again between Nov. 18 and Dec. 14, after hundreds of people had been sued by the recording industry over allegations of file trading.
10. Past surveys showed that many people did not fully understand that they were infringing on the copyright of others by downloading free music. Despite the abuse heaped on the industry for its tactics, the message appears to have gotten through. The result is a change in behavior, though not necessarily a change in attitude.

Unit 11 Traveling to Other Lands

Section I Listening Comprehension

I. Listen to the following passages and then decide whether the following statements are true or false.
1. A new leader with a mandate from his people, ideally a reformist one, committed to the internationally backed "road map" peace plan, would be in a strong position to press Israel to withdraw from the occupied territories and allow the formation of an independent Palestinian state — which, on the road map's original timetable, should happen by the end of next year.
2. As a result of the steady rise in carbon emissions, the amount of carbon dioxide in the atmosphere has increased by 31% since 1750 — a rate unprecedented in the past 20,000 years. Nature usually absorbs a large portion of these emissions in oceans and forests, known as "carbon sinks", thereby slowing the rate of accumulation in the atmosphere. However, recent trends suggest that carbon emissions are outpacing absorption.
3. The French, it seems, do not use the word "brutal" in quite the same way as the English do. Jean-Claude Trichet, the French president of the European Central Bank (ECB), reached for this arresting adjective last week to describe the euro's recent gains against the dollar — the

single currency eventually reached a record price of $1.30 on Wednesday, November 10th. But according to a translator, writing in the *Financial Times*, Mr. Trichet's comments were not as alarming as they sound. When the French describe a change as brutal, they mean it is sudden, not cruel and vicious.

4. Buoyed by higher house prices and a consumer splurge, the French economy was looking quite sprightly in the spring. Indeed, at one point, it seemed as if the French were even outpacing their American rivals. Subsequent data revisions — downwards in France, upwards in America — dispelled that illusion. And figures for the third quarter have punctured French delusions of growth altogether. The French economy crawled along at an annual pace of just 0.4% between July and September.

5. The euro area's finance ministers, assembled on Monday for one of their regular meetings in Brussels, are rattled by the euro's rise. But they have so far refrained from calling on the ECB to do anything about it. Other politicians have been less circumspect. It is not enough, they say, for Mr. Trichet to talk down the euro with carefully chosen adjectives. He should put the ECB's money where his mouth is, selling euros and buying dollars to keep the exchange rate stable.

6. Prices in America are not rising without any limit. Perhaps, then, the federal funds rate is not as far below the natural rate as the original Taylor rule would imply. But other tell-tale signs suggest interest rates are unnaturally low.

7. Europe has not, so far, made the same blunder, but the European Parliament is considering the easing of rules for innovations incorporated in software. This might have a similarly deleterious effect as business-method patents, because many of these have been simply the application of computers to long-established practices.

8. Most current therapies — drugs that were developed during the first golden era, in the 1970s — simply attack dividing cells. That stops tumours, but it also kills all rapidly proliferating cells, regardless of their origin, function or state of health. The action of these drugs on normal tissues causes the side effects, including nausea, fatigue and weakened immune systems, associated with cancer treatment. By contrast, the new generation of drugs, several of which are already in the clinic, attack only deranged cells. These drugs are designed to fix the specific molecular problems in a tumour that drive its growth.

9. Two evolutionary pressures are thought to drive this process of diminution. One is that islands are often free of large predators. The other is that they sometimes have a restricted food supply. The result is that you do not need to be big to defend yourself; and if you are big, you may starve.

10. Going by the numbers, humanity seems to be losing the war on cancer. According to the most recent data from the World Health Organisagion, 10 millim people around the planet were diagnosed with the disease in 2000, and 6 millim died from it. And these numbers are

growing. With an ageing population, the spread of Western-style diets, and increasing tobacco consumption, cancer is on the rise around the globe.

II. Choose the one answer that best fits the meaning of the statement you have heard.

1. The Etruscans were big on tombs — constructing entire cities for the dead to inhabit — but Porsena's was supposedly the biggest of the lot. It was, according to one ancient source, a monument of rectangular masonry with a square base whose sides were 90 metres (about 300 feet) long and 15 metres high. On this base stood five pyramids, four at the corners and one in the center, and the points of these pyramids supported a ring from which hung bells whose sound reached for miles when stirred by the wind. From this level rose five more pyramids, and from these another five.

2. All over the world, more boys are born than girls. Evolutionary biologists believe that this is because boys (and, indeed, males in general) are more likely to die at a given age than their female contemporaries. The imbalance at birth thus means that the sex ratio balances at the age when people are reproducing. But for decades there has been a puzzling trend in the boy-girl ratio. In Britain, as well as in the United States and Canada, the proportion of boys being born is dropping. No one knows why, although it has been suggested, somewhat controversially, that the trend is due to chemical pollutants that are mimicking the effects of sex hormones.

3. No document is safe any more. Counterfeiting, once the domain of skilled crooks who used expensive engraving and printing equipment, has gone mainstream since the price of desktop-publishing systems has dropped. Virtually any kind of paper can be forged, including cheques, banknotes, stock and bond certificates, passports and security cards. For currency alone, millions of dollars in counterfeit banknotes make their way into circulation each year, and 40% of the counterfeits seized this year were digitally produced, compared with 1% a decade ago.

4. As a start, patent applications should be made public. In most countries they are, but in America this is the case only under certain circumstances, and after 18 months. More openness would encourage rivals to offer the overworked patent office evidence with which to judge whether an application is truly novel and non-obvious. Patent offices also need to collect and publish data about what happens once patents are granted — the rate at which they are challenged and how many are struck down. This would help to measure the quality of the patent system itself, and offer some way of evaluating whether it is working to promote innovation, or to impede it.

5. So far, the U. S. Department of Homeland Security has given American states more than $40 million to invest in video security systems. But in March, the Washington metropolitan police department admitted that the dozens of cameras it has had in place since 9/11 have so far netted zero arrests. What the surveillance cameras can do is help investigators piece together the details of plots after they are attempted, gather forensic evidence and identify suspects — all of which deepens their understanding of how terrorist networks operate.

6. The use of modern biotechnology in agriculture has emerged as a potential tool for improving agricultural processes, products, food, and the environment. Along with this promise, concerns about the environmental and human health consequences of transgentic products in agriculture have been raised. The public debate has centered around the potential benefits and risks of the application of transgenic methods to agriculture, the oversight of the products, and their control and distribution. Specific issues depend on the product, its use, and its environment.

7. Federal agents arrested a Florida man Wednesday for registering misleading Internet domain names designed to direct children to pornography. The case is the first prosecution under new "Amber Alert" legislation, which includes a provision making it illegal to use misleading web addresses to entice children to pornographic websites.

8. NASA launched its Space Infrared Telescope Facility early Monday from Cape Canaveral, Florida. The space-based observatory will use infrared technology to see targets such as planet-forming discs around stars and galaxies billions of light-years away, including objects that previously have been undetectable. SIRTF is the last of NASA's four "Great Observatories", which include the Hubble Space Telescope, Chandra X-ray Observatory and Compton Gammaray Observatory. Its mission is expected to last from two-and-a-half to five years.

9. Coral reefs in the Caribbean have declined by 80 percent in the last three decades, according to a report in the online version of the journal *Science*. Coral cover in the region has fallen from 50 percent to 10 percent, the study shows — a rate of decline that exceeds rates of tropical forest loss.

10. Stockmarkets are sliding again; the gold price this week hit a seven-year high of $400 an ounce; and the dollar slumped to a new low against the euro. "So what's new?" you might ask: the world economy clearly remains fragile. What is new, however, is the recent batch of better-than-expected figures on economic growth around the globe. Not only has the American economy rebounded, but Japan and the euro area are also now growing again, albeit more slowly. The news from some emerging economies is even more bullish. Many economies in Asia and Latin America enjoyed their fastest growth for years in the third quarter. Adding it all together, the world economy as a whole probably enjoyed its fastest growth for two decades. So why are the financial markets showing lack of confidence?

Unit 12 The Flowers

Section I Listening Comprehension

I. Listen to the following passages and then decide whether the following statements are true or false.

1. Recent trends suggest that carbon emissions are outpacing absorption. Over the past two decades, atmospheric CO_2 concentrations rose each year, on average, by 1.5 parts per million (ppm), but the last few years have seen unexplained and alarming jumps of up to 2.54 ppm

and beyond. This suggests that the ability of the Earth's natural systems to mitigate the rise in carbon emissions is weakening.
2. As American households have run up ever-larger debts, and as banks and other lenders have given up collecting their own debts because stricter federal and state regulations have made the business more costly, the collection industry's annual revenues have more than tripled in the past ten years, to $16.5 billion.
3. The economic slowdown in the euro area, however, has been both sudden and savage. The 12-nation block grew at an annual pace of just 1.2% in the third quarter, according to figures released on Friday, after expanding by 2% in the second quarter and 2.8% in the first. It seems the recovery in the euro area, which has been long awaited, may already be dearly departed.
4. Community health centers not only should be located in inner cities, but in suburbia as well, since many people there also lack health insurance. These centers would be much more cost-effective than having emergency rooms clogged with nonemergency cases of uninsured patients. Community health centers can be augmented with school-based health programs for children. In addition, the development of national guidelines for cost-effective, private, community-rated catastrophic health insurance for the uninsured could help pay for the treatment of serious illnesses that may require hospitalization or other expensive cures.
5. In France, an abrupt, shuddering stop is described as an arrêt brutal. Brutal is again meant metaphorically, just as the English talk of something stopping "dead". But the slowdown in the European and Japanese economies is, quite literally, brutal and, quite possibly, fatal to their hopes of a sustained recovery.
6. American households saved just 1.2% of their disposable income in the second quarter, and just 0.4% of it in the third. An absence of thrift and explosion of credit were sure signs that money was too easy, i.e., rates were too low.
7. In America, many experts believe that dubious patents abound, such as the notorious one for a "sealed crustless sandwich". Of the few patents that are reexamined by the Patent and Trademark Office itself, often after complaints from others, most are invalidated or their claims clipped down. The number of duplicate claims among patents is far too high. What happens in America matters globally, since it is the world's leading patent office, approving about 170,000 patents each year, half of which are granted to foreign applicants.
8. Given the complexity of the problem, then, researchers see a need to combine several drugs into a therapy so that several mutations can be treated simultaneously. That is not, it must be said, a new idea. Combination therapies are standard for most cancers (and also for AIDS). But most existing treatments include several of the traditional, non-specific drugs. The trick now is to work out how to build successful combinations using the new generation of targeted drugs.

9. For decades, community health centers have done a very good job of providing low-cost primary health care to those with and without insurance. Since most of the nation's uninsured actually are employed — but often in low-wage jobs — these centers provide an invaluable cost-effective service and, thanks to government subsidies, some care is free or on a sliding fee scale. This is one government program worthy of expansion. Yet, while touted by the Bush Administration, adequate funding has not been forthcoming.

10. When we meet a stranger, we form an immediate impression of the sort of man he is. Without thinking we take in small details of how he stands, the way he uses his hands, his eye movements and facial expressions. The conclusions we draw may or may not be correct, but they certainly affect our actions. If we start to talk with him, our words are accompanied by other gestures which may elucidate, emphasize, enhance or even contradict what we say.

II. Choose the one answer that best fits the meaning of the statement you have heard.

1. Such a site has not, of course, completely escaped archaeological attention in the past. A dig in an outlying part of it known as Gonfienti has been under way since 1998. Gabriella Poggesi, the archaeologist in charge of the Gonfienti dig, has unearthed the foundations of what was evidently a wealthy settlement on the banks of the Bisenzio river.

2. Although these patterns are invisible to the naked eye, they can be detected and analysed by computer programs, and it is these that the three researchers have spent the past year devising. So far, they cannot trace individual printers, but they can tell pretty reliably which make and model of printer was used to create a document.

3. The National Research Council's (NRC) Board on Life Sciences and Board on Agriculture and Natural Resources have convened a standing committee that will help identify emerging issues in the broad areas of agricultural biotechnology. The Standing Committee on Agricultural Biotechnology, Health, and the Environment (CABHE) will review and discuss scientific guidance for issues surrounding biotechnology as it is applied to food and fiber production, health, and the environment.

4. The University of Michigan unveiled a new undergraduate admissions policy that gives highest priority to academic performance while still including race as a factor, in response to two recent U.S. Supreme Court rulings. While the old undergraduate admissions formula awarded minority applicants an extra 20 points, the new policy does not quantify the contribution of race to admission decisions. The university's application for admission will now include several questions designed to elicit more information about a prospective student's background and achievements.

5. Examining historical and modern species records from Singapore and neighboring Malaysia, researchers found that Singapore has lost 85% of its native forest habitat and nearly 28% of its overall biodiversity since 1819, when the British established a colony on the island. Today, more than half of Singapore's surviving species are concentrated in just one-quarter of a percent

of the country's total area, in land designated as forest reserves.

6. The 2,514 new cases of HIV reported among drug users in 2000 represented a 5 percent increase from the previous year. However, the total number of cases is still lower than those from previous years — in 1994, for example, 4,226 new cases of HIV infection among injected-drug users were reported.

7. Trans fatty acids, often found in cookies, crackers, dairy products, meats and fast food, increase the risk of heart disease by boosting levels of "bad" cholesterol.

8. Early symptoms of infection include fever, headaches, dry cough, swollen lymph nodes, chills and severe sweating. Currently, there is no treatment for the disease, which is fatal in 1 to 10 percent of infected humans. Although smallpox vaccination can protect people from developing monkeypox, it is not foolproof — of the 23 reported cases of the disease in the U. S., one patient had already received the smallpox vaccination.

9. The world's freshwater reserves are shrinking due to pollution, climate change and population growth, according to a United Nations report presented this week at the World Water Forum in Kyoto. In the next 20 years, the average amount of water available for each person worldwide will drop by one-third. By mid-century, anywhere from 2-7 billion people — out of a projected global population of 9.3 billion — will experience water scarcity.

10. This year the mood at the show was unusually gloomy. There was much muttering about the sparsity of both exhibitors and attendees, whose numbers fell to around 50,000 this year from around 200,000 in 2000. Veterans grumbled that a once-sprawling show that used to take five full days to absorb could now be covered in an hour or two. Once the biggest annual show in Las Vegas, Comdex has lately been eclipsed by the Consumer Electronics Show (CES), which earlier this year attracted around 120,000 visitors. This mirrors the shift in the technology industry's center of gravity, away from PCs towards sexier consumer-electronics devices such as mobile phones, games consoles, digital-video recorders and flat-panel TVs.

Unit 13 In Search of Life's Origin

Section I Listening Comprehension

I. Listen to the following passages and then decide whether the following statements are true or false.

1. "Not fit for purpose" is a curiously British phrase, hauled out only in extremism and as good a sign of despair as any. Until recently it was most often applied to the government and all its works: the Home Office, NHS (National Health Service) reform, the country's drug policy. Now it is being hurled at Heathrow, Europe's busiest airport.

2. The drugs business is by far the most profitable illicit global trade, says the United Nations Office on Drugs and Crime (UNODC), earning some $320 billion annually, compared with estimates of $32 billion for human trafficking and $1 billion for illegal firearms. The runaway Afghan opium trade — worth around $60 billion at street prices in consuming countries — is

arguably the hardest problem. Heroin is finding new routes to the consumer, for instance, through West Africa to America, and via Pakistan and Central Asia to China.

3. The figures are, of course, backward-looking. The slowdown they record was not caused by this month's uptick in the euro. But numbers nonetheless bode ill for the future. They suggest that Europe's wakening economies are not in a good position to cope with a strengthening currency.

4. As for Germany, its economy grew by just 0.4% last quarter. Germans had to foot a higher import bill, the statistics office said, no doubt because of higher oil prices. But their export earnings were also down. The stronger euro will temper the rise in the dollar price of oil, but it will also blunt the competitiveness of Germany's exports.

5. A staggering three-quarters of the debt-collection industry's new hires quit after just three months. America's call-centre business — another industry in which hysteria about outsourced jobs has run high — faces the same dilemma. "It's very hard to hire in the U.S.," says Mr. Ginsberg. In Amherst, an Indian firm plans to do its best.

6. Patents, said Thomas Jefferson, should draw "a line between the things which are worth to the public the embarrassment of an exclusive patent, and those which are not". As the value that society places on intellectual property has increased, that line has become murkier — and the cause of some embarrassment, too. Around the world, patent offices are being inundated with applications. In many cases, this represents the extraordinary inventiveness that is occurring in new fields such as the Internet, genomics and nanotechnology.

7. Despite these billions, the rate of death from cancer in the United States has increased from 163 per 100,000 individuals in 1971 to 194 per 100,000 in 2001. By contrast, mortality rates from heart disease and strokes, two other diseases often seen as being associated with affluent styles of living, have fallen.

8. The most promising new diagnostic technology is the DNA microarray (or "gene chip", as it is colloquially known). Gene chips can do two things that are relevant to cancer diagnosis. They can identify mutations in particular genes, and they can monitor the activity of lots of genes at the same time — showing a doctor which genes in a tumour are busier than they should be, and which are less busy.

9. Why human intelligence evolved in the first place is controversial. Many researchers feel that it was not so much to deal with the non-human world (e.g., predators and food-gathering) as to deal with other people. One theory, known as the "Machiavellian mind", is that intelligence is there to analyse, and thus manipulate, the motives of others. Another, known as the "mating mind", is that much of human intelligence is about showing off to the opposite sex in a behavioural equivalent of the peacock's tail. Both could be true. Whether either of these purposes would disappear on an island is moot.

10. Gays who have children — and a quarter of gay couples do — gravitate towards them for the same reason that straight parents do: better schools, bigger gardens, peace and quiet. Mark Strasser, for example, lives with his male partner and their two children in Columbus, Ohio. He says they encounter no hostility eating out as a gay couple or picking up the children from their private school. He has to rack his memory for the last time anyone called him anything nasty for being gay. "That would have been in the late 1980s, I think," he says. His employer, a private university, offers the same health insurance to employees' gay partners as to spouses.

II. Choose the one answer that best fits the meaning of the statement you have heard.

1. Can household arrangements affect the human sex ratio? According to Karen Norberg, of the National Bureau of Economic Research in Cambridge, Massachusetts, they can. In a review of data from almost 60,000 American families, Dr. Norberg found that the chance of a woman giving birth to a boy rather than a girl is higher if she has been living with a man before the child was conceived. To be specific, for parents who were living together, boys were born 51.5% of the time, while when the parents were not cohabiting only 49.9% of births were male. This difference may seem small, but statistically it is highly significant, which suggests it is the result of evolution.

2. In ancient times, counterfeiting was a hanging offence. In Dante's "Inferno", forgers were placed in one of the lowest circles of hell. Today, desktop counterfeiters have little reason to worry about prison, at any rate, because the systems they use are ubiquitous and there is no means of tracing forged documents to the machine that produced them. This, however, may soon change thanks to technology developed by three anti-counterfeiting engineers based at Purdue University in Indiana. The results of their research will be unveiled formally at the International Conference on Digital Printing Technologies in Salt Lake City.

3. Africa lags partly because its population is growing so rapidly. In rural areas, mothers are giving birth to at least six children on average, doubling the population every generation. As a result, Africa's top-line numbers are improving more than its ratios. Millions more African children are going to school, but the denominator is also increasing. According to the UN, in 1990 there were 237 million Africans under 14; today, that figure is 348 million, and by 2015 it is expected to top 400 million.

4. A sudden, massive power surge late yesterday afternoon shut down much of the power grid serving northeastern North America, affecting more than 20 million people in New York, New Jersey, Ohio, Michigan, Connecticut, Pennsylvania, Massachusetts, Vermont and parts of Canada. The blackout stranded travelers at airports and train stations, shut down cash machines and hampered cellular telephone service throughout the region. Although the origin of the

power failure is still unknown, federal officials said Thursday that the incident was not terrorism-related.

5. Estimates of atomic bomb survivors' radiation doses — the basis for current radiation exposure safety standards — are accurate, researchers said Thursday. Doubts about the accuracy of methods used to collect exposure data in 1945, immediately after the bombings in Hiroshima and Nagasaki, prompted the review. The earlier methods were unable to detect radioactive fallout more than a half-mile from each bomb site. The scientists examined copper samples from Hiroshima buildings for trace amounts of a radioactive nickel isotope produced by the atomic bomb explosion. The amount of nickel in each copper sample can be correlated to the intensity of radiation exposure at the site from which the sample was taken.

6. Coral loss can have serious consequences, including the collapse of reef fisheries, a reduction in tourism and increased coastal damage from hurricanes. Coral decline also threatens the estimated 1 million species of fish, invertebrates and algae found in and around world's reefs. Several National Academies reports examine the environmental role of coral reefs and suggest ways to protect these and other marine resources.

7. About 16,000 Americans die each year from AIDS and another 40,000 contract HIV; nearly a third of the 850,000 to 950,000 U.S. residents living with HIV/AIDS are unaware they carry the virus. From 1981 — when the disease was first documented — to 2001, intravenous drug users and their sex partners have accounted for nearly one-third of all HIV infections.

8. Recent news stories excoriating the retirement compensation package for Dennis Collins, former chief of the James Irvine Foundation, make the case for increasing foundation payout rates. A bill before the U.S. House of Representatives — which has met wide opposition from foundations — would require them to give more of their money to charity every year.

9. By referring back to his first Comdex speech in 1983, Mr. Gates reminded his audience just how long (by the standards of the industry) he and his firm have been around, and how willing he is to play a long game. Microsoft's gradual establishment of its dominance in PC software, via its Windows and Office monopolies, owes as much to its ability to outlast its competitors as to clever programming or anti-competitive behaviour. Microsoft's deep experience of the computer industry means it knows what all the mistakes are, and what traps and pitfalls to avoid.

10. The environment minister pledged to boost spending on flood defences from £600 million now to £800 million a year by 2011. The extra money will be welcome, but will not address the fundamental problem: England's penchant for building houses in silly places (Scotland, Wales and Northern Ireland are all much stricter). Some £200 billion-worth of houses, businesses and other infrastructure is at risk from flooding. One in ten new houses are being built in similarly risky places, including 31,000 planned for Ashford in Kent and 120,000 in London's Thames Gateway.

Unit 14 The Little Guy

Section I Listening Comprehension

I. Listen to the following passages and then decide whether the following statements are true or false.

1. Stereo Hits, a radio station in Coban, Guatemala, decided to go global last year. In an effort to boost revenue from its advertisers, which include Coca-cola, Panasonic and PepsiCo, it began streaming its broadcasts over the Internet, allowing anyone in the world with a connection to tune in. Raul Najera Ponce, head of the station's online unit, estimates that this "web-casting" costs Stereo Hits just $100 a month, since it needs neither a frequency licence nor a transmission tower.
2. Thanks to Americans' seemingly bottomless appetite for more debt, Mr. Ginsberg still predicts employment growth in the debt-collection industry at home — if the agencies can attract new workers. As it happens, few Americans seem to enjoy hassling their compatriots to pay credit-card debts or hospital bills they cannot afford.
3. Anxious observers will have to wait until later in the month to confirm which parts of the euro area's giant economy are losing the most steam. But it is likely that both French consumers and German exporters, the euro area's twin-stroke engine of growth in the first half of the year, have misfired since.
4. A widely watched index of their economic expectations, compiled by the ZEW research institute, collapsed in November to 13.9, from a reading of 31.3 the month before. The institute blamed, in part, the euro's appreciation, which it described, not as brutal, but as "very distinct" nonetheless.
5. Some 500 police officers, backed by American's security men with helicopters, raked in about $3 million, according to some officers. They were supposed to destroy 12,000 of the estimated 100,000 hectares of poppy in Helmand. They claimed 7,000 hectares had been ripped up, but the UN verified only half this amount. Ordinary policemen averaged $1,000 each in backhanders. "We do a dangerous job and we get $70 salary a month," said one, "If we are killed there is no money for our families. We just have to make money while we can." One police colonel is said to have treated himself to a new Lexus car.
6. In 1998 America introduced so-called "business-method" patents, granting for the first time patent monopolies simply for new ways of doing business, many of which were not so new. This was a mistake. It not only ushered in a wave of new applications, but it is probably inhibiting, rather than encouraging, commercial innovation, which had never received, or needed legal protection in the past.
7. Cancer is characterized by uncontrolled cell growth. Healthy cells regulate their division into daughter cells carefully, subordinating their own Darwinian tendency to reproduce in favour of

the survival of the body they inhabit. It is one of the marvels of evolution that they are able to do this, and so allow the development of multicellular creatures. But evolution works on many levels, and it is almost inevitable that mutations in some of the trillions of cells that make up a human body will disable the regulatory genes. Then it is just a matter of the survival of the fittest among cells. In a competition between regulated and unregulated cells, the unregulated ones will multiply faster, and win. The result is cancer.

8. Islands are famous for generating indigenous species from whatever biological material pitches up on them. One frequent trend observed in such island species, at least when they are large mammals, is dwarfism. Elephants seem particularly susceptible. The last mammoths, which lived on an island off the coast of Siberia, were, paradoxically, dwarfs. Similar elephantine examples are known from Malta, Sicily and, indeed, Flores itself. And the same thing has been observed in cattle, too.

9. In the classes that emphasized health over appearance, the instructor wore a loose-fitting T-shirt and gym shorts. She also sprinkled health-oriented comments throughout the session. In the appearance-based classes, however, she wore tight-fitting aerobics attire while making comments that drew attention to looks. The instructor's leadership style directly affected the student's attitudes toward the class. The women in the health-oriented class reported that they felt more engaged in the workout as well as revitalized and less exhausted after class than did those in the appearance-targeted sessions.

10. It is well established, in both humans and other species, that successful males have lots of offspring, while unsuccessful ones have few or none. Females, by contrast, show a smaller range of reproductive output, with most having some offspring, but none having as many as the most successful males.

II. Choose the one answer that best fits the meaning of the statement you have heard.

1. Though the approaches of the three researchers differ slightly, all are based on detecting imperfections in the print quality of documents. Old-school forensic scientists were — at least so the movies would have you believe — able to trace documents to particular typewriters based on quirks of the individual keys. The researchers from Purdue employ a similar approach, exploiting the fact that the rotating drums and mirrors inside a printer are imperfect pieces of engineering which leave unique patterns of banding in their products.

2. An ad hoc subcommittee under the purview of the National Research Council's Committee on Agricultural Biotechnology, Health, and the Environment (CABHE) will review and evaluate biological methods used for purposes of confining genetically engineered organisms. The study will focus on biological methods for confining transgenic crop plants, grasses, trees, fish and shellfish, but will also consider methods used for other categories of transgenic organisms. The committee will focus on genetic mechanisms of biological confinement such as induced sterility, but will also identify and discuss other available or possible biological confinement

methods. Methods resulting in significant reductions in the risk of escape into the environment will be identified, and their efficacy for reducing environmental risk assessed.

3. The first cases of a virus related to smallpox have been reported in the Americas. At least 23 cases of monkeypox had been detected in three Midwestern states — Illinois, Indiana and Wisconsin. Although similar in many ways to smallpox, monkeypox is less infectious and less deadly than its more famous relative. The disease occurs primarily in Central and West Africa. Although state and federal officials are still investigating the cause of the Midwest monkeypox cases, they do know that all the patients had direct or close contact with infected prairie dogs kept as pets.

4. Three New England states filed suit against the U. S. Environmental Protection Agency in an effort to force the government to regulate carbon dioxide emissions, citing the chemical's contribution to global warming. Their suit aims to reclassify carbon dioxide as a "criteria pollutant", joining nitrogen dioxide, ozone, sulfur dioxide, particulate matter, carbon monoxide and lead. The Clean Air Act requires the government set and enforce standards for allowable atmospheric levels of these pollutants.

5. More than 190 countries unanimously adopted the first international treaty against smoking at a meeting of the World Health Organization. The treaty calls for an advertising ban and new labeling for tobacco products, indoor air controls to reduce second-hand smoking, and stronger legislation against tobacco smuggling.

6. Windows, just a prototype in 1983, is now the dominant personal-computer (PC) operating system, having seen off a host of rivals. The computer industry has mushroomed in size, gone through several booms and busts, and is now worth around $870 billion. Microsoft has become the world's largest software firm, and Mr. Gates the world's richest man. His firm has also, of course, been through a bruising battle with antitrust regulators. But even as the landscape has changed around Mr. Gates, his position as the industry's figurehead has remained unchallenged. Each year, for two digital decades, he has returned to Comdex to rally the industry, hold court with analysts and journalists, unveil new products and present his optimistic vision of the future.

7. Despite its name, Smugglers' Gulch is one of the toughest places to sneak into America. The ravine near San Diego is bisected by a steel wall and watched day and night by agents of the border patrol, who track would-be illegal immigrants with the help of floodlights, helicopters and underground pressure sensors. Rafael, a cement worker, has already been caught jumping over the fence five times. Yet he still loiters on the Mexican side of the fence, waiting for nightfall and another chance to cross.

8. One shock for many people may be the discovery that EU entry does not in itself bring wealth. The countries of Central Europe will take a very long time to catch up with their western neighbours. The Economist Intelligence Unit has calculated that if the 15 countries of the

current EU enjoy economic growth of 2% a year, and the countries joining in 2004 and 2007 (including Bulgaria and Romania) grow by about 4% a year, then it will take the new members, on average, more than 50 years to draw level with the old ones. If the new members manage only 3% growth, it will take them 90 years to catch up.

9. The ability to remain anonymous and have a choice about when and to whom one's identity is disclosed is an essential aspect of a democracy. The technology a system uses, whether scanning a face or using a smart card, is less important in maintaining privacy than the way the system is designed and the scope of the system. Our report offers good design practices to follow when setting up an authentication system. Using them will improve security for the system and privacy for the users, considerations particularly relevant to ongoing policy debates such as about national identity cards and frequent traveler cards.

10. Net inflows of investment into American bonds and shares plunged from $50 billion in August to only $4 billion in September, the lowest level since the crisis caused by the collapse of Long-Term Capital Management in October 1998. The very suggestion that foreigners might not continue to buy dollar assets in future was enough to make some investors sell this week. A cheaper dollar will help to reduce America's external deficit, while at the same time supporting growth. The risk is that if the greenback falls too fast, bond yields could rise, choking off recovery.

Unit 15 Stretching the Limits

Section I Listening Comprehension

I. Listen to the following passages and then decide whether the following statements are true or false.

Exercise I

Water is essential to life. We need it for drinking, producing food, washing, generating power, transportation, industrial processes, and ensuring the sustainability of the Earth's ecosystem. Yet not only is this life-giving source being rapidly depleted and increasingly polluted — but far too many people lack access to it. That is why this year's World Environment Day focuses on the key message "Water — Two Billion People are Dying for it!"

The challenge we face is enormous. To meet the Millennium Development Goals (MDGs) and the Johannesburg Plan of Implementation, agreed at the World Summit on Sustainable Development last year 2002, which include the targets of halving by 2015, the proportion of people without access to safe drinking water and proper sanitation, the world will need to connect approximately 200,000 people to clean water and 400,000 people to improved sanitation each day.

The United Nations Development Programme (UNDP) is committed to help developing countries tackle all the challenges involved and by doing so help achieve all the MDGs. As a demonstration of UNDP's support for local efforts to achieve these global development targets, this year's World Environment Day also marks the call for nominations for the Equator Prize 2004 — a prestigious international award recognizing outstanding local efforts to reduce poverty while protecting the environment.

Exercise II

In the late 1920s the American astronomer Edwin Hubble made a very interesting and important discovery. Hubble made observations that he interpreted as showing that distant stars and galaxies are receding from Earth in every direction. Moreover, the velocities of recession increase in proportion with distance, a discovery that has been confirmed by numerous and repeated measurements since Hubble's time. The implication of these findings is that the universe is expanding.

Hubble's hypothesis of an expanding universe leads to certain deductions. One is that the universe was more condensed at a previous time. From this deduction came the suggestion that all the currently observed matter and energy in the universe were initially condensed in a very small and infinitely hot mass. A huge explosion, known as the Big Bang, then sent matter and energy expanding in all directions.

This Big Bang hypothesis led to more testable deductions. One such deduction was that the temperature in deep space today should be several degrees above absolute zero. Observations showed this deduction to be correct. In fact, the Cosmic Microwave Background Explorer (COBE) satellite launched in 1991 confirmed that the background radiation field has exactly the spectrum predicted by a Big Bang origin for the universe.

As the universe expanded, according to current scientific understanding, matter collected into clouds that began to condense and rotate, forming the forerunners of galaxies. Within galaxies, including our own Milky Way galaxy, changes in pressure caused gas and dust to form distinct clouds. In some of these clouds, where there was sufficient mass and the right forces, gravitational attraction caused the cloud to collapse. If the mass of material in the cloud was sufficiently compressed, nuclear reactions began and a star was born.

Exercise III

Ideally, development efforts should rest on a mutually beneficial social contract. Such an understanding currently underlies international cooperation on poverty reduction: poor countries understand that aid can help them reduce poverty, and rich countries and international civil society understand that the aid they can promote international economic growth, foster certain foreign policy goals, and make the world more equitable.

If either side begins to doubt the benefits of the partnership and questions this implicit social contract, however, the process will grind to a halt. Several different tensions can disrupt the contract and prevent it from achieving development goals. Donors, for example, sometimes worry that their contributions are not being used for the intended purposes. This fear is commonly reflected in arguments that aid-receiving nations lack the "absorptive capacity" and efficiency to channel resources effectively, or that corruption or politics diverts aid to unintended beneficiaries. Donors are also concerned about burden-sharing — each country being reluctant to provide more aid than it considers its appropriate share. Recipients, meanwhile, sometimes fear that the conditions accompanying aid will force them to undertake unpleasant reforms and accept infringements on their sovereignty.

Donors and recipients can thus end up at odds with one another. Externally imposed performance requirements can sometimes actually help developing country governments and non-governmental organizations (NGOS) overcome resistance to reform among entrenched domestic interests. Still, tension over such conditions lies at the heart of many major development debates today. The more rich countries seek to improve outcomes through rigorous performance monitoring, the more poor nations fear being subjected to the stipulations of international donors. This tension can be finessed but can never be entirely alleviated.

Exercise IV

The habit of reading books is one of the greatest resources of mankind, and we enjoy reading books that belong to us much more than if they are borrowed. A borrowed book is like a guest in the house; it must be treated with punctiliousness, with a certain considerate formality. You must see that it sustains no damage; it must not suffer while under your roof. You cannot leave it carelessly, you cannot mark it, you cannot turn down the pages, you cannot use it familiarly. And then, some day, although this is seldom done, you really ought to return it.

But your own books belong to you, you treat them with affectionate intimacy that annihilates formality. Books are for use, not for show; you should own no book that you are afraid to mark up or afraid to place on the table, wide open and face down. A good reason for marking favorite passages in books is that this practice enables you to remember more easily the significant sayings, to refer to them quickly, and then in later years, it is like visiting a forest where you once blazed a trail. You have the pleasure of going over the old ground, and recalling both the intellectual scenery and your own earlier self.

Unit 16 Getting the Gist

Section I Listening Comprehension

I. Listen to the following passages and then decide whether the following statements are true or false.

Spurred by a quadrupling of carbon emissions during the past half-century alone, Earth's atmosphere is warming at an increasing rate. The hottest 14 years since systematic measurements began in the 1860s have all occurred in the past two decades; the summer of 1998 was the hottest on record, and the winter of 1999—2000 may turn out to be the warmest. Average temperatures are projected to increase further, by 1.2℃ to 3.5℃ (2℉ to 6℉) over the course of the present century — which would melt glaciers and the polar ice caps, raise sea levels and pose threats to hundreds of millions of coastal dwellers while drowning low-lying islands altogether.

Portents of this future are already visible. As the warming trend has accelerated, weather patterns have become more volatile and more extreme, while the severity of weather-related disasters has escalated. The cost of natural disasters in 1998 alone exceeded the cost of all such disasters in the entire decade of the 1980s. Tens of thousands of mostly poor people were killed that year, and an estimated 25 million "environmental refugees" were forced from their homes. The damage wrought by these disasters has been exacerbated by unsustainable environmental practices and the fact that more and more poor people have little choice but to live in harm's way — on flood plains and unstable hillsides and in unsafe buildings.

Reducing the threat of global warming requires, above all, that carbon emissions be reduced. The burning of fossil fuels, which still provide more than 75 percent of energy worldwide, produces most of these emissions. The rapidly expanding number of automobiles around the globe threatens an even greater escalation in emissions. The need to promote energy-efficiency and greater reliance on renewable resources is obvious.

Further development of fuel cell, wind turbine, photovoltaic and cogeneration technologies will help. In the developing world, particularly in rural areas that are not connected to energy grids, the rapidly falling costs of solar cells and wind power have the potential to bring energy to the poor at reasonable costs, thereby also enhancing agricultural productivity and generating income.

Stabilizing levels of carbon dioxide in the atmosphere to a range that is considered safe will require overall reductions on the order of 60 percent or more in the emission of the "greenhouse gases" that are responsible for global warming. Thus far, the international community has not found the political will needed to make the necessary changes.

Implementing the 1997 Kyoto Protocol would mark a significant advance by binding the industrialized countries to verifiable emission limitation and reduction targets averaging 5 percent below 1990 levels, to be achieved over the period 2008—2012. Recognizing the economic roots of the climate change problem, the Protocol seeks to engage the private sector in the search for solutions. It does so by the use of market mechanisms that provide incentives for cutting emissions, and which stimulate investment and technology flows to developing countries that will help them achieve more sustainable patterns of industrialization.

Although the first generation of Kyoto targets represent just one step towards what is needed to reduce global warming, their achievement would result in a sharp reduction in current rates of increase of greenhouse gas emissions by the industrialized countries. Early action is essential. Without success, there will be little incentive for the further rounds of emissions limitations that must follow, in which the developing countries will need to become progressively engaged.

II. Listen to the following passage about Jefferson and Hamilton and their roles in the American history and then write a short summary of around 150-200 words of what you have heard.

As the first President of the United States, George Washington contributed much to getting the new government under way. He steered his country on a sure and steady course. John Adams said that Washington was not influenced by any one man. He listened from all sides and was more independent in his thinking than any man Adams knew. But all was not easy, peaceful and free from trouble, even within Washington's own Cabinet.

Thomas Jefferson and Alexander Hamilton did not get along. The tall, red-headed Virginian had little use for the ideas of the smaller, dark-skinned lawyer from New York. The two disagreed on the idea of democracy. Hamilton was against it, Jefferson in favor. They disagreed, too, on which group the national government should support most — farmers, or those who owned factories and businesses.

To Thomas Jefferson, the best America was an America of independent farmers, with little if any cities. Farmers were honest and close to nature and soil. They were hard-working and could take care of themselves. They needed little help from any government. Cities, to Jefferson, were evil, wicked places. Within their factories, they produced large class of poor people and a miserable way of life. The poor in the cities, said Jefferson, would always need help from the government. "I think our government will remain good for many countries" he wrote, "as long as they remain chiefly agricultural. And this will be so as long as there shall be empty lands in any parts of America. When people get crowded together in large cities, as in Europe, our governments will become as corrupt as in Europe."

To Hamilton, on the other hand, farmers served but two purposes. One was to produce food for people who lived in cities. The other was to produce raw materials such as flax and tobacco for factories. Hamilton's ideal America was one of cities, factories, and trade. He wanted a much stronger national government than Jefferson did. And Hamilton wanted that government to do all it could to help cities, factories, and trade to grow.

Hamilton and Jefferson disagreed over whether there should be a Bank of the United States. Jefferson was afraid that the Bank would help only merchants and factory owners. That is exactly what Hamilton would hoped that the bank would do. The two men disagreed on whether the United States should help a new government in France, one that had come about as a result of revolution. Jefferson wanted to help France because France had helped the United States in their revolution. Hamilton did not. The whisky tax had been Hamilton's idea. He had persuaded the leaders of Congress to pass the law. Any tax that hit farmers was not to Jefferson's liking. Hamilton rode with Washington against the whisky rebels. Jefferson bitterly opposed the government's action.

Jefferson and Hamilton were strong leaders and each had many followers. As their disagreements grew, so did that between the groups that followed them. This was the beginning of political parties in the United States.

Practice Tests

Sample Test One

Part I

Listen to the following short passages and then decide whether the corresponding statements are true or false. There are 10 statements in this part of the test, 2 points for each statement.

1. On a global scale, violence kills 1.6 million people a year. It leaves millions more with injuries, disabilities and mental disorders. Its causes are complex and its consequences are devastating.

2. In order to provide the latest information about violence, WHO launched the World Report on Violence and Health in 2002. This is the first report to provide a comprehensive view of the magnitude of violence around the world, the factors that lead to violence and, at the same time, the potential that exists to tackle this global public health problem. It provides data from around the world on suicide, child abuse, youth violence, sexual violence, abuse of the elderly, violence between intimate partners and other areas of personal and social conflict.

3. The World Report on Violence and Health has three main goals. The first is to raise awareness of violence as a global public health problem. It is not simply an issue for the police and justice departments, for the military or for international security councils.

4. To find out which types of foods require the most fossil fuels and, as a result, release the most CO_2, they considered five different diets. Each equaled 3,774 calories a day, and ranged from the average American diet to red meat, fish, poultry, and vegetarian diets. It came as no surprise to the researchers that the vegetarian diet ranked number one as the most energy-efficient, followed by poultry and the average American diet. It did come as a surprise, however, that fish almost was on par with red meat as the least efficient — a large amount of fossil fuel is necessary for long-distance voyages to catch large predatory fishes such as tuna and swordfish. Moreover, salmon farming is not energy efficient.

5. Deaths are only a very small part of the problem of violence. For each death caused by violence, there are many other people who suffer the social, psychological and physical consequences of violence. Nevertheless, when deaths caused by violence are compared with deaths caused by other global public health problems, the importance of violence becomes alarmingly clear.

6. In 2000, there were over 1.6 million deaths due to violence. This is about half the number of deaths due to HIV/AIDS in that year, and about equal to the number of deaths due to tuberculosis. In 2000, violence took more lives than road traffic crashes and malaria.

7. At the broadest level, violence is divided into three major categories: self-directed, interpersonal and collective. So we differentiate between violence a person inflicts upon himself or herself;

violence inflicted by another individual or small group of individuals; and violence inflicted by larger groups or states.

8. When we speak of violence it is important to understand these different categories. However, it is also crucial to understand that they are closely interrelated. Many risk factors are common to all forms of violence. These include alcohol, drugs, firearms and economic and social inequalities. Reducing these risk factors will reduce all types of violence.

9. Facts and figures clearly demonstrate the enormous impact of violence on public health and health systems. But, behind these figures are individuals and human tragedies. Violence of all types has a dramatic effect on the lives of the victims, the perpetrators and their families, often for a lifetime and sometimes for several generations.

10. To begin to tackle the problem of violence, we need to know its magnitude. Contrary to the impression given by the media, the largest number of violent deaths in 2000 was due not to war but to suicide: 815,000 cases — or one suicide every forty seconds. Interpersonal violence accounted for 520,000 deaths or one murder per minute. There were 310,000 deaths directly due to collective violence.

Part II

Listen to the following short passages and then choose one of the answers that best fits the meaning of each passage. There are ten passages in this part of the test, each with 1 question, which carries 2 points.

11. Winemakers, such as Southcorp, Australia's biggest producer, have sharply raised output in the last 10 years as U.S. wine imports doubled in volume and almost tripled in value. France and Italy increased exports to the U.S. as consumption in their home markets contracted.

12. Now, with the U.S. currency down 26 percent against the Australian dollar, producers face the choice of trimming margins or raising prices in the face of a U.S. glut.

13. Peugeot Citroen, Europe's second-biggest carmaker, and Dongfeng Motor said that they would spend €600 million, or $761 million, to expand their Chinese venture.

14. The partners plan to introduce their first Peugeot model, based on the French automaker's 307 compact car, this quarter and aim to double production capacity to 300,000 vehicles by the second half of 2006.

15. Aluminum Corp. of China, the mainland's biggest maker of the metal, said that it would sell 3.1 billion Hong Kong dollars, or $40 million, of new shares to Alcoa and institutional investors to buy rivals and expand production amid record demand.

16. The easiest way to become an American citizen is to be born there. But for those who fail to plan so far in advance, becoming an American citizen is not so difficult, once you have secured the right to work. Lawful permanent residents are eligible for naturalisation after living in America for five years, unless they have spent too much time out of the country or

fallen foul of the law.

17. One third of the proceeds from the Chalco sale will be used this year to buy smelters that process alumina into the finished metal. A third will be used to accelerate the refining of alumina from bauxite at the company's project in Shanxi. The remainder would be put toward working capital.

18. Chalco is China's only producer of alumina, which provides about half of its revenue. Alumina shortages in China, which relies on imports for about half of the 12 million tons of the material consumed in the country each year, may have cut domestic aluminum production by 700,000 tons in 2003.

19. Britons, an urban people, do not as a rule know much about the ailments of livestock, but foot-and-mouth is an exception. The previous outbreak, in 2001, was disastrous. Government inaction allowed the disease to spread so far that, when steps were at last taken to halt it, large swathes of the country had to be closed off. The sheer quantity of animal corpses, slaughtered to halt the spread of the disease, meant that the army had to help with their disposal atop vast, smoking pyres. The total cost, including compensation, was eventually put at around £8 billion.

20. With 20% of the world's emissions coming from carbon released into the atmosphere via deforestation, one of the more controversial ideas to be floated at the conference will likely be a proposal to create an international carbon-trading system that would, in effect, allow countries such as Indonesia to be paid for not cutting down their forests. Although details have yet to be hammered out, the concept is similar to a European Union carbon-trading system that sets limits on greenhouse-gas emissions, allowing companies exceeding those limits to buy "credits" from companies that produce less than their fair share of pollutants.

Part III

Listen to the following longer passages and then choose the best answer to each of the questions. You may need to scribble a few notes in order to answer the questions. There are four passages in this part, each with 5 questions. And each question carries 2 points.

Passage One

One hundred years ago Henry Ford set up in business and America's love affair with the automobile began. Ford is staging a party that would not have disgraced Jay Gatsby. And why not? The American car market has been roaring, with annual vehicle sales over 16 million. It could be close to 20 million in a decade's time, with another 26 million young Americans clamoring for their first set of wheels.

Yet the ride is not going to be smooth: it will be more like cruising in a Ford thunderbird while ignoring a nasty rumble from its mighty V8 engine. For all the signs are that things are going badly awry in Detroit. Unless something changes, the industry could go broke — with

Ford, the most troubled of the big three carmakers, leading the way. The 100th birthday party could swiftly be followed by a wake.

This quintessential American industry has, admittedly, been written off before, only to bounce back. Chrysler entered the 1980s thanks to a Federal bailout; Ford narrowly escaped bankruptcy around the same time. Washington also came to the industry's aid with restrictions on Japanese imports. Even so, Chrysler nearly came to grief again in the early 1990s, before it was sold to Daimler-Benz. In 1991, the combined losses of the big three topped $7 billion. General Motors (GM) was said to be within an hour of going bust in 1992, with its bosses staring at the fax machine as they waited for a credit-rating downgrading that would have pushed the company over the edge. The downgrade never came, and GM recovered.

Passage Two

Mulick notes that, when he began treating autism in the 1970s, about three children in 10,000 were said to have the condition. Now, reports are one in 166. The number of cases has mushroomed because of better diagnoses and a changing definition of autism that includes a broader range of disorders.

Some of the newer, more popular fad treatments involve special diets or nutritional supplements. Megadoses of vitamin C and B6 are popular, as well as supplements with fatty acids like omega-3s. A casein — or gluten-free diet, which involves eliminating dairy or wheat products, also has gained favor with some parents. While many of these treatments never have been adequately studied, that does not mean they are not promoted. "One of the characteristics of fad treatments is that they are discussed in the media and on the Internet, where many parents can be exposed to them," emphasizes Ann Snow, a psychology graduate student.

While some fads simply are ineffective, others can be dangerous. Chelation therapy, which involves taking medicines to remove the heavy metal mercury from the body, reportedly has led to the death of at least one autistic boy receiving the treatment. Chelation therapy also was touted years ago as a new treatment against some forms of cancer, but eventually was shown to have no helpful effect. Many parents try multiple approaches, hoping at least one will help. One survey suggests that the average parent of a child with autism has tried seven different therapies.

Passage Three

In the early 1970s evidence had accumulated showing that chlorofluorocarbons (CFCs) were damaging the ozone layer in the stratosphere and increasing the amount of ultraviolet B (UV-B) radiation reaching Earth's surface. Since the ozone layer protects humans, animals and plants from the damaging effects of UV-B radiation, the steady increase in CFCs and other ozone-depleting substances constituted a major potential health hazard. But it took a decade and a half of increasingly intensive effort to achieve an agreement that would resolve the problem.

The 1987 Montreal Protocol on Substances that Deplete the Ozone Layer was a landmark international environmental agreement. It has been remarkably successful. Production of the most damaging ozone-depleting substances was eliminated, except for a few critical uses, by 1996 in developed countries and should be phased out by 2010 in developing countries. Without the Protocol the levels of ozone-depleting substances would have been five times higher than they are today, and surface UV-B radiation levels would have doubled at mid-latitudes in the northern hemisphere. On current estimates the CFC concentration in the ozone layer is expected to recover to pre-1980 levels by the year 2050.

Prior to the Protocol intergovernmental negotiations on their own failed to mobilize sufficient support for the far-reaching measures that were needed. But intensive lobbying by civil society organizations, the presentation of overwhelming scientific evidence — and the discovery of the huge ozone hole over Antarctica — eventually created the consensus necessary for the agreement to be signed.

Passage Four

Here is an eye-opening statistic from the Mayo Clinic, Rochester, Minn. By age 80, more than half of all Americans either have a cataract or have had cataract surgery. A cataract occurs when the normally clear lens in the eye becomes cloudy, blurring vision and preventing the lens from focusing an image on the retina, the light-sensitive tissue at the back of the eye. While cataracts do not spread from one eye to another, both eyes commonly are affected.

The only effective treatment for a cataract is surgery to remove the clouded lens. Typically, it is replaced with an artificial one known as an intraocular lens. Made from clear plastic, acrylic, or silicone, intraocular lenses become a permanent part of the eye. Cataract surgery is one of the safest and most effective procedures performed in the U. S. . In the years past, it often was recommended that patients wait for a cataract to turn white before having it removed. Today, there are no set recommendations on the best time to take out a cataract. The standard is to have one cataract removed at a time, allowing the eye to heal prior to the second surgery.

Most cataracts do not disturb vision in the early stages but, as the clouding progresses, a cataract can interfere with everyday life. After successful surgery, patients notice a vision improvement within days. Complete healing generally takes four to six weeks.

Regular eye exams remain the best way to detect cataracts early and monitor their progression. Adults of any age can develop a cataract, but age is the single greatest risk factor. For people over 64, an eye exam at least every other year is recommended.

Part IV

Write a summary of approximately 200-250 words of a passage you are going to hear. The passage is around 500 words in length.

Acupuncture, rooted in a 3,000-year-old tradition of yin and yang, meridians and chi, has to work hard to prove it has scientific validity. But George Lewith, a researcher at the University of

Southampton, in England, who has studied the technique for 25 years, has evidence that it does. In 2004 he showed that real acupuncture has a statistically significant advantage over sham acupuncture in the treatment of arthritic neck pain. Now, he is trying to show why.

It has been known for a decade that merely anticipating receiving acupuncture has an effect on areas of the brain that release chemicals called endorphins. These are natural opiates that are involved in the suppression of pain, and this anticipation-driven response is believed to be responsible for the placebo effect — the fact that merely believing a treatment will help means that it actually does help. What Dr. Lewith has now shown, in a paper just published in NeuroImage, is that inducing a placebo effect with acupuncture has a different effect on the brain from that of receiving actual acupuncture.

Dr. Lewith and his colleagues studied 14 patients suffering from arthritis. Each was subjected, in random order, to three treatments. One "treatment" was to be jabbed with blunt needles. Patients knew in advance that this had no therapeutic value, and was there simply to set a baseline. In another treatment, patients believed they were receiving acupuncture, but in fact they were touched with sham needles that retracted into their shafts like stage daggers. The third type of treatment was actual acupuncture.

While all this was going on, the patients had their brains scanned using a technique called positron-emission tomography, which measures blood flow. During the first type of treatment, the part of the brain that showed most increase in blood flow (and hence, it is assumed, in activity) was the area associated with the sensation of touch. During the second type, there was enhanced activity in the areas responsible for the release of endorphins, too. But during the third type, a zone called the insula ipsilateral also lit up. This is not an endorphin-rich part of the brain; it is, nevertheless, believed to be involved in the inhibition of pain. Dr. Lewith has thus demonstrated for the first time that the neurological effects of acupuncture go beyond the placebo effect.

That was not, however, the case in a second study published this week, in the Journal of the American Medical Association. Klaus Linde, of Munich Technical University, in Germany, was looking at the effect of acupuncture on migraines. He, too, used sham needles as well as real ones, though he did not do any brain scans. Acupuncture did indeed reduce headache frequency in those who received it, compared with those who did not. But it was no better than sham treatment, and therefore seemed to be acting as a mere placebo. A useful technique, then, but not a panacea.

Sample Test Two

Part I

Listen to the short passages and then decide whether the corresponding statements below are true or false. There are ten questions in this part of the test, 2 points for each question.

1. Motorized road transport has changed the face of employment, trade, family life and health

care, bringing benefits that were unimaginable 100 years ago. We can now get patients to emergency rooms, deliver relief at the sites of disasters and take holidays in places we would not have been able to visit before. However, the price we are paying for such benefits is too high. This is why we have chosen road safety as the theme for World Health Day 2004 and why we are launching the World Report on Road Traffic Injury Prevention.

2. During the course of any day, the tragic news of a death on the road is delivered about 3,000 times to families and friends. Fifteen thousand times, people will hear that one of their family members has survived a crash but with serious injury and perhaps lifelong disability. The shock and grief these events cause are all too well-known throughout the world. They are particularly well-known in poorer countries, where 90% of the annual deaths occur.

3. In richer countries, the deaths and injuries are slowly decreasing but, in the poorer ones, they are still increasing rapidly. Victims and survivors are often young, leaving families to cope with the loss of a breadwinner. Most of these deaths, injuries and economic losses can be prevented. In many high-income countries, an established set of interventions has contributed to significant reductions in the incidence and impact of road traffic injuries.

4. France is one such country. It has seen a 20% reduction in road traffic deaths since President Chirac made road safety one of his Government's key priorities in 2002 and introduced a multisectoral approach to tackling the problem.

5. Not everyone is equally affected by the lack of road safety. In high-income countries, most victims and survivors are vehicle occupants. However, in low-income and middle-income countries in Asia the vast majority are cyclists and motorcyclists. In Africa and South America, they are mostly pedestrians and users of public transportation.

6. A variety of approaches are being used to tackle some of the causes, including better legislation, enforcement and information. A number of initiatives, from Colombia to Ghana, from Costa Rica to Vietnam, show that improving road safety is possible even in lower-income settings.

7. Countries need to designate a lead agency in government which can coordinate the national road safety efforts. They also need to assess the problem, prepare a national road safety strategy, allocate financial and human resources, and implement specific interventions that are known to work. These include setting and enforcing laws on seat-belts, child restraints, helmets and drink driving; and promoting daytime running lights and improved visibility of all road users.

8. In addition to setting laws and raising awareness, countries need to formulate policies that promote safer vehicles, safer traffic management and safer road design. The countries that have been most successful have been those that have engaged many different groups from government, civil society and industry in a coordinated program of road safety.

9. Every sector is important — transport, education, health, law enforcement — in tackling the problem. On this World Health Day, I call particularly upon the public health community to

increase its contribution. By strengthening emergency services for victims, improving data collection, contributing to policies, developing prevention activities or simply ringing the alarm bell — as we are doing today — we can all make significant contributions.

10. Everyone can increase road safety in their private capacity as well — as drivers, passengers and pedestrians, and as members of the public who influence decision-makers. Road deaths and injuries are preventable. Let us use this World Health Day to draw attention to this fact.

Part II

Listen to the following short passages and then choose one of the answers that best fits the meaning of each passage. There are ten questions in this part of the test, 2 points for each question.

11. The growing population has been moving steadily into cities. Mechanization of agriculture is one of the factors pushing people away from the countryside. In addition, jobs in manufacturing, bureaucracy, and service industries pull them to the cities.

12. It has been a strange spring, even by British standards. After sweltering through the hottest April for over a century and shivering during an unusually cold May, the country was deluged by the wettest June since records began. Up to seven people died in the subsequent floods; 27,000 homes and 5,000 businesses had to be evacuated. Firemen and paramedics described the rescue efforts as the biggest-ever in peacetime. Insurers gave warning that the final bill would be more than £1 billion.

13. In many of the richer countries, however, in a process termed counterurbanization, cities have turned inside out, and central city populations are actually declining. Poorer citizens remain in the center as the richer avail themselves of the new means of transportation and of communication via phone, fax and the World Wide Web to relocate to the suburbs.

14. Businesses, too, recognizing a new freedom of movement, are leaving the central cities, partly to reduce their overhead costs. Multinational corporations cross international boundaries to relocate their factories, removing them from high-wage urban centers in the first world to new sites offering cheaper labor in the third.

15. Since the building of the first aircraft in 1930 by Wilbur and Orville Wright, and the first solo flight across the Atlantic in 1927 by Charles Lindbergh, international and intercontinental travel has become commonplace. Flights are taken for business and pleasure, and tourism has become one of the world's largest industries. In 1989, 38 million people visited the USA, spending 43 billion. Students, in particular, travel around the globe for formal and informal study and work opportunities.

16. Twentieth-century technology has transformed the quality of daily life as well as its location and density. The automobile, bus, truck, train, airplane, and jet affect transportation for almost all citizens of the world. The revolution in the means of communication — telegraph, telephone, copier, fax machine, modem, Internet, radio phonograph, various kinds of sound

reproduction, photography, motion pictures, television, satellite transmission and cable — have opened visions of the whole world to potentially all its citizens.

17. They have totally transformed work and play as well as the distribution of these activities in geographical space. Air-conditioning has not only changed standards of comfort, but has opened many warmer areas of the world (including the southern United States) to increased immigration and development.

18. The computer has not only affected transportation and communication, but also has transformed data processing, office work, and the further development of both large-scale organizations and of science. With the advent of the World Wide Web it is now quite conceivable that future generations may never have to leave their homes to work, shop, bank and communicate with friends and family.

19. New technology systems such as the automated assembly line production of Henry Ford's automobile factories, the more recent introduction of robotics, and the management techniques of Frederick Taylor have changed the way we work and the efficiency of our production. Scientific research facilities have been established by private corporations, like the Rockefeller Foundations, and, most of all, by national governments all over the world. They have changed our concept and mode of creativity. No longer needing to rely on experienced, gifted artisans tinkering in small shops, twentieth-century technology has systematized invention and promoted an increasing demand for ever more sophisticated and more expensive research facilities.

20. Synthetic fabrics and dyes have changed our wardrobes. Plastics have been the most important new, man-made material of the twentieth century and have replaced metals, rubber, and glass in innumerable uses. They have also increased the world's reliance on petroleum, a non-renewable fossil fuel, from which plastics are synthesized.

Part III

Listen to the following longer passages and then choose the best answers to the questions. You may need to scribble a few notes in order to answer the questions satisfactorily. There are four passages in this part, each with 5 questions. And each question carries 2 points.

Passage One

In a recent 12-month span, carbon emissions from the burning of fossil fuels climbed to more than 7,900,000,000 tons, a record high. Global emissions of carbon have been rising steadily since the late 18th century and rapidly since the 1950s. In fact, annual emissions have quadrupled since the mid-20th century.

Three-fourths of global carbon emissions are the result of burning fossil fuels, namely coal, oil, and natural gas. The rest largely come from deforestation. Of the four major sectors contributing to these emissions, electricity generation — at 35% — accounts for the largest share; transportation and industrial processes, 20% each. The remaining 25% is produced by residential and commercial buildings. Two-thirds of the carbon emissions from fossil fuel combustion are emitted by just 10 nations. The U.S., with five percent of the world's population, is the largest contributor, accounting for nearly one-quarter of global emissions. China is second, with nearly 14%. Other major polluters are Russia, Japan, India, Italy, Canada, South Korea, Germany, and the United Kingdom.

Most of the growth in emissions in the coming decades, however, is expected to come from developing countries. While overall global carbon emissions have risen 13% since 1990, those in China have jumped 47%. Indeed, this one country accounts for nearly half of the global increase in emissions in the last decade.

Passage Two

In the aftermath of World War II, countries in Southeast Asia became more nationalistic as they rejected continued colonial rule for independence. Many adopted indigenous languages as their national languages and the medium of instruction in schools.

Malaysia made Malay its national language and Indonesia did the same. But Singapore — a small multiethnic island nation sandwiched between these two much larger countries — took a different track after it gained self-government from Britain in 1959 and sovereignty in 1965.

Singapore decided to keep English as its working language, partly because it was a neutral bridge between the different races in the country, and partly because it was the pre-eminent language of the international commerce, technology and science and thus offered the fledgling economy the best prospects of success.

Singapore has a mixed population of nearly 4 million people. While 77 percent are ethnically Chinese, they are mainly descendants of people who came from different parts of China speaking different dialects. Another 14 percent of the population are Malays from different parts of Malaysia and Indonesia, while 8 percent are South Asians from different parts of the subcontinent. The rest came mainly from other parts of Asia.

The general literacy rate in Singapore was estimated to be 93.1 percent in 1998, the date of the most recent official survey. For males, the figure was 96.8 percent and for females 89.2 percent.

Passage Three

In the past half-century the world has made unprecedented economic gains. Countries that a mere generation ago were struggling with underdevelopment are now vibrant centers of global economic activity and domestic well-being. In just two decades, 15 countries, whose combined populations exceed 1.6 billion, have halved the proportion of their citizens living in extreme poverty. Asia has made an astounding recovery from the financial crisis of 1997—1998, demonstrating the staying power of its economies — though Asia's poor have not yet regained lost ground.

Chief among the human development success stories since the 1960s are the increase in life expectancy in developing countries, from 46 to 64 years; the halving of infant mortality rates; an increase of more than 80 percent in the proportion of children enrolled in primary school; and the doubling of access to safe drinking water and basic sanitation.

While more of us enjoy better standards of living than ever before, many others remain desperately poor. Nearly half the world's population still has to make do on less than $2 per day. Approximately 1.2 billion people — 500 million in South Asia and 300 million in Africa — struggle on less than $1. People living in Africa south of the Sahara are almost as poor today as they were 20 years ago. With that kind of deprivation comes pain, powerlessness, despair and lack of fundamental freedom — all of which, in turn, perpetuate poverty. Of a total world labour force of some 3 billion, 140 million workers are out of work altogether, and a quarter to a third are underemployed.

Passage Four

By creating factories, the industrial revolution drove a wedge between the home and the workplace that dramatically affected both men and women. Wives who had been accustomed to working alongside, or at least in proximity to, their husbands on the farm or in the shop or workshop now found that the major source of employment was away from home. The industrial revolution, perhaps even more than the political revolutions, forced redefinitions of identities. What should the woman's role and place be now? In a world that expected most females to be under the protection of males, how were single women to define, and fend for, themselves? In what voice should the feminist movement address these complex issues?

As the industrial revolution began in semi-rural locations, its labor force was drawn primarily from young, unmarried women, frequently daughters of local farmers. Some of the early factory owners built boarding houses for the women and treated them protectively, as young wards.

As new machinery became heavier, as factory work became more prevalent, and as economic depression pressed down on both American and British economies, the workforce shifted. Men, often farmers and immigrants, moved into the factories, displacing the women. The men demanded higher pay, which factory owners had previously hoped to avoid by hiring women. The culture of the industrializing world of that time, primarily in Britain called for men to support their families. A young, unmarried woman might earn just enough for herself and that would be adequate. A man required a "family wage". The rising productivity of constantly improving machinery made this "family wage" possible, and it became the baseline standard for industry.

Women were thus displaced from factory work and brought back to the home. By the second half of the nineteenth-century, "domesticity" became the norm for middle-and even working-class women and their families.

Part IV

Write a summary of approximately 200-250 words of a passage you are going to hear. The passage is around 500 words in length.

Writing gives you unique ways to think through ideas deeply, come to know subjects well, and absorb those subjects into your lifelong store of knowledge. Even thirty years later, many people can recall details about the topics and content of essays they wrote in college, but far fewer people can recall specifics of a classroom lecture or a textbook chapter. By writing, you activate brain processes that help you make connections among your thoughts. Such connecting gives you potential access to the pleasures of "shocks of recognition", moments when suddenly your mind leaps from what you know to what you did not "see" before. This access to new insights and increased knowledge are usually unavailable until the physical act of writing begins.

Writing helps you clarify your ideas by having to think about them and put them into words. The ability to "think about thinking" belongs uniquely to human beings. Such reflective thinking permits you to look back at your ideas, reconsider and perhaps rearrange them, and then perhaps revise them in writing — each time getting closer to what you want to say. The writer E. M. Forster said this about writing, thinking, and reflecting: "How can I know what I mean until I've seen what I said?"

Your writing teaches others about your subject. Through writing, you create a permanent record of your ideas for others to read and think about. Reading informs and shapes human thought. In an open, free, democratic society, every person is welcome to write and thereby create reading for others. For such freedom of idea exchange to thrive, writing and reading skills cannot be concentrated in only a select group of people. All of us need access to the power of the written word. In college, you can exercise that power by writing many different types of assignments. Doing so prepares you for today's highly technological workplace, in which jobs demand reading with understanding and writing with skill when creating documents that range from letters to formal reports. Also, the ability to write well identifies you as an educated person, someone who is well-informed and up-to-date and can be depended on to use language clearly and effectively.

Four elements define writing: writing is a way of communicating a message for a purpose to readers. Communicating in writing means sending a message that has a destination. The message of the writing is its content, which originates in your engaging in one or more of the processes of observing, remembering, reporting, explaining, exploring, interpreting, speculating and evaluating. Purpose for writing can be many, as will be discussed later. Readers, also called your audience, are the destination your writing must reach. Taking readers into account as your write is crucial to your success as a communicator.

Purposes for writing concern a writer's goals, sometimes called aims of writing or writing intentions. Purpose for writing originates from the motivating forces behind what is being written.

The purposes of writing to express yourself and to create a literary work contribute importantly to human thought and culture. These purposes offer you the pleasure of writing for yourself as audience and of creatively composing a work of literature for others to read. I concentrate on the two purposes most prominent and practical in your academic life: to inform a reader and to persuade a reader. In the service of these purposes, writers can choose among and even combine many effective writing strategies. These strategies include narrating, describing, illustrating, defining, analyzing and classifying, comparing and contrasting, drawing an analogy, and considering cause and effect.

Sample Test Three

Part I

Listen to the short passages and then decide whether the corresponding statements below are true or false. There are ten questions in this part of the test, 2 points for each question.

1. Many Latin American farm exports, such as sugar, cotton or orange juice, are politically sensitive in the United States, and the Bush team shows little sign of being willing to take on the invested interests involved.
2. To most Canadians, the signs of climate change are all too obvious. Two decades of above-average temperatures have left prairie farmers counting crop losses from droughts.
3. If we understand the current dominance of the English language throughout the world as an opportunity to evangelize English literature, to impose an already existing canon and state, then we shall undertake a task which is both contemptible and futile. If, however, we understand that for the language to live it must begin to find new voices, to articulate different experiences, then we will have a genuine justification for the teaching of literature, that is, the teaching of imaginative writing.
4. International migrants, defined as people who have lived outside their homeland for a year or more, account for under 3% of the world's population: a total, in 2000, of maybe 150 million people, or rather less than the population of Brazil.
5. Canon, the Japanese camera and office-equipment firm reported a 53% jump in profits in the third quarter. It now expects to earn $1.4 billion for the full year.
6. In recent years, the "France-German motor" has been sputtering. The two countries had a nasty showdown at the Nice summit in 2000, and have been haggling ever since about farm reforms and the costs of financing EU enlargement.
7. Proteins are complicated chemicals formed by stringing together simpler chemicals called amino acids. There are twenty-two of them, some rarer than others. The DNA blueprint specifies the order in which these are to be assembled.
8. Although the form of the jury remained the same when it was transplanted to the American colonies, it assumed additional meanings. Jury trial became a symbol of American freedom or popular justice versus the king's justice. Even though the need to establish our independence

has long since passed, jury trial remains at the core of the civil court system.

9. The need for self-reliance, to counter dependence on the news agencies of the superpowers, as well as the need to disseminate an undistorted version of their own experiences, led Third World countries to come up with national, and in some cases regional, alternatives.

10. It is easy to lump all nuclear weapons together, and to dismiss them as equally dangerous. But hydrogen bombs, which derive most of their power from the fusion of light atomic nuclei, are far more terrible than fission bombs, which work by splitting heavy nuclei.

Part II

Listen to the following short passages and then choose one of the answers that best fits the meaning of each passage. There are ten questions in this part of the test, 2 points for each question

11. The French 18th century is a magnet both for researchers and the general reader. France was the centre of that intellectual seedbed of modernity, the Enlightenment. It was a superpower able to spread its influence round the world. It was a motor of economic globalisation.

12. The story of evolution that we have been telling is a very deterministic one. Mutations may be random, but only the winners survive, and winners are those with superior characters. If you ran evolution again, with different but equally random mutations, on the whole you might expect the same winners to emerge.

13. When we speak of "the state", we usually mean the nation state. Whereas it could be argued that both nations and states had existed prior to the expansion of European power, the nation state is a European invention.

14. For more than two years, the federal energy and environment ministers have been talking with provincial counterparts about how to reduce emissions to meet the Kyoto target of 6% below 1990 levels. Since little concerted action has resulted, Canada now faces the task of achieving a 20% reduction by 2012.

15. The discovery phase of litigation serves several important purposes: it can be used to preserve evidence of witnesses who may not be available at the time of trial: to reveal facts; to aid in formulating the issues; and to freeze testimony so as to prevent perjury.

16. In the time when Shakespeare was a young man, almost no one who was not actually brought up speaking English ever bothered to learn it. Now English is in daily use among three or four hundred million people who were not brought up speaking it as their native language. Most of them live in countries requiring English for what we may broadly call "external" purposes: contact with people in other countries, either through the spoken or the written word, for such purposes as trade and scientific advance.

17. Kobe Bryant, 24, is one of the most popular players in the National Basketball Association. He has admitted having sex with the woman, who worked at the plush resort hotel where he was staying, but denies assault. Bryant's first scheduled court appearance is August 6.

Meanwhile, he is free on 25,000 dollars bail. If convicted, Bryant faces probation to life in prison as well as fines ranging from 3,000 to 750,000 dollars.

18. It has already changed most people's lives, but there is more work ahead for the mobile phone. The trusty SIM card can also act as a debit and credit card. That means it may only be a matter of time before mobile phones are used to deposit, transfer and withdraw cash. In the developed world, one of the barriers hindering the switch to mobile cash has been the costly infrastructure developed by banks and credit-card companies. With cash machines and bank branches at every street corner there is less call for an alternative payment system.

19. More rockets continued to rain on the Liberian capital Monrovia today and at least 11 civilians were reportedly killed. The victims are part of about 6,000 displaced people sheltering in the Newport High School. Some of the rockets fell at different locations including the compound housing the UN Children's agency staff.

20. A special report by the two UN agencies dealing with food and agriculture warns that over one million Angolans will still need food aid despite peace and improved crop production. The report says the food needs remain high because of the increase in the number of refugees and demobilized soldiers. The agencies estimate that thousands of metric tonnes of cereal, pulses and smaller quantities of oil, sugar, salt and corn-soya blend will be needed to feed the people until the next harvest.

Part III

Listen to the following longer passages and then choose the best answers to the questions. You may need to scribble a few notes in order to answer the questions satisfactorily. There are four passages in this part, each with 5 questions. And each question carries 2 points.

Passage One

Everywhere, international migration has shot up the list of political concerns. The horror of September 11th has toughened American's approach to immigrants, especially students from Muslim countries, and blocked the agreement being negotiated with Mexico. In Europe, the far right has flourished in elections in Austria, Denmark and the Netherlands. In Australia, the plight of the *Tampa* and its human cargo made asylum a top issue last year.

Although many more immigrants arrive legally than hidden in trucks or boats, voters fret that governments have lost control of who enters their country. The result has been a string of measures to try to tighten and enforce immigration rules. But however much governments clamp down, both immigration and immigrants are here to stay. Powerful economic forces are at work. It is impossible to separate the globalisation of trade and capital from the global movement of people. Borders will leak; companies will want to be able to move staff; and liberal democracies will be reluctant to introduce the strict measures required to make controls truly watertight. If the

European Union admits ten new members, it will eventually need to accept not just their goods but their workers too.

Passage Two

Figures from the Census Bureau estimate that there are 7.9 million illegal immigrants in the U.S. and, in recent years, the number of individuals becoming legal immigrants is around 1,000,000 annually. It is interesting to look at the legal-illegal situation for a moment because both share one thing — the breakdown of where people come from and where they are going. People from the following six countries — in order of numbers — make up most of those trying to get in: Mexico, India, China, Japan, the Philippines, and Vietnam. Where are they all going? Again, ranked by popularity: California, New York, Florida, Texas, New Jersey, and Illinois.

For many, it is the lure of the American Dream, lit by liberty's torch, that attracts them to this country. Yet, it is becoming a dim light as border walls try to discourage illegal aliens from being drawn to the perceived brighter opportunities. In the early 1990s, reforms were announced to deal with the rising problem of immigration, which increasingly was becoming a political matter. The plan was known as "prevention through deterrence"; the aim, to make it so risky and dangerous that there would be no point in trying to sneak into the U.S.. In that sense, the plan is a failure. More than 3,000,000 illegal still try to pour in from south of the border every year.

What the initiative has done, however, is to "militarize" the borderline through a number of operations. These include what were known as Operation Gatekeeper in San Diego, Operation Hold the Line in El Paso, Operation Rio Grande in McAllen, and Operation Safeguard in Tucson.

Operation Gatekeeper was the first and appeared to prove that deterrence worked. One sign of the success is that smuggling costs for this route have risen phenomenally, from $250 per person to more than $1,500. Operation Hold the Line was next, being implemented in the El Paso area in 1993. This produced a 50% decline in apprehensions between 1993—1996. In 1995, the controversial Operation Safeguard was launched. This plan redirected illegal border crossings away from urban zones to comparatively open areas that the border patrol could control more effectively, especially when there were more than 1,100 agents patrolling the area — a fourfold increase from when the operation was launched. After that, Operation Rio Grande gained control of the border in the Rio Grande Valley and then in all of Texas and New Mexico. This saw a massive influx of new border patrol agents — almost 500, which was a 50% increase on previous years' staffing — and they got results. In some areas, immigration flow fell by at least one-third. Crime in cities close to the border also dropped considerably.

Passage Three

Elephants, proverbially, are afraid of mice. Well, it's a nice story, but don't rely on it to frighten the beasts from your smallholding. Poachers aside, the most dangerous thing an elephant is likely to meet is a disgruntled farmer with a rifle. And farmers have good reason to be disgruntled. In many parts of Africa, farms are routinely trashed by visiting elephants. In this case, therefore, prevention is better than cure for both sides. And some recently published research may point the way, using tiny creatures that elephants really are afraid of: bees.

Although elephants are thick-skinned, they have sensitive patches behind their ears, under their trunks and around their eyes. Sometimes, according to bee-keepers, an entire herd can be stampeded by a swarm of bees. Researchers from Wild Animal Protection Institutes based in Kenya have tested the idea that elephants' visits to farms might be discouraged by strategically placed bee hives. It seems they are — and that the hives do not necessarily even have to be occupied.

Passage Four

Tobacco not only kills people, but it also saps national treasuries. Just as there are no safe levels of tobacco consumption, there are no safe investments in tobacco. The economic impact of tobacco has been analyzed in many countries in recent years. Studies from Brazil, China, South Africa and Switzerland complement earlier analyses done in Canada, the United Kingdom and the United States. Their combined message is unequivocal — the alleged economic benefits of tobacco are illusory and misleading.

Most serious analyses of all the economic effects show that a decline in the tobacco industry would not result in less employment. In fact, as employment in the tobacco sector decreases, overall employment may stay the same or even increase. A World Bank study has estimated that the use of tobacco results in a global net loss of US $ 200 billion per year, with half of these losses occurring in the developing world. This cost does not reflect loss due to reduced quality of life of smokers and their families. The same study also estimated that smoking prevention is among the most cost-effective of all health interventions.

Part IV

Listen to the following passage about humanitarian aid to the Iraqi people in war. Write a short summary of around 150-200 words of what you have heard. This part of the test carries 20 points.

As Iraq struggles to recover from conflict and severe economic hardship to a society that is once again able to stand on its own two feet, the United nations has convened a meeting on 23, June to ensure that the Iraqis immediate humanitarian needs are met and the transition to longer-term reconstruction is fully underway by the beginning of the next year.

Indeed, such actions and achievements in responding to anticipated humanitarian needs in Iraq have played a crucial role in averting a much larger potential crisis. Even as the conflict was underway, national UN staff continued to carry out their duties. Aid activities under the Oil for Food Programme in Iraq's three northern govern orates never stopped. National staff of the World Food Programme worked to open corridors from Turkey, Jordan and Iran into Iraq. UNICEF local staff delivered humanitarian supplies and worked to maintain the supply of potable water. WHO local staff supported Iraqi health professionals. Under the Oil for Food Programme, UNDP worked to maintain and restore electric power supplies, especially in the north.

As of today, more than 800,000 metric tonnes of food — enough to feed almost all of Iraq's 27 million people for two months — have been dispatched to Iraq. An average of 3.5 million litres of water per day is being tankered to hospitals, health centres and communities in the south and in the Baghdad area. Basic medicines, vaccines and health supplies have been delivered to facilities throughout the country. Agencies have helped repair and restore water, sanitation and power facilities, as well as schools, which have also been receiving essential education supplies.

But great needs remain. Due to the lack of a functioning economy, combined with prolonged reliance on the ration system, virtually all of the population of Iraq will require food aid in the short run in order to survive. The Flash Appeal for Iraq, asking for $2.2 billion to cover needs for six months, was issued in March. Generous donor funding (approximately $900 million), and access to the resources of the Oil for Food Programme ($1.1 billion), have meant that $2 billion is already available for humanitarian aid for the people of Iraq. The revised humanitarian appeal for Iraq seeks to meet the needs of the Iraqi people up to the end of the year. Given the healthy funding status, only an additional US $259 million is required.

Food aid alone accounts for two-thirds of the aid being requested through the Appeal. While the food sector, accounting for some $1.56 billion, is fully funded, funding is still required for equally important interventions in other sectors. Most essential needs must be still met: health care; clean water and sanitation; electricity; infrastructure repair; shelter; mine action and mine awareness; education; food security and agriculture; assistance for internally displaced persons and returning refugees. Given the urgent needs in other parts of the world in much of Africa, Afghanistan, the Democratic People's Republic of Korea, as well as other places, it is essential that donor countries ensure that contributions to Iraq are in addition to and not in place of — funding for other emergencies.

Sample Test Four

Part I

Listen to the short passages and then decide whether the corresponding statements below are true or false. There are ten questions in this part of the test, 2 points for each question.

1. Peak oil predictions about the impending decline in global rates of oil production are based on scant evidence and dubious models of how the oil market responds to scarcity. In fact, even though oil supplies increasingly will come from unstable regions, the ongoing investments designed to reduce the costs of finding and extracting oil are a more effective response to that instability than trying to fix the political problems of faraway countries.

2. The recent debate over a Medicare drug benefit has publicized the lack of drug coverage among the elderly. However, what is less well known is that although many people with employer-

sponsored insurance have drug coverage, they are being asked to assume an increasing proportion of the cost of their prescriptions.

3. Temperatures in the atmosphere usually drop as altitude increases, but in some settings — though it may seem counterintuitive — the reverse can occur. When this atmospheric inversion in temperature takes place in a valley or other location with minimal air circulation, warmer air up above keeps colder air down below, confined near the ground. It also traps pollution, making cities in these areas more susceptible to poor air quality.

4. Several commercially available materials and technologies can be used now to improve today's Army truck fleet. For example, high-strength steels could reduce weight while maintaining protection, and aluminum and magnesium alloys could replace steel altogether in some components. Also, ceramic-and metal-matrix composites could decrease the weight of braking systems with no sacrifice in performance. These materials and processes are increasingly being used in commercial trucks and trailers, but to a lesser extent in Army trucks.

5. The age of the universe can be derived from the observed relationship between the velocities of and the distances separating the galaxies. The velocities of distant galaxies can be measured very accurately, but the measurement of distances is more uncertain. Over the past few decades, measurements of the Hubble expansion have led to estimated ages for the universe of between 7 billion and 20 billion years, with the most recent and best measurements within the range of 10 billion to 15 billion years.

6. Three years ago, we — the people of the world, represented by leaders and officials from 189 countries at the Millennium Summit — pledged to pursue an ambitious global poverty-fighting agenda, embodied in a set of eight feasible Millennium Development Goals: to halve extreme poverty and hunger by the year 2015; to make primary education available to all girls and boys; to ensure gender equality; to reduce child and maternal mortality around the world; to stop and reverse the spread of HIV/AIDS, malaria and tuberculosis; to strive for environmental sustainability; and to work for global cooperation in terms of aid, trade and debt relief.

7. No one is so safe from this technological revolution. A cell phone can capture the most disgusting or bizarre image and, in seconds, send it around the world. A comic loses control with a rowdy audience and his racial rant makes headlines because someone in the audience captures all of it in a dim-lit video and sends it to a friend who sends it to a friend who sends it to anyone who can call it up on a computer. A pair of minor celebrities indulge in video sex and their private act becomes public in an instant. Nothing is sacred. Bathroom humor reigns supreme.

8. In the early 1970s evidence had accumulated showing that chlorofluorocarbons (CFCs) were damaging the ozone layer in the stratosphere and increasing the amount of ultraviolet B (UV-B) radiation reaching Earth's surface. Since the ozone layer protects humans, animals and plants from the damaging effects of UV-B radiation, the steady increase in CFCs and other

ozone-depleting substances constituted a major potential health hazard.

9. When Ghana beat Australia, 2-1, in the opening match in a doubleheader, it meant that China had advanced to the quarterfinals before it even took the field for its match against Russia. China then beat Russia, 1-0, to claim a first-place finish in Group D. In Columbus, Ohio, the United States advanced to the quarterfinals after beating North Korea, 3-0, to maintain its perfect record in Group A.

10. It's a nightmare scenario that keeps emergency planners and homeland security officials awake at night. Terrorists release a virus or toxic chemicals or detonate a radioactive "dirty bomb" in a major city. One of the first duties of emergency responders will be to determine how a plume of hazardous material may fan out or a virus may spread through a population.

Part II

Listen to the following short passages and then choose one of the answers that best fits the meaning of each passage. There are ten questions in this part of the test, 2 points for each question.

11. One of two Afghan men on a motor-cycle opened fire Sunday on a marked United Nations' car, killing a French aid worker, the first international UN staff member slain in postwar Afghanistan. Police identified the captured assailants as Taliban militants.

12. Britain and Canada advised their citizens to defer non-essential travel to Saudi Arabia, while U. S. and French embassies urged their communities against non-essential movement outside housing areas after suspected Al Qaeda militants on Sunday drove a car rigged with bombs into a residential complex, killing up to 30 people.

13. U. S. Senator Edward M. Kennedy was asked on CBS-TV's "Face the Nation" about his thoughts as the 40th anniversary of President John F. Kennedy's assassination approached on Saturday. Kennedy said he felt a "continued deep-seated sense of loss" from the deaths of his brothers and other family members. President Kennedy was assassinated in Dallas on November 22, 1963. U. S. Sen. Robert F. Kennedy was assassinated in Los Angeles on June 6, 1968. Edward Kennedy's third brother, Joseph P. Kennedy Jr., was killed in World War II.

14. The main parts of a jet engine include a compressor, a combustion chamber, and two turbines. The compressor sucks in air, compresses it, and forces it into the combustion chamber. In the combustion chamber, the air mixes with the fuel and is ignited. The burning gases expand rapidly and rush through and spin the turbines. The compressor turbine turns the compressor; the fan turbine turns the fan. After spinning the turbines, the hot gases rush out of the engine and provide additional thrust.

15. The circulatory system is a network that carries blood through the body to provide nutrition, oxygen, and to remove waste. It consists primarily of the heart, which pumps blood, and a network of blood vessels — arteries, veins, and capillaries. Arteries carry blood from the heart. Veins carry blood to the heart, and capillaries, which are extremely tinny vessels,

connect arteries and veins.

16. Soccer star David Beckham and his wife, former Spice Girl Victoria, denied tabloid allegations that their marriage is strained. A spokeswoman for the couple said Saturday that the story, carried by the Sunday Mirror, was "rubbish" and that a lawyer was looking at the story for possible legal action. The Sunday Mirror reported that Victoria Beckham threatened to walk out on her marriage unless her husband moves back to Britain from Spain, where he plays for Real Madrid. The newspaper said a trial separation had been discussed.

17. China says its current urbanization rate is 32 percent, which means a total of 350 million people live in cities. The real figure, though, is more likely about 17 percent if economic and social indicators of the cities are considered. Only 219 million Chinese, or 17.4 percent of the population, have access to tap water — a basic indicator for urbanization — and only 207 million are registered as non-agricultural population.

18. The U.S. government has decided to refashion its well-known Food Guide Pyramid to help pear-shaped Americans eat less and exercise more. Developed in 1992, the Food Guide Pyramid graphically offers a general outline on how much a healthy person should eat each day from the five major food groups. In the graph, fats, oils and sweets are at the narrow top of the pyramid with advice to use them sparingly. Dairy and meat products occupy the next tier of the pyramid; next are vegetable and fruits. At the bottom of the pyramid is the bread, rice and pasta group, with advice to eat them most.

19. There may well be a conflict between the public's interest in new technologies and efforts by government and employers to restrict coverage of medical insurance in an effort to control costs. With 89 new pharmaceuticals approved by the Food and Drug Administration and almost 4,000 clinical trials for new medicines taking place in 2002, it remains to be seen how many of these new treatments will be fully covered by insurance. In addition, this lack of comprehensive coverage may discourage pharmaceutical companies from developing products that are clinically beneficial but not financially advantageous.

20. Today, people are taking action, across countries and communities — from cartoons to graffiti, from T-shirts to puppets, from TV programmes to bus tours, from postage stamps to reports — for advocacy and awareness building. They have voiced their views on tailoring, prioritizing and localizing the Millennium Development Goals. They have influenced macro-economic and social policies. They are increasingly taking part in monitoring progress and campaigning for progress.

Part III

Listen to the following longer passages and then choose the best answers to the questions. You may need to scribble a few notes in order to answer the questions satisfactorily. There are twenty questions in this part of the test, 2 points for each question.

Passage One

Globalization, defined as networks of interdependence at worldwide distance, is not new. Nor is it just economic. Markets have spread and tied people together, but environmental, military, social, and political interdependence have also increased. If the current political backslash against globalization were to lead to a rash of protectionist policies, it might slow or even reverse the world's economic integration — as has happened at times in the past — even as global warming or the spread of the AIDS virus continued apace. It would be ironic if current protests the positive aspects of globalization while leaving the negative dimensions untouched.

Markets have unequal effects, and the inequality they produce can have powerful political consequences. But the cliché that markets always make the rich richer and the poor poorer is simply not true. Globalization, for example, has improved the lot of hundreds of millions of poor people around the world. Poverty can be reduced even when inequality increases. And in some cases inequality can even decrease. The economic gap between South Korea and industrialized countries, for example, has diminished in part because of global markets. No poor country, meanwhile, has ever become rich by isolating itself from global markets, although North Korea and Myanmar have impoverished themselves by doing so. Economic globalization, in short, may be a necessary, though not sufficient condition for combating poverty.

Passage Two

Be very wary of opinions that flatter your self-esteem. Both men and women, nine times out of ten, are firmly convinced of the superior excellence of their own sex. There is abundant evidence on both sides. If you are a man, you can point out that most poets and men of science are male; if you are a woman, you can retort that so are most criminals. The question is inherently insoluble, but self-esteem conceals this from most people. We are all, whatever part of the world we come from, persuaded that our own nation is superior to all others. Seeing that each nation has its characteristic merits and demerits, we adjust our standard of values so as to make out that the merits possessed by our nation are the really important ones, while its demerits are comparatively trivial. Here, again, the rational man will admit that the question is one which there is no demonstrably right answer. It is more difficult to deal with the self-esteem of man as man, because we cannot argue out the matter with some non-human mind. The only way I know of dealing with this general human conceit is to remind ourselves that man is a brief episode in the life of a small planet in a little corner of the universe, and other parts of the cosmos may contain beings as superior to ourselves as we are to jelly fish.

Passage Three

If a glowing chunk of metal falls out of the sky and onto your house, space junk is probably to blame. On Monday, NASA astronaut Clay Anderson and Russian cosmonaut Fyodor Yurchikhin had a clear-out of the International Space Station, and dumped a 630-kilogram refrigerator-sized ammonia tank and a 96-kilogram camera mounting into space.

NASA said there was no room in the space shuttle's cargo bay to carry the obsolete gear back to Earth. Both items will be tracked by radar until they tumble from space and burn up in Earth's atmosphere. The camera mounting is expected to disintegrate completely, but pieces of the tank weighing up to 17 kilograms could survive re-entry and hit the ground.

NASA hopes the debris will land in the ocean, but says there is a 1 in 5000 chance that it could strike a populated area. The ammonia tank is expected to remain in orbit for at least 300 days, and the agency will issue warnings if it becomes a threat.

There are just 14 missions to the space station remaining before the space shuttles are retired in 2010.

Passage Four

Millions of people around the world would like to heat their homes and run household appliances with solar power. But the cost of doing so puts it out of the question. The first problem is that the cells convert only 10%-15% of the radiation from the sun into energy. The second is that the photovoltaic (PV) material used is a form of silicon that has to be made under high-vacuum conditions and heated in special kilns to 1,400℃. That makes photovoltaic solar cells horrendously expensive.

How to bring the high costs down to a more manageable amount? One answer that is attracting attention is to use carbon "nanorods", superstrong cylinders of carbon atoms that are 75,000 times thinner than a human hair. If scientists succeed in their efforts, carbon-based solar cells could cost as little as a tenth of the price of today's silicon-based versions.

By placing the flexible nanorods in a polymer solution, researchers found it could produce a composite material that had the elasticity and pliability of plastic, but capable converting solar rays into electrical energy. Inorganic nanocrystals behave a lot like polymers. For instance, they can be processed while still in the form of a solution. Scientists had been working with plastics as an alternative to conventional solar cells, but found that they did not conduct electricity particularly well.

Compared with the arduous process of fabricating conventional solar cells, making the hybrid nanorod polymer composite would be more like manufacturing cheap plastic laminates. That could solve the cost part of the solar energy equation. But what about the conversion efficiency? So far, the conversion efficiency of nanorod polymer cells has been little more than 2%. However, researchers are confident that the efficiency can be improved considerably.

Part IV

Listen to the following speech about September 11th attack by the American President George Bush. Write a short summary of around 150-200 words of what you have heard. This part of the test carries 20 points

Today, our fellow citizens, our way of life, our very freedom came under attack in a series of deliberate and deadly terrorist acts. The victims were in airplanes or in their offices. Secretaries, business men and women, military and federal workers. Moms and dads, friends and neighbors.

Thousands of lives were suddenly ended by evil, despicable acts of terror.

The pictures of airplanes flying into buildings, fires burning, huge structures collapsing, have filled us with indignation and resolution.

These acts of mass murder were intended to frighten our nation into chaos and retreat. But they have failed. Our country is strong. A great people has been moved to defend a great nation.

Terrorist attacks can shake the foundations of our biggest buildings, but they cannot touch the foundation of America. These acts shatter steel, but they cannot dent the steel of American resolve.

America was targeted for attack because we're the brightest beacon for freedom and opportunity in the world. And no one will keep that light from shining.

Today, our nation saw evil, the very worst of human nature, and we responded with the best of America, with the daring of our rescue workers, with the caring for strangers and neighbors who came to give blood and help in any way they could.

Immediately following the first attack, I implemented our government's emergency response plans. Our military is powerful, and it's prepared. Our emergency teams are working in New York City and Washington, D. C. , to help with local rescue efforts.

Our first priority is to get help to those who have been injured and to take every precaution to protect our citizens at home and around the world from further attacks.

The functions of our government continue without interruption. Federal agencies in Washington, which had to be evacuated today, are reopening for essential personnel tonight and will be open for business tomorrow.

Our financial institutions remain strong, and the American economy will be open for business as well.

The search is under way for those who are behind these evil acts. I've directed the full resources for our intelligence and law enforcement communities to find those responsible and bring them to justice. We will make no distinction between the terrorists who committed these acts and those who harbor them.

I appreciate so very much the members of Congress who have joined me in strongly condemning these attacks. And on behalf of the American people, I thank the many world leaders who have called to offer their condolences and assistance.

America and our friends and allies join with all those who want peace and security in the world and we stand together to win the war against terrorism.

Tonight I ask for your prayers for all those who grieve, for the children whose worlds have been shattered, for all whose sense of safety and security has been threatened. And I pray they will be comforted by a power greater than any of us spoken through the ages in Psalm 23: "Even though I walk through the valley of the shadow of death, I fear no evil for you are with me."

This is a day when all Americans from every walk of life unite in our resolve for justice and peace. America has stood down enemies before, and we will do so this time.

None of us will ever forget this day, yet we go forward to defend freedom and all that is good and just in our world. Thank you.

Sample Test Five

Part I

Listen to the short passages and then decide whether the corresponding statements below are true or false. There are ten questions in this part of the test, 2 points for each question

1. Population growth has turned out to have an internal check: as people grow richer and healthier, they have smaller families. Indeed, the growth rate of the human population reached its peak, of more than 2% a year, in the early 1960s. The rate of increase has been declining ever since. It is now 1.26%, and is expected to fall to 0.46% in 2050.

2. Environmental groups need to be noticed by the mass media. They also need to keep the money rolling in. Understandably, perhaps, they sometimes exaggerate. In 1997, for example, the Worldwide Fund for Nature issued a press release entitled, "Two-thirds of the world's forests lost forever". The truth turns out to be nearer 20%.

3. The early environmental movement worried that the mineral resources on which modern industry depends would run out. Clearly, there must be some limit to the amount of fossil fuels and metal ores that can be extracted from the earth: the planet, after all, has a finite mass. But that limit is far greater than many environmentalists would have people believe.

4. Reserves of natural resources have to be located, a process that costs money. That, not natural scarcity, is the main limit on their availability. However, known reserves of all fossil fuels, and of most commercially important metals, are now larger than they were when "The Limits to Growth" was published.

5. In the case of oil, for example, reserves that could be extracted at reasonably competitive prices would keep the world economy running for about 150 years at present consumption rates. Add to that the fact that the price of solar energy has fallen by half in every decade for the past 30 years, and appears likely to continue to do so in the future, and energy shortages do not look like a serious threat either to the economy or to the environment.

6. Cement, aluminium, iron, copper, gold, nitrogen and zinc account for more than 75% of global expenditure on raw materials. Despite an increase in consumption of these materials of between two-and ten-fold over the past 50 years, the number of years of available reserves has actually grown.

7. In 1968, Dr. Ehrlich predicted in his best-selling book, "The Population Bomb", that "the

battle to feed humanity is over. In the course of the 1970s the world will experience starvation of tragic proportions — hundreds of millions of people will starve to death." That did not happen. Instead, according to the United Nations, agricultural production in the developing world has increased by 52% per person since 1961.

8. The daily food intake in poor countries has increased from 1,932 calories, barely enough for survival, in 1961 to 2,650 calories in 1998, and is expected to rise to 3,020 calories by 2030. Likewise, the proportion of people in developing countries who are starving has dropped from 45% in 1949 to 18% today, and is expected to decline even further to 12% in 2010 and just 6% in 2030.

9. One form of pollution — the release of greenhouse gases that causes global warming — does appear to be a long-term phenomenon, but its total impact is unlikely to pose a devastating problem for the future of humanity.

10. More than 190 countries unanimously adopted the first international treaty against smoking at Tuesday's meeting of the World Health Organization, after three years and six rounds of negotiations. The treaty calls for an advertising ban and new labeling for tobacco products, indoor air controls to reduce second-hand smoke, and stronger legislation against tobacco smuggling.

Part II

Listen to the following short passages and then choose one of the answers that best fits the meaning of each passage. There are ten questions in this part of the test, 2 points for each question.

11. These environmentalists, led by such veterans as Paul Ehrlich of Stanford University, and Lester Brown of the Worldwatch Institute, have developed a sort of "litany" of four big environmental fears:
    - Natural resources are running out.
    - The population is ever growing, leaving less and less to eat.
    - Species are becoming extinct in vast numbers: forests are disappearing and fish stocks are collapsing.
    - The planet's air and water are becoming even more polluted.

12. The turkey, a "bird of courage" which "would not hesitate to attack a grenadier of the British guards", would have made a much better national symbol than the carrion-snatching bald eagle. So thought Benjamin Franklin, despite the former creature being fat and flightless. The eagle was enshrined on America's Great Seal anyway. But on June 28th, in a move of which Franklin would doubtless approve, the Fish and Wildlife Service announced that it would remove the bald eagle from the list of creatures protected under the Endangered Species Act. The change will take effect in early August.

13. America's economic recovery has become much less "jobless". Non-farm payrolls surged by

308,000 in March, the biggest leap in employment in four years. however, the current economic recovery has produced fewer jobs than any other since the second world war. "Unemployment rose to 5.7% from 5.6%, as previously discouraged workers re-entered the labour force.

14. There's the "Free Trade but Fair Trade" crowd, and the "Level Playing Field" crowd, and the "America First" crowd, all calling for tariffs and other international trade restrictions. Their supposed adversary is corporate America, seeking to boost profits by either importing goods made by cheaper foreign labor or relocating plants in foreign lands to directly take advantage of cheaper labor.

15. Jobs among manufacturers of high-tech products and related services are at least as vulnerable to cyclical downturns as traditional industries. The loss of jobs in San Jose in 2001 and 2002 was huge, second only to New York City — a much larger area that was uniquely wounded by terrorism.

16. With the nation's highest dependence on high tech and IT jobs, San Jose was at the epicenter of the 1996-2000 tech boom, but also of the subsequent shake-out. Few places experienced greater increases in jobs and incomes in the boom era, yet none suffered as great a hangover.

17. In the same two years when San Jose lost more than 120,000 jobs, San Diego added 34,700, Sacramento added 33,900 and Riverside-San Bernadino added 69,300. Employment rose in Modesto, Bakersfield, San Luis Obispo, Visalia, Lodi and Fresno.

18. Although similar in many ways to smallpox, monkeypox is less infectious and less deadly than its more famous relative. The disease occurs primarily in Central and West Africa. Although state and federal officials are still investigating the cause of the Midwest monkeypox cases, they do know that all the patients had direct or close contact with infected prairie dogs kept as pets.

19. The five-page questionnaire asks troops to list any symptoms they developed during their Gulf tours, including cough, rashes, headaches, chest pain or dizziness; and if they are having problems with depression or stress.

20. Smoking-related disease kills five million people worldwide each year, a number that the agency projects will double by 2020 without a concerted global effort to curb smoking, the agency says. Smoking increases in developing countries will account for more than 70 percent of the projected death toll.

Part III

Listen to the following longer passages and then choose the best answers to the questions. You may need to scribble a few notes in order to answer the questions satisfactorily. There are four passages in this part, each with 5 questions. And each question carries 2 points.

Passage One

In 1968, Dr. Ehrlich predicted in his best selling book, "The Population Bomb", that "the battle to feed humanity is over. In the course of the 1970s the world will experience starvation of tragic proportions — hundreds of millions of people will starve to death."

That did not happen. Instead, according to the United Nations, agricultural production in the developing world has increased by 52% per person since 1961. The daily food intake in poor countries has increased from 1,932 calories, barely enough for survival, in 1961 to 2,650 calories in 1998, and is expected to rise to 3,020 by 2030. Likewise, the proportion of people in developing countries who are starving has dropped from 45% in 1949 to 18% today, and is expected to decline even further to 12% in 2010 and just 6% in 2030. Food, in other words, is becoming not scarcer but ever more abundant. This is reflected in its price. Since 1800 food prices have decreased by more than 90%, and in 2000, according to the World Bank, prices were lower than ever before.

Passage Two

In the Supreme Court's 1986 landmark ruling denying the right of adult gay men to engage in consensual homosexual sex, Chief Justice Warren Burger wrote approvingly: "Blackstone (an 18th-century English jurist) described 'the infamous crime against nature' as an offence of 'deeper malignity' than rape, a heinous act 'the very mention of which is a disgrace to human nature', and 'a crime not fit to be named'. To hold that the act of homosexual sodomy", he continued, "is somehow protected as a fundamental right would be to cast aside millennia of moral teaching."

That was fewer than 20 years ago. How things have changed. In 2003 the Supreme Court struck down America's sodomy laws. A few months later, the Massachusetts' Supreme Court became the first state court to rule that gays had a constitutional right to wed. That spark started a bush fire, which has swept the country. Over the past few weeks, renegade ministers and officials in towns and villages in half a dozen states from New Mexico to New Jersey have been doling out thousands of marriage licences to jubilant gay couples.

Horrified conservatives are now working to stamp out the blaze which, they say, is threatening one of the most important foundations not just of American society, but of the whole civilised world. Five American states have already rushed through legislation explicitly banning same-sex marriages. And George Bush has agreed to seek a constitutional ban to the same effect.

Passage Three

Officials at Duke University Medical Center are reviewing the chain of events that led to a teenage girl receiving organs with the wrong blood type.

Jésica Santillán, 17, underwent a heart-lung transplant on Feb. 7, receiving type-A organs incompatible with her own O-positive blood. Her surgeons realized their mistake almost immediately, but could do nothing until a second set of donor organs became available. In the interim, Santillán suffered a stroke and kidney damage. Tests this morning revealed swelling and bleeding in her brain, indicators of severe damage, a day after her second transplant, her doctors said.

Hospital officials have concluded that the donated heart and lungs were typed and labeled correctly, but Santillán's doctors assumed the organs were compatible with their patient's blood type. The United Network for Organ Sharing, which provided both sets of organs, is also investigating the chain of events that led to the mistake.

The incident highlights the serious problem of medical errors. According to a 1999 report from the Institute of Medicine of the National Academies, *To Err Is Human: Building a Safer Health System*, medical mistakes kill 44,000 to 98,000 people each year — more than automobile accidents, breast cancer or AIDS. The report concludes that number could be reduced by 50 percent over five years if serious changes were made to the nation's health care system. Chief among its recommendations is that state governments require hospitals and other medical facilities to report errors that result in serious harm or death. In response to the report, Congress allocated $50 million for a federal initiative to research the causes and prevention of medical mistakes, under the auspices of the Agency for Healthcare Research and Quality.

Passage Four

Perhaps it is no surprise that gays find a hip city like New York hospitable. But two sets of data suggest that America as a whole is becoming steadily more tolerant. First, opinion polls show that homophobia has receded almost as far as Homer Simpson's hairline. As recently as 1982, only 34% of Americans thought homosexuality should be considered an acceptable alternative lifestyle. Now, 57% do. Since young Americans are far more relaxed about homosexuality than their elders — three-quarters of 18-34-year-olds think it is OK to be gay, whereas half of those over 55 think it is not — this trend is likely to continue. This year was also the first since Gallup started asking the question that a majority of Americans have not said that homosexual relations are morally wrong. And a hefty 89% think that gays should have equal rights in terms of job opportunities. If that strikes you as no big deal, recall that a total ban on gays working for the federal government was repealed only in 1975.

Second, and more subtly, one can look at demography. Gary Gates, a Californian academic, has been mining census data to determine where gays live in America. He observes several trends. First, the number of openly gay households is growing five times faster than the population as a whole. The last full census, in 2000, counted nearly 600,000 same-sex couples. Five years later, the American Community Survey (in which the Census Bureau quizzes a statistically representative sample of 1.4 million households) estimated that that number had increased by 30%, to 777,000.

Mr. Gates reckons the bulk of the increase is because as tolerance spreads, more gay couples are willing to be counted.

Part IV

Write a summary of approximately 200-250 words of a passage you are going to hear. The passage is around 500 words in length.

Opinion polls suggest that many people, in the rich world, at least, nurture the belief that environmental standards are declining. Four factors cause this disjunction between perception and reality.

One is the lopsidedness built into scientific research. Scientific funding goes mainly to areas with many problems. That may be wise policy, but it will also create an impression that many more potential problems exist than is the case.

Secondly, environmental groups need to be noticed by the mass media. They also need to keep the money rolling in. Understandably, perhaps, they sometimes exaggerate. In 1997, for example, the Worldwide Fund for Nature issued a press release entitled, "Two-thirds of the world's forests lost forever". The truth turns out to be nearer 20%.

Though these groups are run overwhelmingly by selfless folk, they nevertheless share many of the characteristics of other lobby groups. That would matter less if people applied the same degree of scepticism to environmental lobbying as they do to lobby groups in other fields. A trade organisation arguing for, say, weaker pollution controls is instantly seen as self-interested. Yet a green organisation opposing such a weakening is seen as altruistic, even if a dispassionate view of the controls in question might suggest they are doing more harm than good.

A third source of confusion is the attitude of the media. People are clearly more curious about bad news than good. Newspapers and broadcasters are there to provide what the public wants. That, however, can lead to significant distortions of perception. An example was America's encounter with El Niño in 1997 and 1998. This climatic phenomenon was accused of wrecking tourism, causing allergies, melting the ski-slopes and causing 22 deaths by dumping snow in Ohio.

A more balanced view comes from a recent article in the *Bulletin of the American Meteorological Society*. This tries to count up both the problems and the benefits of the 1997—1998 Niño. The damage it did was estimated at $4 billion. However, the benefits amounted to some $19 billion. These came from higher winter temperatures (which saved an estimated 850 lives, reduced heating costs and diminished spring floods caused by meltwaters), and from the well-documented connection between past Niños and fewer Atlantic hurricanes. In 1998, America experienced no big Atlantic hurricanes and thus avoided huge losses. These benefits were not reported as widely as the losses.

The fourth factor is poor individual perception. People worry that the endless rise in the amount of stuff everyone throws away will cause the world to run out of places to dispose of waste. Yet, even if America's trash output continues to rise as it has done in the past, and even if the American population doubles by 2100, all the rubbish America produces through the entire 21st century will still take up only the area of a square, each of whose sides measures 28km (18 miles). That is just one-12,000th of the area of the entire United States.

全国翻译专业资格（水平）考试问答

问： 什么是"翻译专业资格（水平）考试"？

答： "翻译专业资格（水平）考试"（英文：China Accreditation Test for Translators and Interpreters — CATTI）是为适应社会主义市场经济和我国加入世界贸易组织的需要，加强我国外语翻译专业人才队伍建设，科学、客观、公正地评价翻译专业人才水平和能力，更好地为我国对外开放服务，根据建立国家职业资格证书制度的精神，在全国实行统一的、面向社会的、国内最具权威的翻译专业资格（水平）认证；是对参试人员口译或笔译方面的双语互译能力和水平的认定。

问： 翻译资格考试目前的进展情况？

答： 翻译资格考试从2003年12月开始进行首次试点，到现在已取得了一系列可喜的进步和值得骄傲的业绩，考试的规模稳步增长、影响力不断扩大。

2008年，翻译专业硕士学位教育与翻译专业资格（水平）证书实现接轨，标志着翻译高层次人才培养与翻译行业人才评价标准实现了有机结合。

自2008年起，英、法、日、俄、德、西、阿等7个语种二、三级口笔译共29种58个科目考试已在全国范围内成功推开。各地区、各部门已不再进行翻译系列上述7个语种相应级别职称即翻译、助理翻译专业技术职务任职资格的评审工作。

截至2010年6月，累计报考人数已接近13万人；至2009年底，已有近1万6千人通过考试获得证书。考试的发展得到了社会的认可，并在港台地区和国际上引起了关注。

问： 证书由谁颁发？其有效范围如何？

答： 翻译专业资格（水平）考试合格，颁发由国家人力资源与社会保障部统一印制并用印的《中华人民共和国翻译专业资格（水平）证书》。该证书在全国范围有效，是聘任翻译专业技术职务的必备条件之一。根据国家人力资源与社会保障部有关规定，翻译专业资格（水平）考试已经正式纳入国家职业资格证书制度，该考试在全国推开后，相应语种和级别的翻译专业技术职务评审工作不再进行。

问： 谁负责组织实施全国翻译专业资格（水平）考试？

答： 根据《翻译专业资格（水平）考试暂行规定》的精神，翻译专业资格（水平）考试在国家人力资源与社会保障部指导下，由中国外文出版发行事业局（以下简称"中国外文局"）组织实施与管理。中国外文局组织成立全国翻译专业资格（水平）考试专家委员会。

全国翻译专业资格（水平）考试考务工作，分别由国家人力资源与社会保障部人事考试中心和国家外国专家局培训中心具体承担。即：国家人力资源与社会保障部人事考试中心负责考务工作，国家外国专家局培训中心承担口译考试考务工作。

问： 中国外文局是一个什么样的机构？

答： 中国外文出版发行事业局，简称中国外文局，又称中国国际出版集团（China International Publishing Group, CIPG），是中央所属事业单位，是承担党和国家书、刊、网络对外宣传任务的新闻出版机构，是中国历史最悠久、规模最大的专业对外传播机构。

中国外文局是在周恩来、陈毅等老一辈无产阶级革命家的直接领导下创办的，前身是成立于1949年10月的中央人民政府新闻总署国际新闻局。全局拥有近3000名职工，其中包括近百名外国专家。下属20个机构，包括10家出版社、5家杂志社，以及中国网、中国国际图书贸易总公司、对外传播研究中心、翻译资格考评中心等单位，在美国、英国、德国、比利时、俄罗斯、埃及、墨西哥、日本、香港等13个国家和地区设有海外分支机构，形成了涵盖翻译、出版、印刷、发行、互联网和多媒体业务、理论研究及社会事业等领域的事业格局。每年以10余种文字出版3000余种图书、编辑近30种期刊、运营30余家网站，书刊发行到世界180多个国家和地区，网络受众遍及世界各地。中国外文局对外传播的信息，全面反映了中国悠久的历史文化，真实展现了中国改革开放取得的新进展、新成就，为增进中外理解和友谊发挥了积极作用。

问： 通过翻译专业资格（水平）考试可以实现什么目标？

答： 首先，通过该考试，可以对社会上从事和有志于从事翻译工作的人员的翻译能力和水平作出比较科学、客观、公正的评价。

其次，翻译专业资格（水平）考试，是对全国翻译系列专业技术职务单一评审模式进行的一项积极的、富有改革意义的重大举措。通过翻译专业资格（水平）考试，取得翻译专业资格（水平）证书的人员，用人单位可根据需要，按照《翻译专业职务试行条例》任职条件要求聘任相应的专业技术职务。从2005年开始，英语二、三级翻译专业资格考试在全国推开；从2006年开始，法、日语二、三级翻译专业资格考试在全国推开；从2007年开始，英、法、日、阿、俄、德、西七个语种的考试在全国范围进行。2008年，七个语种的翻译（中级）、助理翻译（初级）职称只能通过考试取得，各地区、各部门不再进行翻译、助理翻译职称的评审工作。

此外，在翻译专业实行资格考试制度，可以规范国家翻译人才资格标准，提高翻译人才队伍整体素质，为翻译市场提供高质量的服务。

问： 翻译专业资格（水平）考试与职业资格证书制度是什么关系？

答： 翻译专业资格（水平）考试已纳入国家职业资格证书制度的统一规划和管理。

问： 翻译专业资格（水平）考试等级与专业能力是如何划分和要求的？

答： 翻译专业资格（水平）考试等级划分与专业能力：

（一）资深翻译：长期从事翻译工作，具有广博科学文化知识和国内领先水平的双语互译能力，能够解决翻译工作中的重大疑难问题，在理论和实践上对翻译事业的发展和人才培养作出重大贡献。

（二）一级口译、笔译翻译：具有较为丰富的科学文化知识和较高的双语互译能力，能胜任范围较广、难度较大的翻译工作，能够解决翻译工作中的疑难问题，能够担任重要国际会议的口译或译文定稿工作。

（三）二级口译、笔译翻译：具有一定的科学文化知识和良好的双语互译能力，能胜任一定范围、一定难度的翻译工作。

（四）三级口译、笔译翻译：具有基本的科学文化知识和一般的双语互译能力，能完成一般的翻译工作。

问：资深翻译、一级翻译取得的方式是怎样的？
答：资深翻译实行考核评审方式取得，申报资深翻译的人员须具有一级口译或笔译翻译资格（水平）证书；一级口译、笔译翻译实行考试与评审相结合的方式取得。资深翻译和一级口译、笔译翻译评价的具体办法另行规定。

问：二级口译、笔译翻译和三级口译、笔译翻译取得的方式是怎样的？
答：二级口译、笔译翻译和三级口译、笔译翻译实行统一大纲、统一命题、统一标准的考试办法。申请人可根据本人所从事的专业工作，报名参加相应级别口译或笔译翻译的考试。

问：翻译专业资格（水平）考试报名条件是什么？
答：凡遵守中华人民共和国宪法和法律，恪守职业道德，具有一定外语水平的人员，不分年龄、学历和资历，均可报名参加相应语种、级别的考试。

问：考试由谁命题？
答：根据《翻译专业资格（水平）考试暂行规定》，中国外文局组建翻译专业资格（水平）考试专家委员会。该委员会负责拟定考试语种、考试科目、考试大纲和考试命题，研究建立考试题库等有关工作。

问：翻译专业资格（水平）考试如何与专业技术职务聘任制接轨？
答：二级口译、笔译翻译和三级口译、笔译翻译的相应语种实施全国统一考试后，各地、各部门不再进行相应语种的翻译及助理翻译专业技术职务任职资格的评审工作。

取得二级口译、笔译翻译或三级口译、笔译翻译资格（水平）证书，并符合《翻译专业职务试行条例》翻译或助理翻译专业技术职务任职条件的人员，用人单位可根据需要聘任相应职务。

问：外籍及港、澳、台地区的翻译人员是否可以参加考试？
答：经国家有关部门同意，获准在中华人民共和国境内就业的外籍人员及港、澳、台地区的专业人员，符合本规定要求的，也可报名参加翻译专业资格（水平）考试并申请登记。

问：此考试设置哪些语种？
答：翻译专业资格（水平）考试现设英、日、法、阿拉伯、俄、德、西班牙七个语种。

问：各语种、各级别考试如何分类？
答：各语种、各级别均设口译和笔译考试。口译考试分为《口译综合能力》和《口译实务》

两个科目，其中二级口译考试《口译实务》科目分设"交替传译"和"同声传译"两个专业类别；笔译考试分为《笔译综合能力》和《笔译实务》两个科目。

问：该考试各语种、各级别的难度如何？
答：本考试各语种、各级别的难度大致为：三级，外语专业本科毕业，并具备一年左右的口笔译实践经验；二级，外语专业本科毕业，并具备 3－5 年的翻译实践经验；一级，具备 8－10 年的翻译实践经验，是某语种双语互译方面的专家。

问：**全国翻译专业资格（水平）考试每年举行几次？**
答：英语二级、三级翻译专业资格（水平）考试每年分两次进行，英语同声传译类考试和其它语种的考试每年只进行一次。每年的 5 月份（具体日期以考前通知为准）举行二级、三级英语、日语、法语、阿拉伯语笔译和口译交替传译类考试；11 月份（具体日期以考前通知为准）举行二级、三级英语、俄语、德语和西班牙语的笔译、口译交替传译类及二级英语口译同声传译类考试。相应级别的职称评审在我国不再进行，即：今后相应语种的翻译专业人员获取助理翻译（初级）、翻译（中级）专业技术职务不再通过职称评审的办法，而必须通过参加相应级别的翻译专业资格（水平）考试获得职业资格，从而获得聘任相应专业技术职务的任职资格。

问：**一个人是否可以同时报考口笔译两种证书的考试？**
答：考生根据本人的实际水平和能力，可以同时报考同一语种、同一级别的口笔译两种证书的考试；也可以报名参加不同语种、不同级别口笔译证书的考试。

问：**各科目考试时间是如何规定的？**
答：二、三级口译、笔译考试均分两个半天进行。
　　二、三级《口译综合能力》科目、二级《口译实务》"交替传译"科目以及英语同声传译考试时间均为 60 分钟；
　　三级《口译实务》科目考试时间为 30 分钟；
　　二、三级《笔译综合能力》科目考试时间均为 120 分钟，《笔译实务》科目考试时间均为 180 分钟。

问：**各科目考试的方式如何？**
答：各级别笔译考试采用纸笔作答方式进行，口译考试采用听译笔答和现场录音方式进行。相应级别笔译或口译两个科目考试均合格者，方可取得相应级别、类别《中华人民共和国翻译专业资格（水平）证书》。

问：**口笔译考试侧重什么？**
答：考试侧重评价考生的实际翻译能力和水平。

问：**考生如何报名？**
答：各语种、各级别考试口译试点城市的 BFT 考点具体负责口译考试报名工作；笔译试点城市的人事考试中心具体负责笔译考试报名工作。详情可登录 http：//

www.catti.net.cn 以及 http：//www.catti.cn 网站查询。

问：报名时须注意哪些事项？
答：参加考试的人员，应符合《翻译专业资格（水平）考试暂行规定》中的条件。由本人携带有效身份证明到当地考试管理机构报名，领取准考证。凭准考证、有效身份证明按规定的时间、地点参加考试。

问：何时能够查询成绩？
答：考试结束后两个月左右。

问：是否有翻译考试培训机构？
答：有。由中国外文局认定的培训机构统一使用"全国翻译专业资格（水平）考试指定培训机构"名义。详情可登录 http：//www.catti.net.cn 网站查询。

问：各语种考试有相关用书吗？
答：各语种考试有考试大纲、指定教材和辅导用书等。中国外文局授权外文出版社独家出版发行相关考试图书，任何单位和个人不得盗用中国外文局指定机构名义编写、出版与翻译专业资格（水平）考试有关的书籍。未经中国外文局授权，不得全部或部分使用翻译专业资格（水平）考试试题作为编写、出版、翻印、复制、发行、培训的内容。

问：考试大纲、指定教材及辅导用书的编写发行情况如何？
答：各语种考试大纲由中国外文局全国翻译专业资格（水平）考试办公室组织专家编写，授权外文出版社独家出版发行；在考试办公室的指导下，外文出版社负责组织专家编写各语种考试指定教材及辅导用书，并独家出版发行。

问：如何能购买到相关的考试用书？
答：参考人员可在全国各大书店购买翻译考试相关图书，或直接与外文出版社联系，网址：http：//www.flp.com.cn，读者服务部电话：010-68995852，68996188。也可登陆中国网（http：//www.china.com.cn）首页"专题库"栏目里的"科教文卫"分类找到相关图书的信息。

问：继续教育与证书登记的目的是什么？
答：实行翻译专业资格（水平）证书定期登记和继续教育制度，是为了适应时代的发展以及社会对翻译专业人员实行规范的行业管理的需要，也是与国际惯例接轨的一种形式。通过继续教育，可以促使持证的翻译专业人员继续努力钻研翻译业务，不断更新知识，不断提高业务能力，保持应有的翻译专业水平，为用人单位使用翻译人才提供客观公正、科学有效的依据。

问：已经通过翻译专业资格（水平）考试并获得翻译职业资格证书的人员，是否必须参加继续教育并办理证书登记手续？
答：是的。2004年1月1日后取得翻译专业资格（水平）证书的证书持有者必须接受相关的继续教育并进行证书定期登记。翻译专业资格（水平）证书有效期为三年，在有效期满前3个月，持证者应到中国翻译协会办理证书登记手续。

问：翻译专业资格（水平）证书持有者继续教育和证书登记由哪个部门负责？

答：中国外文局全国翻译专业资格（水平）证书登记管理办公室为翻译专业资格（水平）证书持有者继续教育和证书登记的管理机构，设在中国外文局全国翻译专业资格（水平）考试办公室。中国外文局委托中国翻译协会负责持证者继续教育和证书登记的具体实施工作。中国翻译协会行业管理办公室是继续教育与证书登记工作的常设机构，联系方式：北京市西城区百万庄大街24号；邮编100037；电话010-68997177。中国翻译协会网站 www. tac-online. org. cn。

问：证书登记和继续教育工作的监督管理单位是哪里？

答：中国外文局全国翻译专业资格（水平）考试办公室负责对继续教育（或业务培训）和证书登记工作进行检查、监督和指导。

问：继续教育的主要内容是什么？

答：继续教育（或业务培训）的主要内容是对证书持有者进行职业道德教育、翻译业务培训。

问：二级口译英语同声传译类考试在何时、何地开始实施？

答：2005年11月12日，二级口译英语同声传译试点考试首次在北京进行。

问：二级口译英语同声传译类考试科目是如何设置的？

答：二级口译英语同声传译类考试设置《口译综合能力》和《口译实务（同声传译类）》两个科目。

问：二级口译英语同声传译类考试对报名资格有何要求？

答：(一) 根据《翻译专业资格（水平）考试暂行规定》（人发〔2003〕21号）和《二级、三级翻译专业资格（水平）考试实施办法》（国人厅发〔2003〕17号）考试报名有关要求，凡遵守中华人民共和国宪法和法律，恪守职业道德，具有一定外语水平的人员，均可报名参加同声传译类《口译综合能力》和《口译实务（同声传译类）》两个科目考试，考试合格可取得相应证书。

(二) 通过二级口译英语交替传译类考试并取得证书的人员，可免试《口译综合能力》科目，只参加《口译实务（同声传译类）》科目的考试，考试合格可取得相应证书。参加《口译实务（同声传译类）》科目考试的人员，在报名时应提交《中华人民共和国翻译资格（水平）证书》（二级口译英语交替传译类）。

问：翻译硕士专业学位研究生必须参加翻译资格考试吗？

答：根据学位〔2008〕28号文件，翻译硕士专业学位研究生，入学前未获得二级或二级以上翻译专业资格（水平）证书的，在校学习期间必须参加二级口译或笔译翻译专业资格（水平）考试。

问：翻译硕士专业学位研究生参加翻译资格考试和其他考生有什么区别吗？
答：翻译硕士专业学位研究生，在校学习期间参加二级口译或笔译翻译专业资格（水平）考试，可免试《综合能力》科目，只参加《口译实务》或《笔译实务》科目考试。

问：翻译硕士专业学位研究生如何报考翻译资格考试？
答：凭学校开具的"翻译硕士专业学位研究生在读证明"（加盖学校公章），根据当地人事考试中心的要求报考。

中国外文局
全国翻译专业资格（水平）考试办公室
2010 年 5 月